A Traveller and Teacher

Crests from the Ocean-World, or Experiences in a Voyage to Europe

A Traveller and Teacher

Crests from the Ocean-World, or Experiences in a Voyage to Europe

ISBN/EAN: 9783337252267

Printed in Europe, USA, Canada, Australia, Japan

Cover: Foto ©Andreas Hilbeck / pixelio.de

More available books at **www.hansebooks.com**

CRESTS FROM THE OCEAN-WORLD,

OR

EXPERIENCES IN A VOYAGE TO EUROPE,

PRINCIPALLY IN

France, Belgium, and England,

COMPRISING SKETCHES IN THE MINIATURE WORLDS,

PARIS, BRUSSELS, AND LONDON;

TOGETHER WITH

INCIDENTS BY THE WAY, NOTED SCENERY, NATIONAL CHARACTER AND COSTUME, DELINEATIONS OF SOCIAL LIFE, VIEWS OF THE PRINCIPAL PUBLIC MONUMENTS, CHURCHES, PALACES, GARDENS, GALLERIES OF PAINTINGS, MUSEUMS, LIBRARIES, LITERARY AND BENEVOLENT INSTITUTIONS, PUBLIC LECTURES, ETC.

AND WITH THREE NEW FEATURES, VIZ.:

FRENCH LIFE ON SHIPBOARD, REVOLUTION OF FEBRUARY IN PARIS, AND A PROFESSIONAL VEIW OF PUBLIC AND PRIVATE SCHOOLS.

BY A

TRAVELLER AND TEACHER.

BOSTON:
JOHN M. WHITTEMORE & CO.,
1864.

Entered according to Act of Congress, in the year 1853, by
ALONZO TRIPP,
in the Clerk's office of the District Court of the District of Massachusetts.

ANDOVER: W. F. DRAPER,
Stereotyper and Printer

PREFACE.

In presenting this volume to the public, a word or two in explanation of the circumstances which gave it birth may not be deemed inappropriate. The tour which forms its subject was the fortune of a respite from active duties, delightfully spent in breathing a freer atmosphere, and seeking to enlarge the horizon of observation and thought. On leaving home, I truly had no intention of attempting a book. I felt rather to be following the onward spirit of self-culture, united to an early, undying love for travelling, than indulging the hope of ever framing out of what I might see, a picture acceptable to others. But it has been thought, since my return, that the somewhat original manner of performing the journey, the important nature of several subjects, not usually spoken of by European travellers, that naturally came under my observation, and the thrilling scenes of the Revolution of February, were circumstances to justify the publication.

As much as has been written upon Europe, there remain, I am persuaded, rich fields unexplored; and who would not encourage learning more of people with whom our relations are becoming every day more intimate?

I have described things as I found them, or, at least, as they appeared to me; and in recording my opinions, I have not stopped to consider the prejudice of party or sect. The narrative style has in general been followed, as best adapted to interest youth; and if the book shall thereby gain attractiveness to supplant the seductive novel, no healthy-minded reader will, I am sure, regret it. If I have been prolix, it was to impart a more natural and vivid interest to the picture of the route. The next thing to travelling for one's self, is to accompany the author in a faithful reproduction of the incidents of the journey. I have often felt, myself, in reading books of travels, that they not unfrequently leave out much of what would be of greatest interest to the reader; minute incidents, perhaps, but containing the clew to important principles. To discriminate between the puerile and the instructively minute, is the province of a philosophical judgment.

As to the literary character of the book, if not so good as might be wished, it is yet such as circumstances have permitted. Written in the intervals of arduous and engrossing duties, with my right hand always free for the labors of a sacred trust, inequalities of style would be expected. It will be further remembered, that even with the gifted, harmony of structure, and force, and beauty of language, except with the practiced composer, are the fruit of time and pains. Slight errors in the first edition, should such appear, must be attributed to my having been at a distance during the progress of the work through the press. Where my Notes have failed me, I have consulted what I deemed the best authorities.

I desire, in conclusion, to express a lively gratitude toward numerous friends who, since the announcement of the book, have in various ways testified to me their kindly sympathy and encouragement. That it may not disappoint any reasonable expectations they may have formed, and at the same time be instrumental in advancing in the community the true, the good, and the beautiful, is the fervent desire of the author.

ALONZO TRIPP.

Highlands Institute, Roxbury, Mass.

CONTENTS.

CHAPTER I.
About Leaving — Thoughts on Leaving Home — Glowing Visions of the Old World — Travelling a Passion with the True Teacher.. .. 9

CHAPTER II.
Departing from the Beaten Track of Travel, the only way to gain Correct Ideas of Men and Things — The Beauty and Fragrance of the Primrose of Domestic Affection — A Nice Welsh Family — A Fastidious Young Lady.................................. 12

CHAPTER III.
Skill of Yankee Captains — Improved Manners of Hackmen in New York City — Appearances in the Streets on Sabbath Morning — My Neat Welsh Hotel — Health-Blooming Landlord and Lady — Smoking and-Beer-Drinking in the Bar-Room — A Mental Glance of New York — Unreserved Kindness of the Boarders — A Stroll among the Shipping — Pleasing Reminiscences of Golden Days of Boyhood — Rolling Tide of Immigration — The Yankee always Travels in the First Style........................... 17

CHAPTER IV.
Thanksgiving to the New Englander away — Observance of the Day by the English and Welsh Boarders — The Advantages of going in a French Vessel — Odd and Inspiring Sensations on Sailing from the Wharf — The Pilot and his French....................... 25

CHAPTER V.
Emotions on Losing Sight of Land — Model of the Vessel, a National Beau-Ideal — Comparative Strength of the Vessels of France and England — Fare, and Style of Living on Board — Sociality at Meals — A Portrait of our Three Apprentices................... 32

CHAPTER VI.
Heavy Weather — The Sailor a Stranger to Fear — The Sublimity of a Dreadful Gale — The Accurate Reckoning of the Captain — One not the Best Teacher of his own Language — The Intense Desire of getting in at the Cruel Sport of Fortune — "'T is sweet to be Drowned in one's own Waters" — The Thrill of a Narrow Escape.. 41

CHAPTER VII.
Land upon the Old World — A Moody Fit of the Captain — Sandwich Islanders — Elevating Effects of Ocean Scenery upon the Soul — Sabbaths at Sea — Sports of the Captain — Pig-Butchery — Arrival off Havre — Entering the Port — The French Woman's

Charge for Beef-Steak — French Mode of Living — The Prospect from the Heights of Angouville — Mode of Teaching Children — Improvement suggested for American Mothers.................. 51

CHAPTER VIII.
Reception by Mons. P. — American News a small space in European Journals — Notre Dame — Museum — Virgin Mary — Origin of Havre — New Dock — American Ships.......................... 69

CHAPTER IX.
Honesty of the French to Travellers — Leaving the City — Scenery through Normandy — Picturesque Costume of the Farmers — Arrival in Rouen — Kindness of Landlord and Lady — Market-Women under my Window — Grandeur of Rouen Cathedral — Richness of Interior — Rollo, the Norman — Church of St. Owen — Statue of Voltaire — Palais de Justice — Maid of Orleans — View from the Cote de St. Catherine — An Historical Mental Picture — The Ancient Port of the City — Supper — View of the City............. 77

CHAPTER X.
Annoying Trait of French Landlords — Comparative Excellence of Railways in France — Emotions on Arrival in Paris — Hotel du Havre — A Scene with the Landlady — Kindness of Madame David 95

CHAPTER XI.
Shopping in Paris — Fascinating Manners of the Shopwomen — Beautiful Appearance of the Streets — Fashions Different in Paris, London, and New York — Napoleon Column — Garden of the Tuileries — Library of St. Genevieve...................................... 103

CHAPTER XII.
Letters from Home — The Effect of Contemplating Aright Noble Public Edifices — Boarding School — Pupils out on Promenade — Arc de Triomph de l'Etoile — Minister of Public Instruction in Paris — Cimetiere du Pére la Chaise, the Paris of Cemeteries — Vice Rector at the Sarbonne — Pantheon — Description...................... 115

CHAPTER XIII.
Public Schools — Monsieur Lefebre — Order and Precision of the School — Corporal Punishment Prohibited — Mode of Teaching the Alphabet — Drawing — Singing — Advantage of the System — Its Defects — Municipal School Français — The Principal and his Professor — Plan of the School — Preparatory Department — Notre Dame de Lorette.. 135

CHAPTER XIV.
Communal School — Character of the School — Private Day and Boarding School by the Frères — Plan of the School — Singing —

CONTENTS. vii

Municipal School Superior — Arrangement of the Building — Drawing — Church St. Eustache — Cathedral de Notre Dame, compared with the Rouen Cathedral — Bell — Splendid Interior — Coronation of Napoleon — English Episcopal Church — Muddy Streets — Practice of the Ladies — Hotel des Invalids — Exterior — Interior — Military School — Woman among the Lower Orders.............. 147

CHAPTER XV.

Palace of the Louvre — Former Richness in Art — Characteristics of the several Schools of Painters — Sunday at the Louvre — Influence of the Art upon the Masses — Sculpture, Petrified Beauty — Marine Museum — Royal Institution for the Blind — Benefits of the Noble School — Professor-Lecturer of Chemistry — Garden of Plants — Description — Adult and Juvenile Evening Schools.............. 168

CHAPTER XVI.

Palace of the Luxembourg — Rich Paintings — Institution for Deaf-Mutes — Mode of Teaching — Teachers of French — Palace of the Fine Arts — Church of the Madeline — Its Magnificence — Nuns at the Church of St. Germain l'Auxerrois — Rural Restaurant — Madame David — Reunion of Ouvriers — Bishop of Paris............ 202

CHAPTER XVII.

To Versailles — Chateau — Vastness — Splendid Grounds — Sumptuous Interior — Hotel de Brissac — Condition of Domestics — Normal School.. 221

CHAPTER XVIII.

Revolution of February — Cause, Reunions — Italian Independence — Just Milieu of Mr. Guizot — More Remote Causes — Louis Phillippe — Stormy Session of the Chamber of Deputies — Evening School for Journeymen and Apprentices — Palais de la Bourse — Fortifications of Paris — Place de la Concorde — Parisian Cafés — Dancing — Model Office — Theatre Français — Orchestra — Lectures at the Sarbonne — Monsieur Frank....................... 231

CHAPTER XIX.

Gen. Scott under Arrest — An Ambiguous Character — Parisian Morals — Loveless Marriages — Left-Hand Marriages — Legalized Vice — Hospice d'Accouchement — Hospices des Enfans Trouvers — Causes, etc. — Manufactory for the Crown Tapestry — Palais Royale — Sumptuous Interior — Chapel of St. Ferdinand............ 256

CHAPTER XX.

The Grand Banquet at Paris — Opinions of the Approaching Crisis — The Gloomy Eve of the Fated Morrow — Sudden Tacking of the Ship of State — Mental Scenes in the Bosom of the Government —

Madame the Duchess of Orleans — Monsieur Guizot — Paris in a Posture of Defence — Thrilling Scenes of the 22d.............. 269

CHAPTER XXI.
Revolution Continued — Suavity and Kindness of Mr. Rush — Chamber of Deputies — M. Guizot in the Tribune — Resignation of M. Guizot — Reading Rooms — Alarm in the Night — Cause — Departure — Appearance of the Streets — Departure from Paris — Amiens — Appearance of Belgium............................ 286

CHAPTER XXII.
Arrival at Brussels — Officials — A Worcester Gentleman — Appearance of the City — Lady of the American Minister — Palais du Congress — Chambers of Parliament — Belgium — Theatres — Resignation of Louis Phillippe, and Flight of the Royal Family — Cafés and Boulevards — Schools — Hotel de Ville — Palace of Fine Arts 304

CHAPTER XXIII.
Symptoms of Revolution in Belgium — Communal Schools — Cathedral of Gudule — Religious Sects — Lamartine — Marriage in Europe and the United States — Academies — Botanical Garden — Influence of Lamartine — Carnival — Hero-Worship — Shopping — Carpet and Lace Factories.. 316

CHAPTER XXIV.
Departure for Brussels — Canal Boats — Bruges — Cathedral of Notre Dame — Dietetics — Groups of Musicians — Arrival of a Steamer — Embark for Dover — Dover Heights — Custom House — Smuggling — Dover Castle — Leave for London........................ 340

CHAPTER XXV.
London — Beggars — Tower of London — Dungeon — Crown-Jewels — St. Paul's — Sir Christopher Wren — The Thames Tunnel — River Steamers — Trafalgar Square — Nelson Monument — British Museum — West-End — Buckingham Palace — Westminster Abbey — Parks.. 357

CHAPTER XXVI.
Hospitality of the English — Gallery of Paintings — Popularity of Queen Victoria — Disaffection — St. Paul's School — Guildhall — Royal Exchange — Bank of England — Bridges — Houses of Parliament — St. James's Park — Prince Albert — Normal and Moral School — East India Docks — Elihu Burritt — Quakers — National Schools — House of Lords — Shopkeepers — Homeward Bound.... 383

CHAPTER XXVII.
European Schools........   403

CRESTS FROM THE OCEAN-WORLD.

CHAPTER I.

ABOUT LEAVING — THOUGHTS ON LEAVING HOME — GLOWING VISIONS OF THE OLD WORLD — TRAVELLING A PASSION WITH THE TRUE TEACHER.

WHAT a crowd of delightful anticipations throng the imagination of an American, as he leaves his home to visit the Old World! It is there that the human race had its origin, and long has it been the grand theatre of its numberless exploits. Treading the classic ground of his forefathers, he can trace the windings of civilization to their source, and mark the different epochs in the world's history. Character may there be seen variously modified by political institutions, and social life, in its endless phases, keeps the traveller constantly alive with renewed interest. It is, too, on the Eastern Continent, to which his thoughts are now turned, that the human mind has received its widest expansion, its fullest development, and the treasures of intellect so profuse, so infinite in form, which meet him at every step, fill his mind with engrossing and profound interest. But when he comes to the arts — to painting, sculpture, and architecture, he is translated to new worlds of mortal creation, to revel in a sublime existence, which before was but dimly shadowed to his imagination.

If with such feelings the traveller ordinarily looks forward to a tour in Europe, these feelings are doubly intense, when the tourist is a teacher. Accustomed, from the duties of his vocation, to deal with mind; necessitated to learn its conditions, to trace the causes which have led to certain results in its formation, and especially to know the agencies by which it is successfully moved, he hails, with peculiar pleasure, so grand an opportunity to look abroad among the nations of the earth ; to compare their diverse condition ; to observe the peculiar traits of individual character ; to note the changes which the hand of time has wrought in the social fabric; to study the modes of thought, feeling and expression which give coloring to ideas ; and, in fine, to take a general survey of the basis and structure of society, in connection with the causes which have led to its development.

Not only is the teacher to be conversant with mind anatomically and physiologically, to understand its structure and functions, and the conditions of its healthful growth; but he must be familiar with the subjects of the mind, the varied forms of knowledge which incite to action its powers, and constitute the woven fabric of its essence. History, science, language, and poetry are but so much of the teacher's stock in trade. Is it surprising, then, that he should long to gather largely and afresh from the primitive source — that he should pant to tread the very soil hallowed by the most glowing associations, about which he has so often conversed with his pupils, — that he should hasten to view the astonishing and transcendently beautiful combinations of form, in the fine arts, the simple principles of which it has been his daily task to teach, — that he should be thrilled with delight at the prospect of hanging with ecstasy upon the living tones, palpitating with the heart's keenest emotions, and giving spirit and grace to those languages, the bare forms of which have afforded him so much gratification in his daily study, — that his very soul should leap with pleasure as it flies on the wings of imagination to gaze on those sublime scenes in nature, which have lent inspiration to the poet, and moved him to so lofty a flight of song,—sweet numbers which, though stripped of half their glow and beauty, by the absence of the scenes which inspired them, have yet elevated his soul to a loftier existence, and opened to it new sources of purer enjoyment?

Nor is it enough that the teacher should clearly comprehend the mind, and be perfectly familiar with the varied subjects which employ its energies. It is not sufficient that his own mind is an ample storehouse, filled with principle, fact, and apt illustration systematically arranged, ready to flow out at bidding to elucidate every subject as it comes up for investigation. He must possess himself the quintescence, the impalpable of knowledge, obtained not from books, but from large intercourse with men, and free draughts at nature's well. With this, he must permeate the character of his pupils. He must infuse his own spirit into their very being, — distil the dew of his soul into the waters of their life — if he would hope fully to arouse them to lofty purpose, and intense action.

Yes, others may delight to travel; but with the true teacher, the artist, the man whose life is in his work, travelling will be a passion; and though he may suppress a sigh, as with tearful eye and saddened heart he thinks of the endearing ties he is called to sunder, and the changes which inexorable time may work in his dear circle or beloved flock, before he is permitted to embrace or greet them again; yet he will soon rise above these pathetic emotions, his spirit strengthened by the glorious prospect from the fields of intellectual treasure before him, and the increased usefulness which his sacrifices, and sweet and noble toil will give him.

CHAPTER II.

DEPARTING FROM THE BEATEN TRACK OF TRAVEL, THE ONLY WAY TO GAIN CORRECT IDEAS OF MEN AND THINGS — A FASTIDIOUS YOUNG LADY — A NICE WELSH FAMILY — THE BEAUTY AND FRAGRANCE OF THE PRIMROSE OF DOMESTIC AFFECTION — THE HEART-BREATHINGS OF THE HOMEWARD-BOUND EMIGRANT.

Boston, Nov. 20th. I called this morning on board of one of the Cunard steamers, lying at East Boston. These are certainly noble ships, and all honor is due to the genius of him who conceived the grand design of linking the two continents by steam-navigation. Yet, he who journeys abroad with an especial view of gaining a more intimate knowledge of men and things, will not hesitate to turn off from the more beaten roads of travel, and pursue some of the less frequented paths. He will thus gain in delightful interest what he may lose in pleasurable ease; and if he is not swept over the route so delectably, he will have this loss fully compensated, by gaining more vivid impressions of nature, and receiving a more enlarged horizon of thought.

Returning, I stepped on board a ship, the only vessel in port, I learned, soon to sail for England or France. I found the accommodations narrow, but neat and comfortable enough for a person of moderate desires; but the captain, who was pacing the wharf in all the dignity of his profession, replied so *curtly* to my inquiries, and with an air so unmistakable to an eye the least experienced in nautical character, that I bid him good morning at once, resolved to look farther, for the means of a pleasant transit across the Atlantic. A winter passage with a morose captain, was by no means to be ventured upon. The officers of the packet-ships acquire by habit a civil and obliging behavior toward passengers, even when those qualities are not a part of their natural disposition; but the captain of a transient ship is influenced by no peculiar motives to induce him to deviate from his ordinary line of conduct. Indeed, his position on board, in rank above all others, and his relation to the ship's company, clothed with almost arbitrary power, called to govern men accustomed to despotic rule, who would frequently take undue advantage of a mild discipline, he acquires, unconsciously to himself, an imperious temper and stern manner of action, which, when they happen to be united with a naturally passionate and reckless disposition, combine to render him not altogether a most agreeable social companion for a solitary sea-voyage.

New York, Nov. 21st. — Left Boston last evening, in the six o'clock train, to come by the way of Stonington. This route is preferred, I believe, to that by the way of Fall River, by the more timid class of passengers, as being safer at this season, — the distance by water being considerably less. The Fall River route, however, by the superior boats on the sound, the liberality of the Company, and gentlemanly and polite attentions of the officers on the whole route, has justly won the favor of the public; and when we were aroused from our warm slumbers, and hastened into the cold midnight air, to exchange, first from the boat to the cars, then to the boat, then again to the cars, and finally to the boat, we began to feel that we had paid dearly for our choice of routes.

An unusually large number of passengers were along with us;

and, in changing from the boat to the cars, there were the usual tumultuous and hurried scenes exhibited, with more or less confusion; some bustling for bits of luggage, or *toting* or dragging pieces along with them, to the annoyance of their neighbors; others solicitous for their female companions, who were scampering to meet them, or being half pulled along through the dark, or dimly-lighted way; or some father hastily uniting the members of his group, and, with many words of encouragement and caution, uttered in quickening and paternal tones, sees them safely in the right car. The manner and expression of the company were as varied, too, as their character. A few, at the given signal, snatch their valises or carpet-bags, and press right on through the crowd, jostling any that may happen to be in their way. Some others are more deliberate in their movements, and more mindful of the rights of their neighbors; a large number, apparently unused to travelling, or unacquainted with the route, appear anxious — a little disconcerted — put questions to any one, for the resolving of their doubts, and then follow on with the moving tide, sometimes hastening, then retarding their movements; while a small number, adepts in travelling, appear quite at home; and by their loudly repeated commands to the waiters, and dignified movements, seem desirous to attract attention to their vast superiority in matters pertaining to travel.

I could not but notice a delicately beautiful young lady, just before me, exquisitely dressed, and leaning on the arm of her brother. She was fainting, she said, of thirst and would give a kingdom for a single draught of cold water. A sturdy and generous hand quickly extended her some, in a tin vessel. She turned away with an air of disgust; she could not bear to allay even her intolerable thirst from a cup that had been drunk out of by others. A half dozen voices eagerly assured her that the cup was intact, and pressed her to partake. She would not believe them, and passed on with the crowd, bearing an expression of over-squeamishness, that caused a suppressed tittering among the several witnesses of the act. Two or three foreigners near, looked at each other in surprise; and doubtless noted the incident, as material for future use. This little trait, forms of course, no fair illustration of American female character; but it may justly be feared, that among the many excellent qualities of our lovely countrywomen, a false delicacy in matters of form, too often appears, as a blemish.

Travelling alone, on a long journey, the mind, freed from the engrossing details of petty affairs, observes narrowly, noticing incidents that might escape the attention at other times. Near me, in the cars, was an interesting group, whose peculiar accent betrayed them of English origin. Their kindly nature, evinced in the most trivial act for each other's comfort, and the deep affection, modulating the very tones of their voice, linking them in a sweet bond of family union, completely charmed me. How beautiful the flower of love that springs up in the bosom of an affectionate family! It not only delights the eye, but fills the very air you breathe, with fragrance. Seeking the first opportunity for an acquaintance, I learned that they were Welsh, and had been residing in Canada, where the father, employed by the English government in making surveys of the unexplored territories of the British crown, had so improved his former condition, as to enable him to revisit the scenes of his youth, and to take over with them to the New World, some of their relatives. Undoubtedly, the bright anticipation of so soon seeing Old England, and embracing their long-separated friends, had enlivened their hearts, and lent an unusual warmth and glow to their expression. How keen the pleasure of the emigrant, as, improved in worldly prospects, he turns his steps toward the dear home of his fathers! With some of his hard-earned wealth, he gilds the declining years of his aged parents, in ameliorating their physical condition — while he staggers their imagination with recounting the marvels of the New World; and overwhelms their hearts with paternal joy, as he presents for a blessing the youthful scions that have sprung up to him, amidst the fertile lands of the distant West. The political economist, in estimating the advantages that have resulted to the world, by the discovery of America by Columbus, may well take into the account this element of the immigrant's improved condition.

CHAPTER III.

SKILL OF YANKEE CAPTAINS — IMPROVED MANNERS OF HACKMEN IN NEW YORK CITY — APPEARANCES IN THE STREETS ON SABBATH MORNING — MY NEAT WELSH HOTEL — HEALTH-BLOOMING LANDLORD AND LADY — SMOKING AND BEER-DRINKING IN THE BAR-ROOM — A MENTAL GLANCE OF NEW YORK — UNRESERVED KINDNESS OF THE BOARDERS — A STROLL AMONG THE SHIPPING — PLEASING REMINISCENCES OF GOLDEN DAYS OF BOYHOOD — ROLLING TIDE OF IMMIGRATION — THE YANKEE ALWAYS TRAVELS IN THE FIRST STYLE.

APPROACHING the city, the beautiful scenery that skirts the East river, was shut out from our view, by the dense mist, occasioned by the change of temperature in the air during the night, that hung over the rippled bosom of the stream, through which we were noiselessly gliding with the speed of an arrow; while the raw morning air, and the feeling of loneliness that involuntarily creeps over one, on entering a new place, kept most of us within the cabins.

Now the engine ceases; all the passengers crowd upon the deck; there are one or two backward turns, some little manœuvreing, when our floating palace shoots in by the pier, directly to the spot marked out for her, with a precision and ease, that mark the dexterity of our Yankee captains, in whatever craft they undertake to manage. Then comes the bustling of passengers, accompanied with the confused noise of the cabmen, who almost deafen you with their repeated importunities for your luggage. This is not a little embarrassing to those who travel for the first time, and annoying enough to every one. In justice, it must be observed, in passing, that this feature of travelling life has materially improved in the State of New York, within a few years. The time was, when it had become absolutely intolerable; when passengers approached New York or Albany with feelings akin to those of seamen, when passing through the famous Straits of Caraccas, at the time the buccaneer held sway in those seas.

Accepting the invitation of my new acquaintance, to take rooms at the hotel kept by a friend of his, in Walker street, I leisurely strolled along thither, with my valise in hand. On leaving the pier, what was my surprise! It being Sabbath morning, the foreign population were out; and the German and the French languages greeted my ear with as much frequency as my own; and then so densely thronged were all the streets, that I should really have supposed myself in London, rather than in New York, as I formerly knew it. And here let me say, for the benefit of those who intend travelling abroad, and who would go in a simple style, and be free from the trouble and expense of looking after, and removing much luggage, that it is better in all respects to leave your trunks and extra suits at home. A few changes of linen, and an extra coat, with the articles of toilet, all of which can be put into a valise, will answer all the purposes of comfortable travelling. In any of the cities, and especially in those of Europe, articles of clothing can always be purchased, when needed, with the advantage of being in the latest style; while the anxiety and trouble avoided, and the expense saved, which would be something of an item in a long journey, are really of considerable importance.

Arrived at the hotel, I found the landlord and his lady, a charming young couple, with countenances blooming with health and vivacity. They were extremely neat in their persons and dress, and the most sociable and obliging people in the world. I was immediately shown my room, which was both commodious and airy, and contained an ample bed, as clean and voluptuous as I should have expected to find in the house of a friend. The warm breakfast was awaiting us; and we found the fare, though simple, both excellent and abundant; while the clean, sanded floor of the dining-room, the snowy-white napkins beside our plates, and the gleaming knives and forks, all served not a little to heighten the relish of the meal. Indeed, the whole house was a pattern of neatness, in wide contrast with the shabby elegance of some of our so-called genteel boarding houses. There was, withal, pervading everything, an antique quaintness and simplicity, which brought to one's mind some of the better sort of English inns, described by English writers, inducing a feeling of home, so congenial to the heart of a stranger. The only material drawback to the pleasantness of the house to a traveller, was the smoking of pipes, drinking of beer, and fierce and boisterous conversation, that was ever going on in the bar-room. It really seemed that the genius of the immaculate weed and the glorious old ale, had usurped absolute possession of that part of the edifice, and was having things entirely his own way. But, aside from this feature, the house was greatly to be commended for its many excellent qualities. Thus noting the salient features of your hotel, may seem trivial to the reader; but let me assure him, that should he ever travel, he will find his personal comfort and disposition of mind so greatly to depend upon the qualities of his hotel, as hardly to forbear making mention of that part of the path of his travel, ever afterward.

To sketch the details of a week's sight-seeing in New York city, would form a long, and what might justly be considered an inappropriate chapter in a book professedly of foreign travel; although not even an American, in a visit to the emporium of the New World, would fail of ample material for the employment of his pen. The almost fabulous growth of the city in wealth and population; the gigantic spread of its commerce, with ships whitening every sea; the ever-rolling tide of foreign immigration, crowding the shores of its majestic harbor; and, at the same time, the equally increasing domain of those sublime institutions, the School, the Church, and Asylum, generously encircling the empire of mind, — and, on the one hand, rapidly assimilating the foreign population, as it reaches its shores, to the elements of republican character; and, on the other, antagonizing the sordid power of wealth, combined, form a series of agencies, so grand in outline, so rapid in march, so unceasing in action, and, moreover, so powerful in results, as to astonish and elevate the mind of the beholder. In their contemplation, surrounded as he is by the evidences of their greatness, he feels as if living in an age of powerfully quickened energies, and of high moral grandeur; and the pulses of his life beat fuller and quicker. The ineffectual struggle of the fine arts for a seat upon the throne of mind; the vicissitudes and fate of authors and other literary men in their rugged and toilsome ascent up the hill of fame; the unbounded success of the gigantic printing press; the cosmopolitan phase of the city, in which are represented the costume, physiognomy, and specific character of almost every nation upon the globe; the phantasies of public amusements; the caprice of fashion; the sombre aspect of vice and crime; the abject state of destitution; and the sore annoyance of petty larceny and deception, together form so many features in the physiognomy of this life-beating metropolis, for the study of the traveller; and unsusceptible indeed must be that mind which is unmoved in their contemplation. But I must not dwell on these and many other features in the physiogmy of this magic-growing city,—topics rich in reflections. I will, therefore, skip a few pages (as the schoolboys say), taking permission, however, to glance at a topic or two in connection with the incidents of the way, just to keep up the thread of the narrative.

Most of the boarders at our house were of the better sort of English, Scotch, or Welsh people, on their way to the mother-country, or home, as they call it, to visit their friends. They were, as might be expected, in the best of spirits,—cheerful and lively, with hearts overflowing with emotion, in confident anticipation of the happiness that awaited them. Happy souls! might no cruel turn of the treacherous wave over which they were soon to be wafted, disappoint their hearts' fondest wishes!

The conversation naturally turned upon a passage. They had nearly all secured theirs, in different ships; and they all solicited that I would make mine, each in his particular vessel; and the invitation was extended with that unreserved cordiality which left no room to doubt of its sincerity. It would have afforded me sincere pleasure to accept, especially had they all been going in one ship,—for who does not love to be with open and warm-hearted people, particularly when they are, as in this case, sensible and intelligent? but I feared that my plans would not permit. A stroll among the shipping in port, with me a favorite way of spending a leisure hour when in the city, awakened the usual reminiscences of that period of my early life, when, with golden scenes overhead, and flowers beneath my feet, I danced gaily over the bounding billow, not only of fleeting life, but also of the ocean. There is much in a sailor's life, to captivate the imagination of a bold and spirited youth. Its changes; its thrilling scenes; the varied scenery of countries; the peculiar costumes and manners of different nations; with that *abandon* mode of life, so charming to the undisciplined character,— all render it in consonance with the fire and buoyancy of free and careless life. There is something in the calling, too, that enlarges the mind, and elevates the character, making ample amends for the rough and angular points it leaves upon its apprentices. Our glorious sea-captains, for their noble bearing, enlarged views, and generous impulses, may well thank old Neptune for his efficient influence.

The large number of packet and other ships in port, and soon to set sail for England or France, appeared thronged with passengers. Indeed, the tide of travel setting toward Europe from the United States, if not so great as that rolling from Europe towards the United States, is still not inconsiderable; and fully merits to be taken into the account, in estimating accurately the aggregate of immigration to this country. A very large proportion of the passengers that go out in these ships, are those that, having formerly immigrated to this country, are now on a visit to their friends in Europe; and after a transient stay there, return, bringing perhaps with them others of their friends and acquaintances, to advance the Western stride of empire. It is evident, therefore, that if all who land upon our shores be set down as so much immigration, there will be some included who have already been reckoned. The rates for passage in the first class of the packet-ships, were about as follows:— in the first cabin, one hundred dollars, including board and wine; in the second cabin, twenty dollars, and found in bread, tea, and coffee; for deck passage, twelve dollars, with bread, and access to the caboose to prepare the meals. In many of the ships, the second cabin was as commodious as need be, — being provided with state-rooms and comfortable berths. Indeed, the second cabin in these ships was formerly the first cabin, and used as such, until the falling off of the first-class passengers, who now mostly go by steamers, and the increase of travel with the second-rate passengers, made it for the interest of the company to divide the cabin, and provide for a large and respectable part of the travelling community, who are better satisfied with moderate charges, — provided they can have, at the same time, comfortable quarters. Among the passengers in the second cabin, and even on the deck, you will frequently meet with persons of considerable wealth, and of high intelligence. But you will rarely see an American there. The habits of the Yankee and the European, are widely different in this respect. The latter is accustomed to accommodate himself to his pecuniary circumstances, or to his position in life; while the former never thinks of this. He rarely travels but in the first style, — ordering the best of everything, at least so long as he has money to foot the bills. Brother Jonathan may be close and hard-fisted on his own soil, in trade with his fellows; but when he travels, there is not a more liberal soul. He parts with his money as freely, and with the grace of a titled millionaire, used to the thing from youth. This trait of our countrymen is so well understood upon the continent of Europe, that an American traveller is expected to pay more for everything he orders, than any other person; and the charges on the route are not unfrequently graduated in conformity with this expectation. When an American ship is telegraphed to one of the cities of the north of Europe, it usually throws the entire city into a state of rejoicing, not seen on the approach of the ships of any other nation. Not unfrequently, salutes are fired, and the church bells rung, in expression of welcome. This may be owing in part to the favor with which the Americans and the United

States are regarded by these people; but it will not be doubted that the principal thing which moves these impulses, is the golden anticipation of the money that is to be cast among them by the generosity of the crew and officers.

CHAPTER IV.

THANKSGIVING TO THE NEW ENGLANDER AWAY — OBSERVANCE OF THE DAY BY THE ENGLISH AND WELSH BOARDERS — THE ADVANTAGES OF GOING IN A FRENCH VESSEL — ODD AND INSPIRING SENSATIONS ON SAILING FROM THE WHARF — THE PILOT, AND HIS FRENCH.

Nov. 25th. Thanksgiving! What pleasing reminiscences it awakens! Sweetly embalmed in memory are gladsome scenes of the past. Linked with the present, they glide before the mind, drawn thither by the silver chord of association; while fancy, aided by the mellowing hand of time, smilingly interweaves her golden threads. You are at once transported to the venerable domicile of an aged grandfather. Once a year, at least, his heart bursts the bands in which the sordid aims of life, the rest of the year, so narrowly confine it; and the austere and wrinkled countenance, darkly shaded, by carping at the folly and extravagance of the age, now expands with a generous and benignant smile. The doors in the parental mansion have been thrown wide open at an early hour, and the halls now ring with the merry voices of youth, mingled with the deep tones of middle life, and the pleasing garrulity of old age. Soon comes the long-anticipated event. A table of ample dimensions, with the time-honored turkey, and other rich viands, prepared by the good old grandmother, assisted by some of the more skilful aunts, greets the eye with its rich burden. Around the festal board gather uncles, aunts, cousins, the beloved grand-parents, and, peradventure, an invited guest or two,—when genial mirth and conviviality heighten the pleasure of the annual feast. The evening glides off, enlivened by story or song; while the younger members of the family group, one by one, silently withdraw to enjoy the youthful pleasures of the social party, or dance where soft eyes look love to eyes, which speak again in the unmistaken language of the heart. But if Thanksgiving-day awakens pleasing recollections, these are not unfrequently accompanied with those of a sadder hue. When memory turns the shroud of departed joys — of endearing ties ruptured by the ruthless hand of death, it strikes the key-note of the dirge of our remembrances. Over the spirit of the New Englander, distant from his home, a lonely feeling creeps, on the recurrence of this day.

We dined plainly to-day; and I began to think that we should have nothing to recognize the observance of the hallowed event. In this, I was agreeably mistaken. In the afternoon, we were favored with a visit from ———, the celebrated harpist. He had the kindness to entertain us with some of his sweetest pieces; and it is needless to say, that we were highly delighted with the performance. The harp is rarely played in the United States; but, from the classical associations connected with the instrument, and its sweet tones, it never fails to please, when its strings are gracefully and skilfully touched. In the evening, after tea, the gentlemen boarders of the house, with some of their acquaintances, assembled in the dining-room; and, after drinking two or three glasses apiece of beer, chose one of their number chairman, and held a convivial meeting, in honor of the day. The motion that each should tell a story, sing a song, or make a speech, passed by acclamation,—whereupon, the company set themselves to work in lively earnest, and they gave what the French would style a *me-*

lange of noble sentiments and graceful turns of expression, mingled with puerile thoughts and coarse allusions. I could not but admire, however, the deep and melodious tones of several who sang, although not so much could be said in favor of the general character of their performance. Many of the old English ballads, naturally sung, are very effective, and somehow stir up emotions within, quite irresistibly. It was all strongly English,—the full tone, broad accent, sluggish manner, and thorough frankness, except being softened with more generous sentiments than is usual with the English in their sentiment toward America, their adopted home. "America as she is, and England as she was," met a hearty, right English-fashioned reception. The evening closed with a brief speech from the president, who, in a touching and really eloquent manner, contrasted the unhappy condition of some of our fellow-men in foreign lands, with the favored lot of the masses in this country; and concluded, by expressing the fervent wish that the suffering everywhere might be speedily relieved. On the whole, this was not so bad a substitute for a Thanksgiving!

Nov. 29th. I was so fortunate as to secure an arrangement for a passage across the Atlantic, in the Union, a small French brig, Capt. Pavé. As the vessel was by no means heavily built, and was deeply laden, a person in the least timid, might have hesitated to venture his personal fortune in so inferior-sized craft, across the vast Atlantic, at so boisterous a season; but one at all versed in nautical affairs, well knows that it is not the largest ship that is the safest, or most comfortable, even in a severe gale at sea. Besides, the beautiful model of the Union revealed her an excellent sea-boat.

The captain appeared intelligent and well-disposed, and desired my company for the aid I might be to him in improving his knowledge of the English language. The accommodations in the cabin were very superior, for a vessel of the size; and being the only passenger, I should be the object of exclusive attention with the officers and crew, and be freed of the annoyance arising too often from the qualms and peevishness of landsmen at sea. I anticipated much advantage, moreover, from the fine opportunity it offered, of gaining a more intimate and familiar acquaintance with the idiomatic French, — an excellent preparation for an advantageous tour through the country. So near proximity would reveal intelligibly to my mind more of French character, taste, and peculiar ideas, than I could otherwise gain, — as well as enable me to learn something of French history, not written in books; and to find out where to go, to travel to the best advantage; and what objects to examine as the most interesting and instructive. The boarders at our house congratulated me on my good fortune, and approved my judgment in the choice I had made. I retired to my state-room, on board, at a late hour, with a racking pain in my head, arising from undue exhaustion, — having been in the streets most of the day and evening, in the bustle that attends the eve of a journey. Tossing on my pillow during the night, I had but just closed my eyes, when the noise of ropes and strange voices over my head, aroused me; and when I reached the deck, the captain had just ordered to cast off, — when the ship, with topsails hanging like the roundabout of a boy just decked in his holiday gear, was yielding to the gentle breeze, and noiselessly gliding toward the stream. The city, like a huge animal just aroused from its nightly slumbers, was beginning to beat with pulse and energy. The rays of the rising sun were gilding the summits of its lofty spires; and as I stood upon the quarter-deck, and gazed upon the receding city, the separating link in the golden chain of home and its endearing associations, and yielded to the gentle inspiration imparted by the motion of the vessel, I felt seized with emotions that must enkindle more or less the bosom of every traveller, as he leaves his native shore for a distant journey.

I was diverted from this momentary reverie by the novel-sounding and energetic commands of the pilot, which were instantly passed by the officers from him to the crew, and obeyed by them with the utmost alacrity. Being nautical phrases, they struck my ear as oddly as if modulated in a language quite new to me. A light wind wafted us along during the day, but so sluggish was our movement, that on the change of tide setting in, we came to anchor in the mouth of New York bay. The sky became deeply overcast, and there was strong indication of a gale; but this did not disturb the equanimity of the captain or pilot, who were yielding to the agreeableness of the enchanting domino, and fragrant Havana, in the comfortably warmed and lighted cabin, while master Joseph, one of the ship's apprentices, most delightfully regaled us with the silvery tones which he drew from his violin, with the skill and grace of a Paganini. But in the latter part of the night, the wind increasing, the hands were mustered to find a shelter for the vessel near Staten Island. Here we remained snugly sheltered from the wind, which blew furiously from the north-east, the following day and evening.

This part of the island was dotted, here and there, with tasteful country residences; and the pilot, who was extremely obliging and communicative, related to me incidents in the life of the gentleman who possessed the cottage that adorned so smilingly the bluff of land near us, which aptly illustrated the capricious nature of fortune, especially in rapid-growing New York.

A wealthy gentleman in the city, at his death, left his property to be equally divided among his children, excepting the youngest son, who, being a little too racy in his habits, had allotted, for his share, some acres on the uninhabited islands in the vicinity of the city, at that time nearly valueless. In process of time, — thanks to the improved taste of our merchant-princes for country palaces as summer resorts, — his lands became so enhanced in nominal value, that he was now able to give a dinner to his poorer brothers.

The pilot spoke French with remarkable fluency, and so as to be readily understood, not only in conversation, but by the crew in his orders; but then, he made a perfect homicide of the French grammar, mixing up the particles and accidents of the verbs in pretty Babel-like confusion, — and then his pronunciation, and the cadences of his sentences! As they struck the ear, you were rather reminded of the meeting of the cross-currents of a shallow, than the wavy undulations of the true French melody. This was not surprising, however; the greater wonder being, that in so short a time as he had attended to the study and practice of the language, and the meagre opportunity he had had for its acquisition, that he should have been able to speak half as well. It went to prove, that quickened by the force which interest imparts to our energies, we may often make astonishing acquisitions. It may suggest, too, a valuable principle in the education of youth. A scholar, with no stimulus to excite his powers, will often lifelessly drift in the dead-sea of study for months, and even years, to the no small vexation of his teacher, and real mortification of his parents; but by some means awaken or reanimate his sleeping faculties, and he darts off, like a thing of life before the freshening gale, to the astonishment and delight of the beholder. The pilot informed me that there were no less than one hundred and eighty pilots in the city, and that they were organized in independent companies, each being left free to compete with the rest in securing the greatest amount of pilotage. If a vessel is spoken in the offing, or entering the harbor, the captain is obliged to pay, at least, half-pilotage. The old pilots complained, and with some justice, of the act of Congress, which some three years ago removed all restrictions to free competition. They were about petitioning the law-makers for a reënactment of the same, securing the privileges of the craft to such as by due knowledge and experience have claims to them. This largest liberty, though certainly unjust, and quite annoying to the duly qualified, is not wholly unproductive of good results. To it may be, in great measure, attributed the vast superiority of our Yankee pilot-boats, in point of beauty of model, and quality of speed, over those of any other nation.

CHAPTER V

EMOTIONS ON LOSING SIGHT OF LAND — MODEL OF THE VESSEL
A NATIONAL BEAU-IDEAL — COMPARATIVE STRENGTH OF THE
VESSELS OF FRANCE AND ENGLAND — FARE, AND STYLE OF
LIVING ON BOARD — SOCIALITY AT MEALS — A PORTRAIT OF
OUR THREE APPRENTICES.

Dec. 4th. On coming on deck in the morning, I met with a clear horizon, and a piercing wintry-air. With anchors weighed, and bellying canvas set to a brisk gale from the north, the brig was gallantly ploughing her way out of the harbor, in company with numbers of other craft with prows set in different directions. The scene was enlivening. At eight o'clock, with a moistened eye, we shook hands with the pilot, and bid him good-by, intrusting to his care our last missives of love and friendly affection to dear friends that we were fast leaving behind. At nine o'clock, the captain and mate regulated the ship's chronometer, and noted the bearings and estimated distance of Sandy Hook, — when the ship's bow was fairly turned toward beautiful France. At eleven o'clock, P. M., the hills of Neversink were just merging below the horizon. We were now indeed launched upon the glorious Atlantic, with a broad expanse of three thousand miles before us. As my eye lost the lingering vestige of my native country, and "reflections thick" rushed upon me, I could scarcely repress a sigh. As I turned away, the captain, in a sympathetic tone, observed: *Vous êtes triste, Monsieur, vous regrettez votre pays.* To turn the subject without a reply, I cast a glance at our short canvas,— top-gallant-sails being furled, — and then pointed, inquiringly, at a large ship near, that was ploughing by us under top-gallant studding-sails— a perfect cloud of canvas. He caught my meaning with the quickness of a Frenchman's apprehension, and giving a true French shrug, exclaimed, *Ah, Monsieur, on presse;* then, turning on his heel, he gave me a hint in respect to such matters, that served as a guide for the rest of the voyage.

We continued rather slowly our watery path, amidst variable and not particularly propitious winds, steering first broadly off to the south-east, under that sentiment of dread which all foreigners have of our American coast, and then gradually hauling up nearer our course, so as to pass near the south point of the great Bank of Newfoundland. We soon lost the sharp, nipping air of the land, which, under the double influence of the agreeable power of the ocean upon the superincumbent atmosphere, and the radiating force of the Gulf-stream, that ocean-caldron upon our coast, softened down to so genial a temperature as to remind us continually of the balmy month of June, rather than frosty old December, wrapped in furs and icicles pendant from his hoary beard. We were quite comfortable without fire in the cabin.

The first few days from port are not the most sociable in an ocean passage. The crew are necessarily busily employed in stripping the ship of her land-hamper, and snugly reducing her to a sea-dress. This, with noting the ship's departure, keeping her reckoning, and writing up the log-book, neglected by the ex tra labors in port, require the constant attention of the officers, while the captain is absorbed in his accounts, or distracted by the ever-rising images of his wife and children, or the voluptuous form of his mistress, making a captive of his mind, and bearing * to the endeared family-circle, or to the hall sounding with mirth and revelry. Even the steward is a little out of humor, bustling in the cabin in setting to rights things disarranged in the hurry of leaving, and broadly hinting to you some of the rules by which he expects you will be governed, if you desire to be on good terms with him. While the passengers, strangers on board and strangers to each other, and swelling with past memories and future hopes, will feel no disposition to be communicative.

One who has been a sailor will be interested in nothing relating to maritime scenery more than in observing and comparing the model and build of the vessels of different nations, as well as those of the same. He will easily trace a striking resemblance between the physical conformation of a nation, and the architecture of its ships. The ideas of beauty which seem derived from the human form, and which constitute the basis of style, are so faithfully transferred to ship-building, that one could easily tell the physical conformation of the people of a nation, even before seeing them, if favored with an inspection of its ships. Who would not, for instance, come at a pretty good idea of the style of beauty among the Chinese, after seeing one of their elaborately-constructed junks? The thick and rounded form of a Dutch craft is an unvarying model of the captain's bulky frow at home. The Englishman is heavily built, and slow in his movements; the Frenchman, lighter in mould and more graceful in action. About the same difference may be seen in the form and construction of the vessels of the two nations. The Americans, who are a medium between the English and the French, not so heavy as the former, nor so light as the latter, have maintained the same characteristic in their ship-building. They have combined the peculiar excellences of the two nations most happily, while under the force of an original genius, and an energy imparted by free institutions, they have improved upon all models.

and may now be considered foremost in the march of ship-architecture.

Our ship, although of fine model and graceful finish, was yet of slight build. The timbers were smaller than they would have been in an English or even American vessel of the same size. The captain assured me that she was as strong, having the inferiority in this particular more than made up by superiority of material, and better fastenings. This might be true, yet the imagination has something to do with the comfortable feeling of security on ship-board, and the reflection of the passenger that a single plank separates him from the watery caverns below, is greatly consoled when the eye everywhere meets great solidity and apparent strength. And, unfortunately for the arguments of the captain in the case of our vessel, the frequent dismal sound of the pumps, when she rolled heavily, increasing as the sea increased, with the unharmonious cracking and creaking of the partitions and wainscoting in the cabin, spoke a language not quite so unmistakable, saying to the feelings, at least, that greater solidity would have better resisted the enormous straining to which she was exposed, heavily laden as she was, and surged to and fro by the powerful waves of the heavy ground-swell.

I was forcibly struck with the indifferent manner of working ship, by our sailors. There was not the promptness and celerity of movement, seen on board of an American ship; yet the crew yielded all due respect to the captain's commands. It may with some reason seem strange, that a people naturally so ingenious in design, and dexterous in execution, as are the French, should not excel in a profession calling for quickness of apprehension and facility of adaptation; yet, I think that the inferiority of the French, as sailors, even to the English, Dutch, and Swedes, is generally admitted. They seem to lack the boldness, the physical hardiness, and even nautical skill of those people. It is true that we now have few ships manned fully by American seamen. In our marine, all who are not soon promoted to officers, are so intemperate and quarrelsome, as to render them undesirable for crews; and it is now becoming a pretty general practice, to supply our ships with sailors from the northern nations of Europe, — particularly from Denmark and Sweden. These sailors, naturally rather slow and methodical, when transferred to our ships, have their energies so quickened by the spirit of American enterprise, as to answer even a superior purpose. For, manned with them, our ships invariably make shorter passages with smaller crews, than the French ships of equal tonnage. The fare of the sailor is an item of some note in the bill of the aqueous part of his amphibious life. Cut off from the variety of shore-life, and doomed to a dull routine of duty, eating and drinking constitute about all of his physical comforts and mental recreations. In this respect, as well as many others, the condition of the sailor has become much improved of late years, not only in our own marine, but in that of all other nations. Yet we are still greatly in advance. We give sailors better quarters, better grub, and better pay, than others; and, it may be added, we require them to work a little more vigorously. I observed that the living, with the crew, was much after the American fashion, — three meals a day, and coffee and tea, — except that the bread was of an inferior quality; and that dinner was invariably preceded by soup, — the Frenchman's staff of life. In the cabin, on the contrary, the style was an obsequious imitation of the French, — two meals a day, — breakfast at ten o'clock, A. M., occupying at least one hour; and dinner at five o'clock, P. M., at which we sat not less than one hour and a half, whether the weather was stormy or fine, whether it blew high or low, whether you could sit upright, and swallow your food with some degree of decency, or whether the reeling and lurching of the ship obliged you to hold on with one hand, to retain your position, and to make the other serve the three-fold purpose of steadying your knife and plate, and, in the interval of a lull, steering the scanty and indifferently-prepared food in the channel to the welcome vortex of so many edible things. Claret-wine was freely served as beverage, — taking the place of tea and coffee. This I was never particularly partial to, even in my more wine-drinking days; but, by frequent tasting, and the contagious example of the captain and others, I found such influences to have their usual effect; and, in a little time, I began to quaff with something of the smack of a relish of the thing. We had coffee served at breakfast, after the courses, but very sparingly. I thought it of sufficiently high quality, in all conscience, being so highly concentrated as nearly to overpower my sapient nerves; but the captain, of different gustatory education, would frequently scold the steward for the insipidity of the dish, — when, to supply the deficit, he would add a little strong brandy, or perhaps a slice of butter, or even both at the same time. Tea we never indulged in, except some one who was ill, or had been trying to quicken the sluggish physical man by a dose of medicine. Even then, it was prepared so economically, and sipped so mincingly, that you would have supposed it the rarest and most expensive of exotics.

I must confess that at first it required a little effort to come to like some of the French-prepared articles of diet, such, for instance, as our classic dish of codfish and potatoes, prepared *in olive oil*, and other like departures from American modes of regimen; but taste in matters of food, as well as in the fine arts, is so much a matter of education and habit, that the opinions and ways of those of the society in which we are accidentally cast, soon greatly modify our own; and in a short time, I found little difficulty in conforming, in a degree that astonished myself, to almost whatever was served. Our time at meals was always spent, French-like, very agreeably. The captain was always then in the best of spirits, particularly communicative, striving to draw out conversation from others, and interest all. Our meals thus served to enliven the mind, as well as refresh the body. They were really green spots in our otherwise rather dreary passage, and served to make us better satisfied with ourselves, and more pleased with each other. This feature of French life deserves more than a brief mention. It merits being imitated by Americans on ship-board, who rapidly devour their meals in moody silence, then quickly rush on deck, as if eating was a sad and desperate duty, the quicker done, the sooner over.

The only exception to this, was the captain's stereotyped fault-finding with the steward. This was carried to a point absolutely intolerable to every one, I will venture to say, but himself. The dishes at meals followed each other in course; and as each was brought into the cabin by the steward, it was subjected to a careful inspection by the captain, who was sure to find something wrong,—whereupon would follow a volley of French derogatory expressions; while the culprit, a fine fellow, by the way, quite accustomed to the ordeal, would submit with the utmost calmness, replying respectfully, but occasionally dropping an expression so adroitly, and with so much *sang froid*, to the captain's absurdities, as to make it difficult for us oftentimes to suppress our risibilities.

We had on board three boys, the ship's apprentices. Foreign vessels usually carry more or less of these cabin appendages, according to the tonnage of the ships. They are bound to the captain or ship for a series of years, to be inducted into the mystery of seamanship and navigation. They live in the cabin, and are exempted from some of the drudging of the common sailor, but are more directly under the control of the captain. One can hardly expect to rise to the station of officer, who has not served a regular apprenticeship. Many, however, before their period of service expires, run away to America, where a more propitious field awaits them.

The character and tastes of our apprentices were extremely diverse; and their cases illustrate most strikingly the folly of not duly considering the natural aptitudes of boys, before making choice of their pursuits in life. The youngest, whom I will call François, was a puny stripling; and from constitutional temperament, and gentleness of disposition, as unfitted for the rough career of a sailor, as it would seem possible for one to be. He was, moreover, at times, dreadfully sea-sick, though he had been on board six months. He would then lie around under foot, utterly indifferent whether his head was up or down, or what fate befel him. In these fits of physical and mental prostration, if you had deliberately thrown him into the sea, I verily believe he would have manifested no opposition to the act. Yet, when the sea became smooth, and nature recovered a little, he would manifest a degree of intelligence and spirit, which showed that he was by no means destitute of the elements of success, if the right calling had been chosen for him. As it was, he was incessantly moaning complaints at the wretchedness of his lot, and even calling down imprecations on the heads of those whose mistaken zeal for his welfare, had placed him in his present situation. Joseph, one of the other lads, was quite as averse to a sea-life, as was François, although his dislike arose from different causes. The son of a priest, educated, and accustomed to the refinements of society, there was no congeniality between his cultivated tastes, and the coarse, unintellectual life on ship-board. His mind having been strengthened by discipline, he evinced more fortitude than the other, and was wont to put the best side of things outward. How ever clouded his spirits by tempestuous weather, on the first abate ment of the storm, a gleam of sunshine would arise from his clas tic spirit, even before it appeared in the heavens over our heads We called him our moving barometer; but he was even more than this, — for the captain referred to him all disputed points in literature, with the expectation of a satisfactory explanation; and he more than once, on our passage, cheered our drooping spirits with the exquisite tones which he knew so well how to draw from his favorite violin, and as often amused us with graphic sketches with the pencil, — some of them so supremely droll, as to defy the gravity of the most imperturbable of our company. His hatred nevertheless, to a sailor's life, was so unconquerable, that, with un usual moral integrity, he would, I have no doubt, have run away, had an opportunity offered; and it did seem too great a sacrifice thus to misemploy his fine intellectual powers and rare accomplishments

The third boy, Pierre, or Peter, was just the antipode of the others. He was a true son of Neptune; and was never more happy than when engaged arduously in ship-duties. His consti- tution appeared of iron, resisting alike the effects of heat or cold; and, wet or dry, cold or warm, he was ever the first at his post,— while no murmurings escaped him, however severe the task, or great the privation. Notwithstanding his boldness and undaunted spirit, a smile of goodly nature was ever playing around his coun- tenance; and your every request was promptly and willingly complied with. In the absence of the ship's steward, the captain had assigned the place to Pierre, who, in addition to this, stood his night-watch, and steered his *trick*, and was always up in taking in sail or reefing. He appeared to have no idea of selfishness, and was only satisfied in doing all in his power. Success to his ca- reer! He deserves to be one day a commodore.

CHAPTER VI.

HEAVY WEATHER — THE SAILOR A STRANGER TO FEAR — THE SUBLIMITY OF A DREADFUL GALE — THE ACCURATE RECKONING OF THE CAPTAIN — ONE NOT THE BEST TEACHER OF HIS OWN LANGUAGE — THE INTENSE DESIRE OF GETTING IN AT THE CRUEL SPORT OF FORTUNE — "'TIS SWEET TO BE DROWNED IN ONE'S OWN WATERS" — THE THRILL OF A NARROW ESCAPE — ECSTASY OF THE CREW ON DESCRYING LAND.

THE winds were variable, and the weather so mild in the first of our passage, that I began to conclude that crossing the Northern Atlantic in the winter was not, after all, the dubious affair that I had made up my mind to its being, on leaving New York, — but, after passing a little to the eastward of the Grand Bank, and reaching a more northern latitude than we had been sailing in, the wind set in to blow from the west, veering from that point to the north-west, when we had a succession of gales, so furious and constant, as indeed to speed us quickly across the ocean, but which, at the same time, were near ingulfing us in the fearful surges of the deep. During this time, our brig could bear but little canvas, or none; and she labored so severely from the cross-swell, occasioned by the veering of the wind some three or four points, as to require very frequent and protracted duty at the pumps. Such weather as we experienced is a trying ordeal for a vessel to pass through, when deeply laden with certain kinds of cargo, — such, for instance, as loose grain ; and many a craft, in passing it, has, doubtless, met a sad fate. As for our barque, she behaved most of the time manfully, although she appeared like a tiny bauble, a sport to the fury-lashed waves around. I must confess that, at times, I was somewhat apprehensive, lest an overstrained part might give way, and we all be hastened to the awful depths below us; and imagination, with no direct object of contemplation, easily conjured up phantoms of dread and doubt. Even the captain,— who, to sport with our fears, one day, at the table, jocosely remarked, that our hopes were certainly freighted in a fragile barque, that but a single plank separated us from eternity, and that if but an inch's length of oakum should loosen from a seam, then adieu to the bright scenes of this world, — wore an anxious and thoughtful expression. More even, I thought to detect at times, a lurking of fear in his varying expression. But the sailors evinced not the slightest concern. They attended to their duties with the utmost composure, and when their work was done, hastened below, threw themselves into their berths, and slept as soundly as if in a snug chamber at home.

The sailor, when on ship-board, is a stranger to fear. The most tempestuous weather, such as would overwhelm the mind of a passenger, filling it with the keenest apprehension, he regards as only a natural occurrence, which he does not, if possible, allow even to interrupt his hours of rest. To illustrate how familiarity with scenes of danger gradually removes from the mind the fears with which they are naturally accompanied, I might attempt a faint description of an awful night which we experienced, and such as occur at rare intervals, even in the stormiest sea-going life, furnishing to the traveller who may witness such, vivid reminiscences in his entire after-life.

The wind, which had been steadily increasing for several days, had now (December 16th) reached a degree of force, which it seemed impossible to pass. It actually bellowed and screamed around our hull and through the cordage, as if old Boreas himself was present, goaded to madness by some unseen fury. It would frequently come in irresistible gusts, hurling off the ridge of a wave, and bearing it with electric speed, in the form of spray, far off to leeward. The smallest piece of the foresail possible to be set, just to steady the direction of the vessel, was more sail even than she could well bear; and, under the herculean force of the gale, she reeled, staggered, yet pressed on, with a celerity absolutely thrilling. Under the pressure, the masts seemed straining from their base; and, as she darted off with alarming speed on the ridge of a mountain-wave, the hull would quiver like an aspen-leaf.

The sublimity of the scene presented to our view was in faithful harmony with the terrific grandeur of the occasion. The entire canopy of the sky was deeply overcast. Several degrees from the horizon, quite around us, it was dark and impervious,—but as the eye ascended the vaulted arch of the heavens, the clouds became more transparent, until, at the zenith, the full-orbed moon shed down her placid rays, which, after struggling through the broken, and light fleecy clouds over our heads, were reflected broad around, illumining ocean and sky. The broadly crested waves, in all directions, as far as the eye could reach, was a feature entirely new to me, and they contrasted fearfully with the inky-blackness of the horizon.

Ropes had been drawn diagonally across the quarter-deck, to cling to in a heavy lurch of the brig, or when an unlucky sea should break over. The captain and officers, in storm-sea rig, tarpaulin north-westers tied around the body, and spray dripping from moustache and beard, resembling half-drowned rats, were posted on what resembled the weather-side of the quarter-deck, while I alone had the other. Here we remained during the night, scarcely a word being spoken, except the few necessary to complete the commands. The brig behaved manfully, scudding being her forte; but two or three seas tumbled over on our quarter during the night, threatening to ingulf us. So strained was every part of the vessel, that the water rushed down through the seams of the deck, at other times perfectly tight, to the discomfiture of the boys in the cabin, who sent up their shrieks, feeling, doubtless, that it was the signal of their departure from this world. Occasionally a sea of gigantic proportions would heave up almost directly over our heads, then in a playful, fantastic manner would topple and threaten to bow its briny crest full upon us; but the good brig would some how or other manage to get the audacious monster beneath her, when, pressed in each other's embrace, they would move on together for a moment with intense celerity. The night was one long to be remembered, and the scene fearful and thrilling in the extreme; but fear was not the predominant feeling in my own breast. The sublimity of the occasion elevated the soul above the grovelling emotions of ordinary life, and entranced it in the regions of Nature's splendid domain.

But how did the sailors on board view the matter? They appeared to regard it with little more than ordinary concern. The watch on deck were kept most of the time at the pumps; but as soon as relieved, they tumbled into their berths in the forecastle, and slept soundly until called again. The only complaint they made the next day, when the wind had abated, was, that the deck over their heads leaked so badly during the night, as almost to drown them in their cots.

As we neared the English coast, it was with no reluctance that we parted with the incessant westerly gales, that we had fully experienced in their terrific violence, and came into the variable winds and shifting weather of the coast. The dreary views that we had been so long accustomed to, were now relieved, and our hearts gladdened by the constant appearance of vessels bound to sea. Some of them I recognized as our noble American ships, which, with a white cloud of canvas, were majestically speeding their way to the "land of the brave and the home of the free." Within a few miles of the coast, we spoke an English ship which had left sight of land a few hours before; and, by exchange of reckoning, we found the longitude of the two captains to differ but a few miles. On expressing my surprise at this accuracy, the captain assured me that he rarely came wider of the mark; and I had good reason to credit his statement. Added to good general scholarship, he possessed a thorough knowledge of navigation, and the collateral sciences serviceable to a complete elucidation of all the principles of the noble science. His ample state-room, on board, was liberally provided with nautical instruments, and he evinced a pride even in keeping the most complete and accurate account possible, of the ship's reckoning, by the several methods revealed by modern science.

The captain showed his superior education and taste in nothing more pleasingly than in his choice private library; and he exhibited a knowledge of literature, that would have done honor to a professor of *bellelettres*. He translated English with ease, but was not able, however, to speak a word of it; and his attempts to pronounce were surprisingly awkward, and, at times, supremely ludicrous. He often expressed a high idea of the value of the English language. With a complete knowledge of it and the French, he could travel, he used to say, and be understood the world over

The plan of mutual instruction, by set lessons, was not carried out by us with the same enthusiasm with which it was commenced. Frequent interruptions, occasioned by the duties of his post, and the want of habits of regular application, soon shook the captain's confident resolutions; while myself enjoying just the advantages I most coveted, of continually hearing the spoken language, in its varied phases of tone and accent, and freedom to converse at pleasure, I readily yielded to the example of the captain, of appearing at lesson-hour at first rarely, and, finally, not at all. It was, doubtless, not the first ardently-formed plan, soon neglected. Besides, we found ourselves not so competent teachers of our respective tongues, as we imagined ourselves to be; and I became thoroughly convinced of what I had long believed, that a person is not so successful a teacher of his native dialect, as of a foreign language that he has mastered. The reason is obvious. Having acquired his own language principally by imitation, he understands it little more than practically; and he is surprised at his own ignorance, when asked to explain some of its simplest elementary principles. In learning a foreign language, on the contrary, he necessarily begins at the basis, and learns by general rules, in a short time, much that would otherwise be tedious to acquire, and at great expense of time. Besides, having gone over the precise route himself, he knows by experience the difficulty of the way, — which cannot be apparent to the native, who has reached his haven by quite a different passage. He thus becomes a better pilot in the literary sea. As an illustration in point, of the woful ignorance often existing even among the learned, respecting the simplest elements of our language, the amusing spectacle was exhibited, a few years since, at the "Literary Hill," over which gleams one of our "Twin Stars of the East" of venerable professors, hoary with classical and oriental learning as well as age, actually submitting to the pupilage of a famous Professor Bronson, devoting several hours a day of their hallowed time, to tugging away with most commendable docility and perseverance, and for what, — why, wonderful to say, to learn the powers of the letters of the English alphabet. The ear of the facetious student, at this time, while passing through the halls of the buildings, to his recitation-room, was wont to be greeted with certain explosive groans, produced by the "dorsal and abdominal muscles," reminding him of the awful travail of the spirit, oppressed by the mountain-weight of ancient lore; and striving with desperate energy to discover the neglected paths which lead to the oozing rills whence issue the tiny streams that form the ocean of all science and literature. And if he chanced to stroll through the groves about the "Hill," at almost any moment of the day, his ear was sure to be struck with strange, inhuman sounds, as if the very rocks and vales were vocal, and there were airy tongues on every side. It is unquestionable, I think, that with the exception of pronunciation, a person will not succeed so well in teaching his native tongue, as a foreign language which he has mastered.

Our delightful anticipations of soon reaching land, were now most cruelly sported with, by a period of light head-winds and calms, — so that, at the expiration of several days, the captain informed me that we had not advanced during the time, the distance of two miles towards the end of our route. Such bitter experiences are by no means unfrequent. Indeed, it often occurs, in crossing the Atlantic, as elsewhere in passages, that a ship, after having been most agreeably wafted to within a day's sail or so, of port, and when the most intense gladness pervades every heart on board, with the joyful expectation of soon embracing long-separated loved ones, and of sweetly enjoying the blissful emotions that arise in the breast from all the endearments of home, native country, and friends, that these keen anticipations are suddenly doomed to a most tantalizing and provoking reverse, by a succession of head-winds, calms, or even adverse gales, — sometimes blowing the vessel back half the distance of her course, causing long and dreary days, and even months, to elapse, before actually reaching the eager goal of affection's wishes. There are probably few things in life more trying to the spirit's fond desires, than such disappointments!

While we were thus languidly reclining on the smooth and voluptuous surface of the circular expanse, of which we were the centre, yielding a slight motion to the gentle heaving of its majestic breast, the air became oppressed, and the entire sky gathered up in lowering presages, admonishing us of the certain proximity of a storm. From the dangerous nature of the European coast in this latitude, and its exposure, especially at this season, to sudden and irresistibly violent gales, these dark omens conveyed no very comfortable feeling to my own mind, — although the rest on board seemed too much carried away with joyous anticipations of home, to share my apprehension.

As I had fully expected, the wind, on the 29th, set in from the south, steadily increased in force, accompanied with rain. We continued ploughing steadily our way, under the pressure of a twelve-knot breeze, it being so thick that we were able to see but a short distance. To some casual remark of mine, in respect to the propriety of running for land, under so unfavorable circumstances of seeing it sufficiently far ahead for safety, the captain playfully remarked that, *running* as we were, was indeed dangerous, but then it was "sweet to be drowned in one's own waters." Despairing, however, of making point d'Ouessant, the headland run for usually by French vessels coming from the West; and, determining our precise situation, by means of exchanging signals with an English ship beating out, at 11 A. M. we squared away, and ran directly up the channel. By 8 P. M., the gale was at its height; and it being dark, and dangerous running, the captain very prudently deemed it best to heave the ship to, or, as the French express it, to put the ship *en cape*. But, if it is dangerous running under such circumstances, the channel being commonly thronged with vessels going in every direction, it is no less so, lying to, — the vessel quite unmanageable, and liable to be run into by others. Of this we were made sensible, by a most thrilling incident. The brig had no sooner been placed in her situation to the wind, and everything properly secured, when the watch on deck cast up a most piercing shout, that a sail was bearing down close upon us. We all sprang upon deck, bellowed to the top of our voices; and while the mate, with French celerity, placed the ship's lantern in the rigging, others set up a drumming on barrel-heads, and tin vessels, with whatever they could seize hold of. All this, which transpired in a moment, caused no change in the course of the approaching vessel. She was coming directly for our midships, and was nearing us with awful quickness; but while revolving in my own mind, what I should do for safety in the moment of the expected terrible concussion of the two ships, there was all at once heard a confusion of voices on board of the other, a creaking of yards, in the act of changing the position of the sails, — when her towering prow, dimly defined by the white foam of her forefoot, gleaming through the blackness, gradually turned toward our stern, and, in a moment, she thundered past us, within a stone's toss of our taffrail, a ship of gigantic size. It was a hair-breadth escape, and thrilled my nerves to their very extremities. How often is the sailor called to witness such scenes, when he is suddenly hurled upon the very brink of existence, with the fearful chasm of sudden death yawning full before him!

At one o'clock, the next morning, the wind changed to the northwest, and when we came on deck, at sunrise, we were greeted with a bright sky, and the frosty air from the land. Our men experienced a night of hardship, but they conducted bravely. Several vessels during the day passed us, bound out the channel. At eight o'clock in the evening we were called up to see Guernsey light. As the bright blaze, gleaming over the water, broke upon our vision, it sent a thrill of delight through every heart. For several hours, the most tumultuous joy reigned on board. The boys jumped and capered in wild ecstasy. This was quite natural. It was their first voyage,— six months far away from home. We had just completed a tempestuous passage. The long-anticipated day had arrived. They were soon to tread again the sunny soil of their beloved country, and embrace affectionate friends. It is true that the word *home* is not found in the French language, and that many of the delicious associations which its name calls up in the breast of an American or an Englishman, are unknown to the French; but no people are more enthusiastically attached to their country than the latter,— more proud of its glory, more passionately wedded to its bright scenes and delectable life. Their ardent and impetuous temperament gives liveliness to their expression. It was not surprising, therefore, that our boys appeared a little intemperate in manifesting their emotions.

CHAPTER VII.

LAND UPON THE OLD WORLD — A MOODY FIT OF THE CAPTAIN — SANDWICH ISLANDERS — ELEVATING EFFECTS OF OCEAN SCENERY UPON THE SOUL — SABBATHS AT SEA — SPORTS OF THE CAPTAIN — PIG-BUTCHERY — ARRIVAL OFF HAVRE — ENTERING THE PORT — THE FRENCH WOMAN'S CHARGE FOR BEEF-STEAK — FRENCH MODE OF LIVING — FURNISHED ROOMS — THEIR AGREEABLENESS — THE LAND-LADY'S DAUGHTER — MISTAKE IN GETTING INTO MONS. P.'S SCHOOL — THE PROSPECT FROM THE HEIGHTS OF ANGOUVILLE — THE ENGLISHMAN AND HIS DAUGHTER — MODE OF TEACHING CHILDREN — IMPROVEMENT SUGGESTED FOR AMERICAN MOTHERS.

EARLY the next forenoon we saw in the mellowing distance, Isle d'Aurigny. Land upon the old world! How strong the emotions it awakens! At 3, P. M., Cape de la Hogue was visible, and at 7, P. M., the light of Harfleur became distinct to view. We were now gently rippling through the water with a leading breeze, — our course direct for Havre, which we expected to see in the morning. As I paced the deck, I musingly reviewed the brief stage of life just passed. My passage had been, on the whole, as pleasant and profitable as could reasonably have been expected.

I had been treated with kindness, even indulgence, by all on board. This might have been owing in part to the disposition I cultivated of giving the least possible trouble to others. By conversing freely with those on board, I had learned much of value to me, of their intimate sentiments and mode of thought and feeling. I gained a glimpse of how much can be accomplished by the mind, when nerved by strong determination and resolute energy. In the short space of four weeks, I had nearly completed writing and pronouncing aloud, as a review, the exercises in Ollendorff's French Method, besides reading through a number of French and English books, and gleaning an armful of old numbers of Knickerbocker and English reviews. This, with writing my journal, and several hours a day spent in earnest conversation, I thought quite successful for my poor brain.

The captain was in general reasonably forbearing in disposition; but one evening, at table, he was moody and lowering. He muttered some deep-toned ejaculations, and then mentioned a *dernier* resort, a horrid necessity of using arms; and questioned the boys about their pistols. I then more fully comprehended the meaning of the two bright muskets, standing at the head of the table, and remembered with no feeling of pleasure, that quite a serious mutiny had broken out on board, in their outward passage, and that the captain had encountered difficulty with the commander of a French ship in Boston, and was expecting to be obliged to settle the dispute by the falsely-honorable mode of a duel, on reaching Bordeaux. The meal was swallowed in almost general silence, and when the officers and boys had retired, the captain observed to me, by way of explanation, that the crew had become indolent, and that he feared he should be compelled to make use of his pistols. He seemed aware of no other means of spurring their energies than by such barbarity. The facility with which a Frenchman, Spaniard or Italian glides from the most amiable and placid state of temper to the most intense hate and fury, on the slightest provocation, is a marked feature in their character, and a Yankee in their company, if he desires to give no offence, is obliged to exercise the utmost caution of manner.

ELEVATING EFFECTS OF OCEAN SCENERY.

Two of our crew were natives of the Sandwich Islands. They were very green when they came on board, in New York, having been to sea only in their passage from the Islands, and comprehending not a word of the French language, and but a few sentences of English. Their progress was very marked. Before arriving at Havre, they could understand any order given, perform with facility most of the ordinary duties, and even speak some French. They were quite intelligent, and if a fair specimen of their race, furnish cheering evidence of the capacity of this class to reach an advanced stage of civilization.

Many complain, and with some justice, of the irksomeness of an Atlantic-passage; and yet, to a contemplative mind, the ever varying scenery is full of the deepest interest. The immensity of the ocean, wrapping the extent of the globe; its infinite changes, — at one time a glorious mirror, then, swelling in gentle, undulating waves, rolling their silver volume, and again, in wrathful spleen lifting their angry foreheads to the sky, impress the mind with awe, and elevate it to a larger conception of the Infinite Power, which can hold the waters in the hollow of his hand, and with his breath fan the languid air into the furious tornado. The imagination is busy in fathoming its unknown depths, and in figuring the unseen monsters that lurk beneath its treacherous bosom.

Bright aurora, sending her glittering shafts across the eastern sky; the orb of day springing from his briny couch, and casting a flood of light into illimitable space, careering through the vaulted arch, and then plunging into the sparkling waves; the gorgeous tints of the western sky; the refulgent splendor of the starry night, like angel's eyes in azure robes; the placid beauty of the queen of night, walking with graceful majesty through the heavens, and shedding her silvery light upon the smiling face of the ocean; the fantastic aurora borealis gaily illumining the northern heavens; the water-spout, charged with the colors of the prism, raising itself from the sea like a column of crystal, supporting the canopy of the sky, — each, and all, are infinitely beautiful, and furnish food to the mind and the eye.

But the purest and highest pleasure derived from a sea-passage, to a mind imbued with deep religious feelings, is found in the circumstances which heighten the enjoyment of its Sabbaths. A Sabbath on the ocean, when all around is grand and lovely, may be made a most refreshing season to the spirit. There is something in the situation, and the surrounding scenery, to open the soul to an intimate communion with thoughts of the spiritual world. Man's loneliness, his feebleness, and utter dependence upon a supreme power, is then more forcibly realized; while the boundless expanse which everywhere meets his eye, the immense vault of heaven over his head, and the fathomless deep beneath his feet, are striking emblems, and heighten the idea of the vague and infinite future, towards which he is speeding. What can be really more profitable, as well as spiritually fine, than a silent promenade, on some beautiful Sabbath evening, with a serene sky, propitious breeze, and moon and fleecy clouds overhead? The movement of the ship, darting forward in graceful celerity, quickens the sentiment of existence; while those majestic creations of Nature's handiwork, floating in the azure vault, with an illimitable background of space, seem to elevate his soul, and beckon it to worlds where faith points to infinite happiness. I must say, that to me, the Sabbaths were not the most uninteresting features of our passage. Promenading the deck, and yielding to the inspiring influences spread out all around, in such benificent profusion, or seated in some nook of the brig, studying the Scriptures, the hours came laden with golden treasures. The grand and simple language of the inestimable volume was greatly heightened by the sublimity of surrounding nature, while the blessed thoughts seemed to breathe a purer and holier flame. I was certainly conscious of an awakening influence upon my own mind by the powerful appeals therein made to the wandering and fugitive soul, and of revelations of more intimate and broader views of the true purposes of human life, of the wisdom of Divine Providence, and of the holy attributes of an Eternal Father.

The captain, differently educated, and under the influence of associations quite dissimilar to mine, in respect to the claims of the holy day, chose to while away the time, when the sea was sufficiently calm, in a more amusing manner; but he had the politeness to allow perfect freedom of opinion, never seeking by his manner to annoy me in what must have been considered by him, peculiar habits, nor ever alluding, in the slightest manner, to sentiments which led us to manners so different. One day, he exercised his skill with his rifle, in essaying to shoot upon the wing some sea-birds that had been hovering upon our wake. This, I felt to be a double wrong, being not only a sacrilege upon the holiness of the day, but an inexcusable barbarity, thus to torture the inoffensive creatures which, like winged-messengers of friendship and gladness, had come to soothe and enliven the drear loneliness of our way. On another, he spent the forenoon in testing the trueness of his aim, at pistol-firing, at a target, the distance of the brig's length; and I must confess that, so often did he pierce the centre of the paper aimed at, that I should have felt a little reluctant to be his antagonist in an affair of honor, if I had possessed the slightest repugnance to receiving an inconvenient piece of lead among the delicate machinery of the physical man.

One Sunday, the captain announced that the day would be noted by the death of one of our quadrupeds, and facetiously ob served to me that the mate, who was a true hero in such matters, would be the executioner. The slightest incident in a sea-voyage, becomes a matter of real interest and importance, in arousing excitement. All were soon upon the scene of action. Presently the mate, duly armed with a most fatal looking knife, gleaming in the wintry air, made his appearance. The ill-fated quadruped, as if inspired with a prescience of approaching doom, precipitately fled, and remained ensconced under a part of the long-boat, — and there, with a sullen but plaintive grunt, seemed to beg us to desist from our cruel and unnatural designs upon his life. He resisted successfully for some time the adroitness of the several persons who, by turns, sought to dislodge him from his retreat; but finally Jack, more successful, secured him by the hind legs, and drew him forth, — the little fellow kicking, uttering his piercing shrieks, and pulling back with true piggish pertinacity. It was all of no avail. He was laid upon his back on a table; one boy held fast his extremities; and the mate with one hand held fast his muzzle,— the knife gleamed, the blood spirted up, then flowed gurglingly into a basin held by one of the boys, he quickly stirring it all the time to prevent its coagulating. At the spectacle, I involuntarily turned away, ejaculating an anathema at the barbarity of man, and breathing a sigh of commiseration at the fate of our fellow-voyager. Poor fellow! He was not allowed the humble privilege of squealing in his agonies. After contributing much to amuse us by his antics, during the voyage, he had fallen a victim to man's cupidity and heartlessness. Thus it is with life; those whom we have most befriended, are often the first to aid in our downfall and ruin! As to the butchery, it was done with a dexterity which showed, that in matters relating to the *cuisine*, certainly, the French can challenge competition with the entire world beside.

But to return. The bright morning of the next day (January

1st, revealed to our eager view the port of Havre. Soon, a small boat was seen approaching us, from the harbor, and rowing alongside, the pilot jumped on board of the brig, and nodding to me as he passed along, greeted cordially the captain; when, descending to the cabin together, they were in a moment engaged in earnest and voluble conversation. The basket of news was quite emptied, when a lively discussion of its contents ensued between them, which lasted several hours.

Being a little too late in the tide, we were obliged to reconcile ourselves to a delay, the more irksome, as it was fête-day in the city. I was however offered a passage ashore in the boat, but preferred remaining to finish my letters for home.

We were notified late in the afternoon of the flood, by the departure of the Southampton steamer, when, after a "hasty plate of soup," we squared away for the entrance of the port. In a few minutes we were sweeping gaily along, between the massive granite piers, that stretch far out into the harbor, forming a wide and deep canal, leading into the inner basin. The western pier was covered with people, attracted thither by the pleasures of an evening's promenade. They gazed on us with lively interest, as we sped past them; while on my part, being thus suddenly ushered into the presence of so many human beings, and the novelty of their mien and costume, filled me with pleasurable curiosity. The gates of the noble canal were soon opened, and we passed quickly into the wall-locked harbor, making fast in a magnificent basin in the very heart of the city.

Declining an invitation from the captain to visit some acquaintances of his, in town, I experienced more pleasure in promenading the deck alone, yielding to reflections ushered in by the transitions of the scenes of a day. Later, however, I stepped ashore, and cautiously threading my way through parts imperfectly known to me, soon found myself bending over a Parisian journal in one of the principal Coffee-houses of the city. It being New-year's day the city was better lighted than commonly, and the promenades and café's were unusually thronged. As I passed along, the animating movement of the crowd, the silvery tones of the females, the wild and merry laugh of the children, kindled within me emotions which were greatly heightened by the change from the monotony of a sea-passage, to the full and social amenities of a city.

I was not permitted, the next morning, to remove my luggage from the brig, although the captain exerted his influence for me, as it would have involved some informalities in the custom-house regulations. These government restrictions, so different to an American, from what he ever meets with at home, and so contrary to his idea of civil freedom, are annoying enough to him. But the better policy, as well as the better morality, is to submit to them with the utmost frankness and good humor. Much unpleasant feeling, if not petty trouble, is thus prevented.

The captain took me early to the office of his consignee, who gave me the address of Mr. Stanton, then our consul at Havre. The latter gentleman received me with all due kindness, and had the goodness to loan me late journals from the United States. He made me a certificate of American citizenship, to enable me to procure from the French authorities a passport,—I having inadvertently neglected to procure one in New York, before taking leave. On learning that one principal object of my visiting Europe, was to inspect the schools and educational establishments, he had the politeness to give me a note of introduction to the Principal of the most distinguished private school in the city, of which his son was pupil. At the same time he observed, that the schools in Havre were inferior to the best in the United States.

On leaving the house of the American consul, I met the captain, who kindly offered his services to aid me in finding comfortable rooms. We entered a house of respectable appearance, the landlady of which was an intimate acquaintance of my companion. She took us hastily through her unoccupied rooms, briefly expatiating upon their several peculiar excellences, — but the remainder of the time she was engrossed in the most lively conversation with the captain. As she was naming the price of meals, he ventured to observe that her charge was too much. *Ah, mon Dieu, non, Monsieur* (she replied, with inimitable French exclamation), "the Englishman eats so much beef-steak for dinner." " But," replied the captain, "you are not so dull as to take my friend for an Englishman. He is, you must know, on the contrary, a true-blooded American, — a Yankee from the United States of America." *Eh, bien*, retorted the woman, "it is all the same, Englishman or American, they both like much meat for dinner, and that is very expensive." We left, — I promising to return within a mentioned time, if I decided to take rooms at her house.

The agreeableness of one's stay in a foreign city, as well as his personal comfort in the time, will greatly depend upon the eligibleness of his quarters, and the particular amenities of his hotel. As I could not remove my luggage from the brig till evening, I felt that the interim might not be spent in a more pleasing and instructive way to me, than in choosing my quarters in the city, with the utmost deliberation, — examining things leisurely, with the double view of making a favorable selection in a room, and of casting a scrutinizing glance into this department of French life; and my researches were crowned with curious interest. It will be well here to state, that the French mode of living, in cities, as practised by a large part of the inhabitants, differs widely from that with us, and forms a marked feature in French life. Instead of thronging in boarding-houses, and eating in great haste, at a specified hour, it is a common practice to hire a furnished room, with the services of a domestic to keep it in order, and to brush your clothes and polish your boots, at a moderate price, and to take your meals at the *restaurants, cafés*, or even to have them brought to your room in quantity and of a quality to suit your palate or pecuniary disposition. Not only does the bachelor of small means and retired habits, live in this way; but it is followed even by professional men, by respectable merchants, often by wealthy citizens, and not unfrequently by ladies of character and reputation. This peculiar way of living, compared with our mode, practised by the same class of society, has a forbidding feature, it is true; but it also has its charms. If it lacks the glow and endearment of the fireside circle, it can claim the complacent gratification of luxurious ease and perfect independence. To the traveller, it is certainly most convenient and agreeable. He can thus rise and retire when he pleases, take his meals when his appetite prompts, and where he chances at the time to be, — with the privilege of selecting his dishes, and paying for such only as he orders.

After leaving the brilliant *Rue de Paris*, which extends to the north, quite through the city, I soon perceived the object of which I was in quest. Furnished rooms were seen advertised all around. *A louer* (to let); *chambres à louer* (rooms to let); *une petite chambre garnie à louer* (a small furnished room to let), were so frequent as to remind you of the sign-boards of the most business-thronged part of the city. The rooms were of every variety of size and furnish, adapted to the varying wants of different applicants. I examined each, as I passed along, making the most minute inquiries, and asking all pertinent questions that I could possibly think of. The apartments bore a faithful, but often au humble imitation of furnished lodgings in Paris, to which, in matters of taste, not only the provincial towns, but even the seaports, still look up with obsequious deference. The two prevailing peculiarities in the rooms here, as elsewhere in France, were ampleness of space, and the number and variety of useful and ornamental articles with which they were fastidiously furnished. The size of the rooms varied of course with the price of rent; but even the cheapest possessed a degree of spaciousness that plainly told that, in a practical knowledge of the laws of hygiene, the French are, in this respect, greatly our superiors. They were not only furnished, as often with us, with an empty secretary, a clothes-press, ample means for ablution, etc., but with many other articles either of convenience or mere ornament, such as a mantel-clock, sofa, shower-bath, writing-desk and apparatus, library-case, and mere adornments of mantel-vases, pieces of statuary, pictures, and the more trivial and purely ornamental articles. The floors, either paved with wide, smooth bricks, or blocks of hard wood, set in mosaic, and of highly polished surface, were rarely covered with carpeting, or more than a mere hearth-rug or two. The beds themselves were luxuries. They usually stood in a recess of the room, being of the easy and voluptuous form of a couch, and having curtains not unfrequently of damask or silk, gracefully canopied over them. The mattress, which in France is always of wool, is neater, and, speaking from experience, infinitely more comfortable than either feathers or hair. The *bed-linen* is never of cotton material, and the covering of the pillow is sometimes silk. A French bed-chamber thus possesses an air of grace, luxury, and even oriental splendor, that is quite captivating to the senses. But it must be acknowledged, that a severely simple taste is sometimes shocked at the incongruous medley in the articles of furniture, and the profusion of trinkets used as ornaments. There is sometimes a most ludicrous contrast between the rich, second-hand furniture, magnificent mirrors, and the coarse and homely appearance of the walls and wainscoting, that reminds you of pride in rags. The way to these miniature elysiums, too, is often through a wet and squalid court, up, for several stories, a crooked, narrow, dismal, rough-stone stairway, so dark, as often to require the presence of a light to thread your way along it, even in the day time. Unless you select one of the very few, comparatively speaking, of the rooms that look out upon the street, — as you glance through your window, your eye meets smoky, tiled roofs, roughly cut, and ungraceful angles of buildings, or recesses and narrow alleys, unseemly with accumulated filth; while, if you move from the immediate splendor that surrounds you, your spirits are chilled with the damp, lugubrious, and prison-dreariness that pervades all around. Thus situated, you are quite alone, although there may be scores of human beings half-imprisoned in the same house, separated only by walls. You will see none of the inmates of the same general dwelling, except you accidentally meet in passing to and from your apartment, some one of the indwellers who have to pass through the same general inlet. If a gentleman, he politely makes a passing recognition; or if, perchance, the garrulous maid, with tidy cap and coarse petticoat, or the good-natured male domestic in *blouse*, both clubbing in wooden shoes over the stone steps, cracking their jokes in merry simplicity, they will step aside with deference to let you pass, or with alacrity comply with your demands.

I finally secured a pleasant room, at a reasonable price, of a very agreeable woman; and it may be observed, by the way, that females transact all such business in France. Her only child, a simple-hearted girl, of perhaps fifteen or sixteen years of age, had lately been married to a young man, a little her senior in age, and

VISIT TO A SCHOOL.

greatly her superior in intelligence and style of manners. He gave me with apparent pleasure such information as I desired, and from him I learned that although he honored the family with his company at breakfast, in their narrow tea-parlor, yet he invariably took his dinners at a restaurant, either alone or with some friends. He followed no particular business, but managed to pass as a kind of second-rate gentleman. The good woman, his bride's mother, seemed proud of her son-in-law, and perfectly doated on her daughter. She lived in the most frugal manner imaginable,—thus husbanding her earnings, which were destined, doubtless, to maintain the newly-acquired dignity of her fond and loving daughter. The ancient idea of marriage in France, by which wedlock was entered upon out of motives of ambition, or of personal aggrandizement, or as a mere arrangement of convenience, is not yet quite freed from society.

Having become fairly domiciled, I took an early opportunity, as might be supposed, to visit the school of Monsieur P——, to whom I had a letter of introduction from Mr. Stanton. Accordingly, the next day, at an early hour in the forenoon, I reached the school-building, but by some mistake, strayed into the *cusine* of the establishment, instead of the drawing-room of the principal. My unexpected appearance among some dozen female cooks and laundress-women (for it was a boarding establishment), produced some confusion as well as merriment. On learning my errand, however, one of them, clad in a cap of snowy-whiteness, coarse but tidy petticoat, and wooden shoes, bid me follow her; and, leading the way out of the spacious, plain, but exceedingly neat kitchen, up a broad and clean stairway, ushered me into the reception-room of the establishment. The bell rang, and presently the door opened a little way, and a portly face, beaming with expression, and redolent with health, clad in a small velvet cap.

peeped into the room, and excused himself till four o'clock, saying that he was then engaged with some classes. It was precisely what I wished to see, — the principal teacher instructing his classes, — but before I could find time to reply, he had disappeared. As the day was bright, (something quite rare at this season in Havre,) I decided to make a visit to the Coté d' Ingouville, which is a suburb directly north of the city. It is situated on the steep declivity of a ridge which overlooks the town, and is adorned with beautiful mansions, embowered in shrubbery and surrounded with gardens, which rise in terraces one above the other. At the gate of Ingouville, you have a partial view of the fortifications of the city. They were begun by Louis XII, continued by many succeeding sovereigns, but only completed by Napoleon. They are about three and a half miles in circuit, and consist of bastioned ramparts surrounded by trenches.

The prospect from the heights of Ingouville, if it be a clear day, well repays the somewhat toilsome ascent, by the parallel streets of the village, which run horizontally along the side of the declivity, and communicate by narrow cross-streets. From the elevation upon which you stand, there stretches far away to the north and east, quite beyond sight, an uninterrupted verdant, grassy plain, in appearance, not altogether unlike some humble prairie of the West, in the early mantling of spring. As you turn towards the west and south, your eye falls upon the broad estuary of the Seine, embraced in arms of bold shores, moving its breast towards the stormy North Sea. Below you is the life-throbbing city, with its grand basins, forests of masts, glittering spires, and dingy edifices, surrounded by bastioned walls. A little farther, just across the stream, peers the little village of Honfleur, nestled in harmonious surroundings, while far away to the south-east, sweeps in graceful curves the noble Seine, till perhaps a steamer swiftly gliding upon its gentle bosom. The view is no less extensive than picturesque and lovely.

In descending, I overtook an aged gentleman whom I had the good fortune to enlist at once in conversation. A little way on was his daughter, accompanied by a merry group of children, to whom she was the admired governess. They were improving the lovely afternoon in a stroll, and right heartily did they appear to enjoy the healthful pleasure. They bounded along in a wild excitement of joy, innocently vieing with each other in their attempts to heighten the enjoyment of their devoted teacher. The father, in his wandering loquacity, touched upon the many excellent qualities of his beloved daughter with all a parent's partiality, and recommended her superiority as a teacher, in a manner only pardonable in age. They were French children, and she was their instructor in English. According to my informant, they had enjoyed scarcely no other advantages of learning to speak English, except in their intercourse with their teacher and with each other; and yet in the very short space of time which she had been their governess, they had learned to speak astonishingly well. To convince me of the truth of his assertions, he called to him a little boy of the number, who replied to my questions with such natural expressions, and with a pronunciation and accent so accurate as quite to surprise me, although I was fully aware that very young children will readily learn to speak with idiomatic ease as many languages as they are accustomed to hear spoken around them.

You hear English very commonly spoken in Havre. The large number of Americans and English always in the city, and the immense trade carried on with those people, make some practical knowledge of the language indispensable to the mercantile portion of the French residents, and to such others as have business with those who speak the English. But, besides this, the English language is cultivated by all classes, as a useful and fashionable accomplishment. The remark is applicable, with slight modification, to other cities and large towns in France.

These children whom I met, illustrate the mode pursued generally in France, by the wealthier classes, to give their children a thorough and efficient knowledge of a foreign tongue; and it is based on correct principles of action. Instead of leaving their children to grow to an age when their minds are capable of more severe studies, and then giving them a dictionary and grammar, to learn practical language, they adopt a plan simpler, and more in accordance with nature's teaching,— that of placing their youth at an early age in a situation to hear the language spoken, which they then acquire with the utmost ease, and almost intuitively; and at an advanced age, they are set upon the grammar and philosophy of the language, and attracted to explore the riches of its literature. In this way, the student gets such an apprehension of the language he is studying, as to be of positive utility to him in the practical pursuits of life;— and further, of immense advantage in the harmonious development of his powers, —and so intimate and thorough, as to be a real source of refined pleasure. By the other way, he rarely gains more than a smattering; his knowledge being so cumbersome, as to prove of little use or advantage, ever subjecting its possessor to vexation and chagrin.

The period of childhood and early youth, too, is altogether the most favorable for acquiring a certain part of a language, which can never be learned half so well at a more advanced age, if, indeed, it can then be learned at all. It is at this period that the ear is peculiarly delicate in discriminating sounds, and the vocal organs flexible to execute their form. At this time in life, the faculty of imitation is in active play, and the memory is quick and seizable. Pronunciation of words, accent, idiom, which most stubbornly resist all laws of analogy in language, are mastered so easily and rapidly by the child in habitual intercourse with a correct model, that he is almost unconscious of his acquisition. It has been more a sportive exercise, than a task. Now, it is just this part of a language which the adult finds it most difficult to learn; which, in fact, he never does learn, except in rare instances, with any high degree of success. And what is more, all this is done by the young pupil, when he could not be accomplishing much else in learning, — thus converting comparatively valueless time into golden moments, laden with the rich treasure of future years.

The practice abroad, of employing, at great expense, a governess, as teacher of young children, might with us be very pleasantly improved upon, at least in this branch of education. In the respectably-educated families of New England, certainly, the time of the mother is not, in general, so completely engrossed with the forms of empty etiquette, as to leave absolutely no time for familiar intercourse with her young children. Let but such a mother possess the power of speaking fluently, and with correctness, one or more of the prevailing languages of Europe, which she might as easily have learned from her own parent, and her tender offspring, only from hearing it used in daily intercourse, will glide into its acquisition as naturally, and with as much ease, as it learns its own tongue, or reflects the tone and manners of those by whom it is surrounded. And is not this a consummation to be desired? How much of the learning sagely prescribed in school requisitions, is not really much less practical and useful, in the average lot of life, than a speaking acquaintance with one of the most extensively-used languages of Europe.

The gigantic improvements in the facilities of travel, which are fast bringing the nations of the earth in actual contact, and the spirit of the age kindling a desire for an enlarged intercourse of man with man, together with the rapidly increasing and intimate business relations of the mercantile world, seem to make a knowledge of some of the modern languages quite indispensable to such as venture beyond the narrow circle of village life; and this need is every day fast increasing.

My new acquaintance, to whom I was indebted for several items of information, admitted most fully, that the view from the heights was grand and lovely; but it was not quite equal to that from the Downs in England. This I considered an altogether natural reservation for an Englishman to make, who, whatever beauty he is forced to admit in a superior object abroad, always thinks of something in "Old England," which a little surpasses it. Many of the mansions, he said, were the residences of wealthy English families, attracted thither by the eligibility of the location, or, perhaps, from motives of economy, — but that there was little social intercourse between them and the French, even when circumstances favored such intercourse. It seemed that the inveterate hatred which has from time immemorial existed between the two countries, had sent its roots so deep into the soil of the national mind, as never to be eradicated. He remarked, that the trade at Havre was enormous, and that many merchants had become ruined the past winter, by excessive speculation.

CHAPTER VIII.

RECEPTION BY MONS. P———. — AMERICAN NEWS A SMALL SPACE IN EUROPEAN JOURNALS — NOTRE DAME — MUSEUM — VIRGIN MARY — ORIGIN OF HAVRE — NEW DOCK — AMERICAN SHIPS.

PUNCTUAL at the hour appointed, I was back at the door of Mons. P's school. A waiter at once showed me into his private library, where he was standing in conversation with a gentleman. Without offering me a seat, he drew from his pocket my note of introduction, which I had left in the morning; and, after glancing at its contents, and observing that he did not read English, begged that I would inform him of my desire. To my request of the favor of seeing his school, he replied with an embarrassed air, that as the entire intercourse was in the French language, that I might not well understand everything. To this, I ventured to say, that I should doubtless be amply compensated for any loss that I should have to forego, on account of an imperfect acquaintance with his language; and I observed further, that perhaps the eye would prove an auxiliary. Whereupon he frankly stated, that he had made it an invariable rule, never to admit strangers to witness the recitations of his school. It embarrassed the pupils, and interrupted the exercises; and then commenced a series of bows, so full of meaning, that I found myself unconsciously moving toward the door, where I encountered his professor in English. The latter gentleman passed out with me, appearing chagrined at my reception. As a partial amends for my disappointment, he evinced toward me the kindest manner imaginable, and, on parting, gave me his card, and begged that I would accept of his services while in the city.

This was my first visit to any European school, and I with some reason felt it to be anything but flattering to my hopes of a free and minute inspection of the modes of instruction pursued abroad. As to Mons. P——, he was doubtless governed by ideas which we, reared among free institutions, hardly know. Further, his splendid library, genteel dress, and aristocratic air, all bespoke a flourishing condition of his school; yet I could not quite dispel a lurking suspicion I always entertain in respect to the entire thoroughness of that instruction which is so carefully veiled from public examination. There may be cases, where the school-room door should be closed to all visitors; but in general, I would have even the walls of the room of the transparency of glass, that the passing, every day world may look in upon the miniature empire within.

President Polk's late message to Congress was reviewed by the leading Parisian journals, in a spirit of candor quite different from the tone of the English press, and especially that of the London Times' school of politics. American news, however, occupies but the shortest space imaginable in the European columns.

Havre has not many public edifices of particular interest. Among those deserving of mention are the Tower, of Francis I; a heavy, round edifice of free-stone, built by that monarch, nearly seventy feet in height, and eighty-five in diameter, which guards the entrance of the harbor on one side, and a small battery, mounting six pieces of cannon, on the other. The citadel, constructed by Richelieu, in 1564, comprises the barracks, military arsenal, residence of the governor, etc. Some of the other public buildings are the marine arsenal, new theatre, commenced in 1817, exchange, custom-house, *entrepôt general*, and Royal tobacco manufactory. Among the churches, the principal is *Notre Dame* a singular edifice of the sixteenth century. I entered this church in the midst of a funeral ceremony. The coffin, of narrow dimensions, and of plain, unpainted wood, was covered with a pall of richly embroidered black cloth, and surrounded by a number of burning wax tapers, perhaps six feet in length. In a part of the nave, near the altar, were the choristers and musicians, in solemn and funereal dirge, chanting a requiem to the departed spirit. An ecclesiastic, in sacerdotal robes, conducted the impressive exercise, accompanying the music with the deep and peculiar tones of his voice; and all the time pacing to and fro, before the altar. A number of religious devotees, or friends of the deceased, were promiscuously scattered in different parts of the nave of the church, either in the attitude of sitting or kneeling, and with a manner and expression of the deepest religious veneration. Presently, an officer with the insignia of office, accompanied by a number of boys, perhaps twelve or fifteen years of age, appropriately costumed, escorted some half-dozen ecclesiastics, who passed before the altar, crossed themselves, and then retired. The entire ceremony was by no means wanting in religious awe and impressiveness, though of course destitute of the simplicity of worship which characterizes our protestant forms.

But the main object of interest in Havre, to the lover of art, is the Museum, which stands at the head of one of the principal quays. It is an edifice of considerable architectural merit, dedicated to sculpture, natural history, painting, and literature. The principal hall of the *Rez-de-Chaussée*, or ground-floor, is filled with statues and bass-reliefs. Among them is *The Pedagogue*, and *A son of Niobé*. The galleries, extending quite around the hall, are filled with a respectable collection of specimens in the several departments of natural history. The saloon, or principal hall of the next story, is embellished with paintings. The number is not less than four hundred, and taken together, illustrate the ancient and modern condition of the art, as well as the several schools. Among them, are fine specimens from the immortal pencil of *Reubens, Vandyke, Raphael, Poussin, Gerard Dow, Murillo, Rembrandt* and others, familiar to fame. This important collection had been recently greatly enriched by the munificence of Mr. Stephens, of Paris, who had given a marked proof of his benevolent disposition toward the city of Havre, by placing at its disposal for the museum, a collection of choice paintings. A further trait of noble generosity, which will be appreciated by artists, was his granting permission to this class to make studies from the sublime creations. It is a characteristic of the fine arts, that while they ennoble the mind and refine the heart, they also awaken the desire to share with others the exalted pleasure they afford.

I made notes of the paintings that struck me most favorably; but as I cannot hope that the reader would obtain a very intelligible idea of them, by any description of mine, I must refrain from the attempt. Let me not omit to speak briefly, however, of two or three of these triumphs of human genius. On entering the principal gallery, the eye is at once arrested by a painting of unusual size, by a modern artist, representing Christ driving out of the Temple the Money Changers and Merchandize Venders. The sketching of the piece, denotes boldness of design; and the attitude and expression of the actors represented, are quite natural. It has, moreover, the high coloring of the French modern school, united with admirable finish of detail. *Chastity* is represented as a female of exquisite form, and a countenance of angelic expression. She is gently spurning the approaches of Furio, at the same time pointing to heaven in admonition for aid. The conception of the painter is most successfully embodied upon the canvas. There is another painting in the collection, by a living artist, which goes far to prove to my uncultivated eye, that modern art is by no means waning. It is a representation of the Virgin Mary, with the Infant Christ sleeping in her arms. As you stand gazing in mute rapture upon the lovely forms before you, you unconsciously bend forward, almost in expectation of hearing the gentle and delicious breathing of the heavenly child, so perfectly life-like is it delineated; while the soft and tender lustre of the slightly upturned eye of the mother, so full of Divine hope and pious resignation, but lends irresistible effect to the angelic expression of her face. The painting possesses points of excellence, that I did not find surpassed in the collection; and I felt almost to worship the genius that could transform to the living canvas, conceptions so beautiful and heaven-like.

In an adjoining room is a collection of manuscripts, and also the Madeline, by Gayrard, in marble. In another, is the Library, which has twenty-two thousand volumes. It is open to the public nearly every day in the week,—and not only warmed, lighted, furnished with table, seats, writing materials, but there is always in attendance a courteous librarian, who promptly provides you with whatever book in the room you may call for, and seems almost to be able to anticipate your desires. This is entirely free, as they are elsewhere in France; and illustrates the noble care of the government of the claims of literature upon the community at large. Among other busts, are those of Voltaire and Rousseau, in the archivault of the gallery. The French mind universally, as well as that of the entire continent, bows with lowly reverence to the almost omnipotent sway of these powerful but singular departed spirits. They were to French literature, what Napoleon was to its military glory; and neither the one nor the other can be spoken of before a Frenchman, without exciting in his breast the most burning enthusiasm.

The origin of Havre is quite obscure, it having been for some time an unimportant fishing-town. The present site was successively occupied by the Gauls, the Celts, and the Romans; but the Northmen were the first people to whom the present city is indebted; and Francis the First has the honor of being its founder. One of these bold invaders, Rollo by name, the Dane, as he was called, though a native of Norway, and chieftain by birth, being of a wild and adventurous disposition, and having with his followers committed many piracies and robberies, were at length expelled the country by the king. They took refuge on some of the islands that form gloomy and mountainous groups on the western coast of Scotland, which have been, in many different periods of the world, the refuge of fugitives and outlaws. Thence they made several fruitless attempts to land upon the English shores, but were everywhere repulsed. This was in the time of Alfred the Great. They afterwards made a descent upon Flanders, defeated Hainault, its king, and compelled the countess his wife, to raise and pay an immense sum for his ransom. Coasting upon the north-western shores of France, after many attempts to land, which proved unsuccessful from the nature of that part of the French coast, they at length effected an entrance of the river Seine, and sailed up the river as far as Rouen. The haven at the mouth of the river being on the whole the best and most commodious on the coast, was called *the* harbor, or as the French expressed it in their language, *le Havre*, the word *havre*, meaning harbor. In fact, the name was in full *le havre de grace*, as if the Northmen, or Normans, considered it a matter of especial good luck to have even such a chance of a harbor as this at the mouth of their river.

Havre, from the circumstances of its situation, is necessarily a great commercial emporium of France. It is the only respectable harbor on this part of the French coast. The river-mouths, and natural indentations along the perpendicular ranges of cliffs that form the coast, which might form harbors, are so exposed to the generally prevailing north-west winds, driving such a continual swell of rolling surges in upon the shore, as to choke up all the estuary openings with shoals and bars of sand and shingle. It is the seaport of Paris; and, in regard to its importance, is to France, what Liverpool is to England. Indeed, it was a remark of Napoleon, that "Paris, Rouen, and Havre, form only a single city, of which the Seine is the great street." In the year 1836, Havre received seven-tenths of the cotton imported into France, more than half of the tobacco and wood for cabinet-work, half the potash and indigo, more than two-fifths of the rice and dye-woods, and more than one-third part of the sugar and coffee. It is built on a low, alluvial tract of ground, formerly covered by the sea, and is divided into two unequal parts, by its outer ports and basins, which stretch into the town, and insulate the quarter of St. Francis. There are nine quays, which, with the high street, form the favorite promenades. It has numerous public fountains, and is well supplied with water, conveyed by pipes from the vicinity. The port consists of three basins, separated from each other, and from the outer port, by four locks, and capable of accommodating about four hundred and fifty ships. These accommodations being inadequate to the growing importance of its trade, in 1839, the French government demanded six millions of francs for its augmentation and improvement. The entrance being too narrow to admit the passage of large steamers, they were formerly obliged to remain in the outer port, imperfectly sheltered from high winds; but a new basin is being constructed on the south-east, near the entrance.

It is to be spacious, and of splendid construction. I was told that it would be completed in three years longer, — it having already been in progress two years. A large body of water being retained by a sluice, and discharged at ebb tide, clears the entrance of the harbor, and prevents accumulation of filth. The rise of the tide is from twenty-two to twenty-seven feet; and by taking advantage of it, the largest class of merchantmen enter the port. The water in the harbor does not begin perceptibly to subside, till about three hours after high water, — a peculiarity ascribed to the current down the Seine, across the entrance of the harbor, being sufficiently powerful to dam up for a while the water in the latter. Large fleets taking advantage of this circumstance, are able to leave the port in a single day, and get to sea, even though the wind should be unfavorable. The pier which forms the western entrance of the harbor, is about fourteen hundred feet in length, to the Tower, and extends into the ocean about three hundred and fifty feet. It affords a most delightful and romantic promenade, and is much frequented as such, by all classes. The principal part of the numerous shipping in port, were large American ships, which brought hither cotton, and were to take emigrant passengers chiefly to the United States, in return, and colliers from England. The week in Havre was improved most agreeably by me, — my curiosity and interest not flagging for a moment, although I had before passed a winter there, and was in consequence quite familiar with its general *physique*.

CHAPTER IX.

HONESTY OF THE FRENCH TO TRAVELLERS — LEAVING THE CITY — SCENERY THROUGH NORMANDY — PICTURESQUE COSTUME OF THE FARMERS — THE SANG-FROID OF A FRENCH WOMAN — HISTORICAL RECOLLECTIONS — ARRIVAL IN ROUEN — KINDNESS OF LANDLORD AND LADY — MARKET-WOMEN UNDER MY WINDOW — GRANDEUR OF ROUEN CATHEDRAL — RICHNESS OF INTERIOR — ROLLO, THE NORMAN — CHURCH OF ST. OWEN — STATUE OF VOLTAIRE — PALAIS DE JUSTICE — MAID OF ORLEANS — VIEW FROM THE COTE DE ST. CATHERINE — AN HISTORICAL MENTAL PICTURE — THE ANCIENT PORT OF THE CITY — SUPPER — VIEW OF THE CITY.

ON Friday, the 7th, at 2 o'clock, P. M., I left for Rouen. A slight incident occurred in the omnibus on the way to the depôt, which illustrates the perfectly honest disposition of the French people, and the honorable treatment shown to strangers, by the agents and attendants on the travelling routes. On paying my fare to Rouen, at the office in Havre, I had also paid it to the depôt, in the omnibus. This latter, it seemed, was not generally done, — the omnibus line being in the hands of another company. Before reaching the depôt, the attendant came round and took the fare from the passengers, and I paid with the rest. In a moment after, I bethought myself that I had thus paid the same fare twice, and stated the fact to the gentleman sitting near me, and to the attendant. The latter at first looked a little incredulous, but in a moment promptly refunded me the price of fare, while all in the carriage looked and spoke as if they expected he would do so as a matter of course.

The train of cars comprise three classes. In the first, or superior, travel the aristocracy and the wealthy; the second class of cars is filled with the middling and respectable sort of people; while the third is thronged with the peasantry and those of the poorest condition of society. The first, and second class of cars, which differ from each other in little more than name and rate of charge, are separate carriages of neat construction, and fitted up interiorly in a comfortable manner. The distance from Havre to Rouen is fifty-five miles, and the fare in the different grades of cars, respectively, is ten francs, seven francs and fifty centimes, and five francs. A slight additional charge is made for your luggage; and the company hold themselves responsible for its loss within a limited value.

The utmost precaution is taken by the several officers of the lines, to prevent mistakes; and the arrangements to avoid embarrassments in passing to seats, in the carriages, are admirable. There is seen but little of the confused and hurried movement, so often witnessed among us, in scrambling for seats in the cars, when the bell rings, although we are wont to associate with the French physical man a tendency to impulsive movement.

As we sped from out of the dense and gloomy walls of the city so suddenly into the smiling suburbs, — gladdened by the pleasing aspects of rural life, I was filled with rapturous emotions Doubtless, the dreary mantle of Nature's drapery which had now for several weeks enshrouded my mind, being thus suddenly removed, had a positive influence in the effect which the grateful scenery produced; but there was something so unusual in winter-scenery in the pervading verdure, enamelling the gardens and pastures, as to create a most pleasing surprise ; while the picturesque combination of narrow walks fenced with shrubbery, broad and majestic avenues lined with hoary elms, variegated plots of ground fastidiously arranged, and highly cultivated, and beautiful villas and mansions mellowed by time, with now and then a church-spire, moss-grown, peeping above the surrounding trees, were well calculated to inspire the mind with delightful emotions. I must say that the associations the scenery called up were mixed with the romantic, and my mind naturally reverted to the sylvan scenes so often the staple of the poet's imagination.

It is a common observation, that the track of a rail-road does not, in general, lay through the most interesting part of a country ; but the remark I imagine is more applicable to new countries like our own, than to those like France, in which nearly all the land is under a high state of cultivation. Travellers, too, differ in their admiration of the scenery in France, some extolling its beauties in broad terms, while others see in any part of the country little to be praised. Speaking for myself, from the few glimpses caught through the windows of my carriage, in a ride from Havre to Paris, and through a few other sections, less pleasing, I must acknowledge its claims most decidedly to the beautiful, as it impressed my own mind. To be sure its beauty is of a specific kind, but none the less real, for all that. If it does not affect the mind in precisely the same manner as do the roughly embosomed lakes of Scotland, the precipitous and wild mountain-views, which flank portions of the Rhine, or the more sublime and dizzy peaks of the grandly awful ridges of Switzerland, it must not, on that account, be considered destitute of the necessary elements agreeably to move and elevate the mind of the true lover of Nature. It has its phase of beauty, which, regarded from its legitimate point of view, possesses high capabilities. Its predominating characteristic, as it struck my mind, is that of placid loveliness, combined with the classic symmetry of the French character, heightened by the mellowing hand of time.

What constitutes a peculiar and pleasing feature in the landscape is, that the land is not enclosed. With the exception of an occasional graceful lattice partition a few inches high, to mark the separation of the lots, there were neither hedges, fences, nor walls, to break the continuity of the scene,— but vast tracts were spread out in every direction. These were divided into plots and squares of various forms and sizes, by the varieties of cultivation. The whole resembled an extensive garden but lately escaped from the shears and roller, displaying a vast carpet of an irregular tessellated pattern, variegated by numberless hues of brown and green. Occasionally, vast forests meet the eye, filled with trees of venerable age, and mathematically arranged. They were the royal demesnes, and hunting-grounds and parks connected with the country palaces of the kings, or, perhaps, the chateaux of the ancient nobility. Rarely is a habitation seen, except an occasional chateau, — the farmers residing in the compact villages, whence they issue every morning to go miles, perhaps, to their daily toil. The roads, which cross these lonely scenes, smiling with the appearance of fertility, are broad and straight avenues, bounded by majestic trees, between which, may be seen both before and behind, an interminable vista.

At one of the way-stations, we received a small accession to our party. It was two neatly dressed and agreeable young women, in style belonging to the better class of French peasantry. At once, and without ceremony, they entered into lively and quite intelligent conversation with any one in the carriage who chose to reciprocate their social favors. Yet there was nothing in their manner that could displease in the slightest, even the most fastidious taste. Although evidently belonging to the humbler class in society, yet there was a natural grace, and even delicacy, in their address and manners, so inimitable, as to make you forget what you might have learned simply of the etiquette of politeness. In a few moments one of them evinced symptoms of illness, whereupon the other requested that the gentleman, by me, would have the goodness to seat himself near and opposite the swooning woman to hold in his, her convulsed hand. The fit lasted a few minutes, when, coming out of it, she engaged in promiscuous conversation, as if nothing had happened, appearing as animated as before, abating an unpleasant dullness of the eye. This, I thought, was treating the ills of life as trifles, indeed.

The historical associations which crowd upon one in passing through Normandy, lend a thrilling interest to its scenery. Every height has its legend and story. The Romans, to whom it was known before the time of Julius Cesar, and by whom it was afterwards conquered, have left here the traces of their powerful domain. In the fifth century it became the prey of the Germanic nations, who, pouring from their Scandinavian hive, like a relentless torrent, tracked their course in blood through the fairest regions of Europe. This portion was especially subjected to the ravages of these maritime freebooters. In the indolent reign of Charles the Bald, who vainly relied on the efficacy of gold, rather than on that of the sword, to oppose their progress, erroneously believing that by gratifying avarice, he could purchase its absti nence, these indomitable semi-barbarians penetrated into the very heart of the country. At length, in 912, the Norwegian Rollo, or Raoul, ascended the Seine, and obtained from Charles the Simple, cession of the whole of maritime Neustria and the hand of Gisla, his daughter, in marriage. Rollo subsequently received Christian baptism in the cathedral of Rouen, and became the first duke of

Normandy. It was annexed to England when William, duke of Normandy, obtained the English throne, in 1066, and subsequently became the battle-ground of France and England. It is not surprising then, that the traveller goes through this beautiful part of France with a feeling of enthusiasm.

At length the cars stopped; and the bustling among the passengers told, plainly, that we had reached the ancient and curious city. The passage occupied two and a half hours, and the rate of travel averaged twenty-two miles to the hour, including several way-stoppages. As it was evening before we arrived, I missed the unique and pleasing views which break upon the eye of the traveller, as he enters this renowned place. On leaving the cars, I was at once surrounded by porters, soliciting my baggage to take to any hotel I might name. One, a lad, followed me some distance, and entreated with so much persistence that I finally yielded my valise, more as a reward to his perseverance than from any need I actually felt for his services. After threading our way some distance through the narrow, crooked, and imperfectly lighted streets, we entered a broad square, then passed through a gateway in a high stone wall, crossed a narrow court, which brought us to the *hôtel du Havre, Place du Marche, Neuf. No. 21*. The landlord, a large man of lofty but courteous bearing, received us with apparent pleasure. With a single word, uttered in an under tone, he dismissed the porter, which I endorsed, by handing him ten sous for his service to me. I was at once shown the different rooms in the house, not occupied,— the landlady, a most voluble and amiable soul, and so insignificant in appearance as to be taken sooner for one of the domestics of the establishment than for the lady of the hotel, leading the way and only stopping to exhibit the distinctive claims of the several apartments, which she did with all the ingenuity peculiar to a French woman. Indeed, in each room that we entered, she favored me with a brief dissertation of its merits, but in so measured terms as to convey the idea of its being a recitation, rather than an original essay. I engaged an unpretending room at thirty sous per day, without fire or attendance. The meal I had ordered, consisting of tea, bread and butter, and omelet, was now ready. It proved most excellent in quality and preparation, and I despatched it with a zest sharpened by the fatigues of the day. The remainder of the evening was spent by me most agreeably, in the society of the gracious landlord, and his sweet-toned, chatting wife, who, with the greatest good-nature and kindness imaginable, opened to me their private boudoir, and gratified my eager curiosity in recounting startling events preserved in the legendary annals of that portion of the country. He, swelling with ancestral pride, related many a daring deed of some chivalrous Norman knight; while she, more superstitious, dwelt upon some strange and blood-curdling event, wrested from the mysteries of the dark age of the past. They also gave me a verbal sketch of the noted objects and places, in the city and its environs, worthy of a special visit, — thus condescending to become for me a very agreeable and convenient guide-book. Their thrilling and captivating narrations so haunted my imagination during the night, that I turned ever and anon on my pillow, awaiting, with impatient desire, the first glimmering of the dawn that was to reveal to view so many venerable relics of a wild and heroic age. Even before daylight, my ears were saluted by the clattering of wooden shoes over the rough pavement under the window of my room, and the confused commingling of garrulous and shrill tones of the human voice; and the first view that my eye embraced was the square, filled with market-women, in their picturesque costumes, each at her stall in the open air, supplying the thronged customers with the essential elements of the day's dinner.

There are many memorials of antiquity in Rouen, all of deep interest to the intelligent traveller; but among them, the Cathedral stands preëminent. This celebrated edifice is, by general admission, one of the noblest religious structures in France, or even in Europe. Of the wonderful architecture of the vast pile, I shall hardly attempt a description; for, although some idea may be formed of its magnificent proportions, by a verbal account, yet the grandeur and awe with which it strikes the mind of the beholder, can never be conveyed by words.

We stand before the immense mass! The mind at first is almost overwhelmed with its vastness, its grandeur, its inexplicable power. The breadth is one hundred and three feet, while its length is no less than four hundred and thirty-four feet. Its elaborate and richly-ornamented front, has three fine portals, over the central of which is a square tower, and a beautiful spire of ironwork, reaching to the dizzy height of four hundred and sixty-four feet eight inches, only thirty-eight feet less than that of the pyramid of Cheops. This is flanked by two lofty but dissimilar towers. One of these towers, being older even than the remainder of the building itself, is in a simple and unadorned style; but the other, built at the end of the fifteenth century, is justly admired for the beauty of its architecture. As you gaze upon the complicated pile, amid the mazes of its inextricable details, your eye is lost among niches, corners, points, and pinnacles, ornamented with images of apostles, saints, or, more frequently than either, of the Virgin and Child. These, however, are no unmeaning ornaments, but they served as a volume of religious history, conveying to the unlettered masses, real facts of Scripture history, and fixed them in the minds of the people with a vividness and reality that could not have been secured so well in any other way.

We will enter the gloomy Gothic structure. Our sensations admit of no description. It is not the religious sentiment which seizes the mind, only so far as that feeling is always inspired by the works of genius; but an indefinite and almost supernatural awe. The vast space, the silence that reigns within, the grandness of the architecture, the solemnity of the monuments, the impressive power of the pictures, and the effect of all these objects immensely heightened by the light which comes streaming in from one hundred and thirty windows, the glass being stained with every shade of color, from fiery red to the soft tints fading into white, until nave, and choir, and aisles, seem magically illuminated; while they elevate the soul, — fill it with vague and profound impressions. Indeed, you leave the church, for the first time, with an oppressive feeling. The idea was too vast and complex to be received into the mind at once. We reach the sublime but by degrees; and it is only after a number of visits, and indefatigable studies, that the soul is expanded to anything like a just comprehension of the vast and magnificent proportions of the wonderful edifice. Its contemplation awakens a new sphere of ideas. Its immense vaults within, enlarge the thoughts of man, — while the sublime works of genius around, lend to it a spiritual glow and fervency,—and the summit, losing itself in the air, seems to bear the bright image of the soul direct to heaven.

The interior is truly rich in monuments, although many of these sombre relics have been much mutilated by the numerous religious and revolutionary wars which have from time to time distracted the country. You see there the tomb of Richard I. (Cœur de Lion), many dukes of Normandy, and seventeen archbishops of Rouen; also, the fine mausoleum of the two cardinals d'Ambrose. There, too, lay the form of Rollo, stretched out on his magnificent tomb; and, as I gazed on the mouldering urn, containing the last ashes of the stern chieftain, I could not but recall many a striking incident in his life, indicative of his indomitable spirit. It was in this very church, if I remember rightly, that was performed the ceremony of the nuptials of Rollo with Gisla, the daughter of Charles the Simple. Here, too, took place the ceremony of his profession of Christianity, and of feudal homage to the king. In regard to the renunciation of his own faith, in favor of that of the Christian religion, history informs us, that little difficulty was made either by the rude warrior, or by his ignorant followers; for the dark mythology of Scandinavia does not, on any occasion, appear to have entwined itself with much strength around the affections of its votaries; but when, upon formal investiture with the duchy, he was instructed by the attendant prelates to kiss the feet of his liege lord, the indignant spirit of the veteran revolted from so humiliating a testimony of subjection; "Never, by God," exclaimed he, "will I bend my knees to, or kiss the feet of, a brother man!"

The church of St. Owen, is another of the interesting religious edifices of Rouen, and belonged to the oldest conventional establishment in Normandy. It is situated in the *Palais Royal*, and occupies a larger extent of ground even than the Cathedral. It is a most admirable specimen of the pointed Gothic, — its fine octagonal tower, rising from the centre of the building, is two hundred and fifty-five feet in height. There are several other churches in Rouen, well deserving of notice, and some of them of high antiquity.

The Town Hall, adjoining the Church of St. Owen, was originally a portion of the conventional edifice. It is now appropriated to various public offices, and contains the museum and public library. In the latter, which consists of 80,000 volumes, and about 12.000 manuscripts, I was shown several objects, which, from the associations connected with them, possessed peculiar interest to me. Preserved in a neat mahogany case, are the keys of the city which had been presented to Napoleon. This is only one of the numerous evidences which the traveller is constantly meeting with in France, of the almost perfect adoration in which the great captain is held by the entire nation.

Several of the manuscripts are very old, and are musty with the damp of years. I was shown more than one, said to have been from Voltaire, one of the master spirits of modern literature. As I turned over the leaves, I could hardly realize that the lines before me were traced by the pen of a genius so powerful as to have moved to its centre the entire world of thought and opinion. A little further on, is a bronze statue of Voltaire. I was told that it was an uncommonly faithful likeness. I must confess that, at the first glance, I was filled with disappointment and chagrin. It was some time before I could reconcile the apparently insignificant figure before me, with the splendidly grand beau ideal image which my imagination had pictured to my conception. A few moments' reflection, however, and a more careful study of the face, rectified measurably my first illusion. The countenance was remarkably expressive,—and, in the angulation of the muscles, bore indisputable marks of that steadiness and intenseness of thought, which is a condition of clearness of conception and acuteness of discrimination, qualities rare, of great excellence, and withal so prominent in the style of the eminent writer. He was sitting in an armed chair, the body slightly inclined forward, in an easy position, and the hands holding firmly the sides. The impression which I carried away, was not altogether pleasing, though it was distinct and profound; and has haunted my imagination at times ever since. The statue was rather below the medium height, I should judge; the body lean even to gauntness, while the sharp, prominent atures, skinny hands, impending eye-brows, and deep, hollow eye-sockets, gave a cadaverous aspect almost shuddering to the feelings. There was, besides, a mysterious air enveloping the whole face, impossible to be satisfactorily revealed. But the most distinct feature in the character of the remarkable physiognomy, was a certain facetious, exulting expression, such as I have not elsewhere seen, and resembling what we may well suppose to have been the look of his Satanic majesty, when contemplating the successful consummation of his foul plot, hopelessly to ruin our first parents, and through them the whole human race. Had Voltaire produced but one work, and that the one he entitled *Candide*, there would have been an exact resemblance between his expressed thoughts, and the most marked point in his expressive face.

A few other objects of note shown me, were, a miniature church, very elaborate and curious in workmanship; a bronze statue of the Chinese emperor, surrounded with his mandarins, in very natural attitude; and one of Napoleon's eagles, bearing this inscription: *Force à la loi, et fidelité à l'empereur*, which may be rendered, strength to the law, and fidelity to the emperor. The museum has been open to the public, since the fourth of July, 1809. The pictures number three hundred, and many of them are very striking. I noted, among others, *A Descent from the Cross, A Scene of Carnage between the Romans and Jews, Portraits of the Sacred Writers, A Fishing Smack, Christ and the Woman at the Well, The Death of Abel*, and a pilgrim in a state of religious ecstasy. There was also a most exquisitely beautiful statue of a Madeline, in marble. From the library, I went to the *Palais de Justice*. This magnificent Gothic palace was built for the parliament of Normandy, at the end of the fifteenth century. *La Salle de Procureurs*, or Hall of Attornies, is a noble saloon, whose dimensions and proportions are striking beyond anything I had before seen, or have witnessed since. It is seventy feet from the pavement, and is unsupported by a single column. The acute arched ceiling springs over your head, like the expanse of the sky.

In crossing the square of *La Pucelle*, I stopped a moment to regard an indifferent statue of the famous Joan d'Arc, or Maid of Orleans, erected on the spot where that remarkable heroine suffered martyrdom in 1431. There is little in the statue to admire as a work of art; but the feelings it awakens, and the reflections it gives rise to, are sufficiently absorbing, to arrest the step of the historic traveller. This remarkable woman was born of obscure parentage, and spent the early portion of her life in serving in a menial capacity, deprived of the advantages of education, and those favorable circumstances which are deemed essential to confer distinction or eminence. But these obstacles did not hinder her from rising to a sphere of influence, hardly equalled in the annals of history, and of handing down her name encircled with a halo of light, to future time. Possessing genius of a high order, her soul panted for something above the lot Providence had assigned her; and her great benevolence naturally led her to look for some way in which she could be useful to her people. This soon appeared. France had been invaded by the English, and the affairs of the French king had become reduced to the greatest extremity. To rid the country of the hated English, would confer the greatest of blessings on her nation, and render her name illustrious in all forthcoming time. Possessing a powerful imagination, united with deep religious fervor, mixed with the superstition of the times, she revolved upon the thought, until she imagined seeing in a vision, St. Michæl, the tutelary Saint of France, who ordered her to raise the siege of Orleans, which the English were then besieging, and to preside at the coronation of Charles VII, at Rheims. Placing herself at the head of the French army, she infused so much ardor and enthusiasm into the French soldiers.

that the English were defeated, the siege raised, and the Fr no. king crowned, just as foretold. She was, however, subsequently wounded at the siege of Paris, and taken prisoner at Compiegne. Instead of treating her honorably as a captive, the English fixed an indelible stigma upon their character, by treating her harshly, and causing her to be burnt at the stake. Her simple manners, purity of sentiment, and the courage and intrepidity with which she walked to the fatal stake, have rendered her name a favorite in the galaxy of female stars of the first magnitude. But while the French regard her as the saint of France, the English, in the spirit of their deep-rooted animosity to the French nation, have characterized her as a sorceress, a *giglot wench*. Even the genius of Shakspeare forsakes him on this occasion, when he represents her in an odious light, entirely disproved by history.

The *Coté de St. Catherine* is a steep declivity of considerable elevation, overlooking the city on the east. I reached the summit by a circuitous route, after no little toil over the steep road rendered slippery by the recent rains. But on reaching the height, I was amply repaid for all my fatigue, by the fine view spread out before me. The city, comprising 100,000 inhabitants, with its angular and dingy roofs, and its numerous lofty spires and towers, piercing the murky cloud that partially enveloped it, lay below me. The verdant and delightful country by which it is surrounded, adds to the pleasing aspect. The Seine, by which it communicates with the Capital on the one hand, and with the flourishing seaport of Havre on the other, is here crossed by a bridge of boats and one of stone, and divides it from its large suburb of St. Sevier. The boulevards which are planted with trees like those of Paris, and the fine broad quays and *cours*, which extend along the banks of the river, are in striking contrast with the narrow, crooked streets of the old city.

As I stood gazing on the scene before me, I could not help falling into a musing mood. The wave of history was rolled back, and the mind, quickened by the influence of local association, and sped on by the power of memory, ran rapidly through the events of the past, vividly picturing to the mental eye, the renowned exploits of a chivalrous age. I could almost fancy to see drawn out in martial array before me, on some plain, those stern Norman knights, who were the terror even of the kings of France, heavily mounted on war chargers, and clad in steel armour; and either meditating some expedition of blood, or recreating in the desperate feats of chivalry for the amusement of the softer sex. The Normans are proud of their descent, and are ever recounting some striking feat of their ancestors; and well they may pride themselves on tracing their origin to those powerful barons who waged war successfully with France, and held even England in subjection, for so many centuries.

I reached the foot of the hill on the west side, opposite to where I made the ascent, with quite as much difficulty, sometimes sliding, at others, involuntarily running, — and often apprehensive of losing my equilibrium, so steep was the descent, and slippery and difficult the way.

Returning to my hotel through the most ancient part of the city, afforded an interesting view of what renders Rouen a most delightful resort to the lovers of the antique and curious. The streets were narrow, crooked, and without side-walks; the pavement of square stones declining to the middle of the street, from the houses, on either side. Of the quaint old houses which lined the sides of the streets, an American reader can hardly form a conception. Their strong oaken frames are filled in with cement or brick; their narrow fronts, and high-peaked roofs, covered with slates or tiles, while many of their angles so jut over the street as to obscure the sun's rays except at noon-day. Scarcely any two houses are alike, and as for *blocks* of houses, such as we see in our cities, there is no such thing to be found. The garniture of the shops, and the costume and manners of the people who reside in this quarter, are quite in keeping with the oddness of other general features, and render the whole a rare picture by itself. Indeed, you would almost fancy that the entire quarter had been recently dug up, as some ancient Herculaneum, where it had been smothering under the ashes of oblivion for ages. Most travellers go direct to Paris from England by another way, and thus miss seeing, next to Paris, probably the most interesting city in France, if not in Europe.

Outside of the boulevards, the appearance of the buildings is quite different. The streets are wider, straighter, and you often see handsome houses, built of the soft cream-colored stone, that abounds everywhere in France. The old and new quarters present a heightened contrast, for which you are indebted to the increase of population and wealth of the place of late, owing to the concentration of trade at Havre, the introduction of steamboats upon the Seine, and the fine rail-road which has recently been completed, connecting Paris, Rouen and Havre, as commercial cities.

Dined at 5 P. M., the usual hour in France, at the *Table d'hote*, — the landlord doing the honors of the table in a dignified and affable manner. The course was frugal, consisting only of soup, fish, and three kinds of meat, with dessert. The dishes were, however, exceedingly nice, and the whole greatly enlivened by the grace, vivacity, and intelligent conversation of a small number of French gentlemen, who formed part of the company. They at once drew me out in conversation, interested themselves in the object of my tour, — taking much pains to give me all the information in their power that could be of possible service to me. They even praised my French. This, however, I took as an act of *excessive* politeness on their part. I may be allowed to remark, however, that the French never laugh at your mistakes, unless, indeed, they are, what needs sometimes happen, uncontrollably droll. They rather assure you, anticipate your meaning, and, in a most delicate manner, set you right. In this respect, at least, we may take, with advantage, a lesson from this people. One of the gentlemen had an uncle in New York; the landlord had been in England, and spoke English; another gentleman intended soon to travel in America,— so that these circumstances brought out, only increased the interest of conversation, bound us closer in the bonds of social friendship, and it was only till after a late hour that we parted, after exchanging cards.

Rouen has an imposing external appearance. It is oval, or rather lozenge-shaped, and was, for a long time, strongly fortified; but its ramparts are now demolished, and their place occupied by a series of boulevards. The squares, or open spaces, are shabby and irregular, and, except the *Place Royale*, near the centre of the city, are all insignificant in size. Some, however, are ornamented with public fountains, of which the city is well supplied. The *Fontaine de Sisieux* is a curious piece of antique sculpture, representing mount *Parnassus*, with figures of *Apollo*, *Pegassus*, etc.

Rouen is an opulent city, and is so eminent for its cotton manufactures, that it has gained the title of the French Manchester. Formerly, the spinning and weaving were both done by hand; but now, both water and steam-power are largely used. It is stated by Villermé, that in 1840 there were fifty thousand persons, men, women and children, or about half the entire population of the city and suburbs, engaged in the cotton manufacture.

There are numerous institutions of interest in the venerable city; among others, may be mentioned the Royal, and University Academies, a royal College, Bible Society, Schools of Design, and Navigation, and various charitable institutions. But Rouen is particularly interesting to the student, as having given birth to some of the most illustrious individuals of whom France has to boast, among whom may be named Pierre Corneille, deservedly surnamed *Grand*, one of the greatest modern dramatists; also, his brother, Thomas Corneille; Fontenelle, the academician; Bochart, the famous Oriental scholar; Daniel, the historian; Brumoi, and others.

CHAPTER X.

ANNOYING TRAIT OF FRENCH LANDLORDS — COMPARATIVE EX-
CELLENCE OF RAILWAYS IN FRANCE — EMOTIONS ON ARRIVAL
IN PARIS — HOTEL DU HAVRE, A SCENE WITH THE LANDLADY
-- KINDNESS OF MADAM DAVID.

Jan. 9th. Took the morning train for Paris. My bill at the hotel, where I had stopped in Rouen, considerably exceeded my expectations, by which I understood some of the especial politeness shown me by the affable landlord and his amiable wife was not for nothing. As I had made a particular bargain in regard to terms, before engaging rooms, I demurred a little at his charges, — whereupon he condescended to inform me of the usage at first-class hotels, of adding a franc per day for extras, whether the traveller received them or not; and it was expected, further, that the travelling gentleman would hand over something besides for the service of domestics, etc. I convinced him, in a word, that I was not altogether uninformed in the premises, when he at once rescinded the charge for extras, remarking simply that I might give at pleasure.

This practice of taking the advantage of the ignorance or good nature of foreigners, who are travelling in France, is common, if not universal. And I am not sure that it is peculiar to France, but that it prevails on the continent. It is needless to add, that this petty swindling is sufficiently annoying, especially to an American, who, though not entirely unacquainted with a species of over-reaching in business, has no experience corresponding to this. In the United States, one never feels the least necessity for entering into stipulations beforehand, for a night's lodging, or day or two's board at a public hotel, to prevent paying double the ordinary charge. But quite different is it in Europe, where, in fault of a previous understanding as to price, you will pay for the neglect. In other respects I found the French landlords and ladies to merit high commendation, — polite, accommodating, and strictly honest. This alone seems a defect in their admirable manner toward travellers. Like unamiable national traits often met with elsewhere, it has the strength of long usage to plead its innocence. Surprising it is to a stranger, how such perverse dealing could ever become so ingrained with the public, as to render the national conscience blind to the fault. It adds an item to the chapter of human inconsistency.

I found the general reception-room, at the depot, spacious and even elegant. After delivering my luggage, buying a ticket, etc., I passed into a neat and well-furnished parlor, having besides, the very convenient appendages of water-closet, and recesses for arranging toilet. The cars were soon by the door, and we issued for seats, leaving our tickets as we passed out. Each took the coach he fancied, and there was a slight bustle for choice. In a moment the city, with its lofty spires, was receding in the distance, and we were wending our way, with the speed of an arrow, toward the queen-city. I must confess that my feelings were elate at the thought of so soon realizing the splendid dream of my youth. On we bounded, through hill and dale, over river, under massive arched tunnels, — some of them of great length. The French railways have the appearance of being thoroughly constructed, — the motion is even, and the carriages easy and comfortable. The interior of the carriages of the second grade are lined with white linen, and side-lamps are kept burning to abate the gloom that would otherwise seize upon passengers, while passing under the long tunnels, of which there are several upon this route. The road crosses the Seine no less than six times; and this, together with the many deep cuts, the expensive depots, and way-stations, and the superior appointments in respect to officers, must needs render the road an expensive one. Its great cost will be more apparent, when we consider that it runs through the heart of Normandy, cutting into valuable parks, gardens, and sometimes, passing near villages, and even through them. The travel on the road, judging by the number with us, and the moderate rates of charge, would seem hardly to warrant the opinion that the stock is remunerative to its holders, though it must be taken into the account that labor is cheaper, and per-cent. interest less in France than in the United States. But the road is of grand importance to the commercial interest of the three prominent cities of which it forms the connecting chain,— and its stock must continue to enhance in value upon a most durable basis. I noticed one feature in the appointment of the road which I have not observed elsewhere, and which, it seems to me, is worthy of mention. Men were stationed at distances along the road, and as it grew dark I noticed that they held lanterns. I was told that it was their duty to hold themselves in readiness to render aid or succor in case of accident while the cars were traversing the road, as well as to keep the track clear of encumbrances of every kind whatever, whether made by the carelessness of others, or by malicious-minded persons. And when it is considered how often accidents upon railroads happen in our own country,— for instance, sometimes arising from obstructions upon the track, resulting even in great loss of life, this feature would seem imperiously to recommend itself for adoption to all managers of railroads who have it not already, and who feel a deep and lively sense of the important trust of human life committed to their hands.

On the whole, I received a favorable impression of their management of railroads, in France. Their construction is, doubtless, much after the English mode of building, — the English having been, till very recently, principally employed as engineers, and even workmen; but both the construction in the more solid and lighter parts, and the management, are considerably modified by the French genius, and accordingly partake much of the grace and luxury of the national character.

The cars stopped within the rich iron ballustrades of the station at Paris; and in a moment, we were all in the spacious room of the octroi, awaiting the inspection by the officers, of our luggage. This, however, causes but slight delay, especially if you submit to the form required by law with polite acquiescence, and there are no circumstances to render you a suspected person. On my whole tour, I was never detained more than a moment from this cause, — the officer merely unlocking the valise, and casting a glance, for form's sake. All, however, do not escape so lightly. The quick and experienced eye of the officers easily distinguish the class of travellers who would be likely to need watching; and, accordingly, some are subjected to a most thorough, and often exceedingly mortifying search. I more than once witnessed, with feelings akin to commiseration, the cumbersome packages of women of the lower class, undergoing a most tumultuous examination, — the different parcels tumbled about, as if the officers were quite indifferent as to the feelings of the owner, and regardless of her right of property. And I may observe, that while the French government officers are almost invariably polite to the last degree, to those termed gentlemen and lady passengers, they may often be seen treating females of the lower classes, in their official duties, as if not particularly inspired with a true and delicate regard for the sex.

The examination over, I was soon in the city, strolling leisurely a-foot, the better to enjoy undistracted, the profound yet delightful sensations of being really in Paris, so long a bright image of my imagination. What indescribable emotions I felt, as I joined the sweeping throng in the immense and densely-populated capital! What wonders of art were soon to break upon my enraptured gaze! Everything around evinced a marked superiority in exact accordance with the unrivalled reputation of the place. The streets were wider and cleaner, the edifices loftier, and more grand and beautiful, than is met with in the provincial towns. Even the persons in the streets, in their costume, gait, and general air, partook of the pervading character, exhibiting a polish of manner, and an easy and elevated style of movement, not elsewhere to be seen.

A few rods from the depôt, I came to the *Hotel du Havre*. As I entered, a neatly dressed and agreeably-mannered female domestic accosted me in bland and insinuating tones, then seized my portmanteau, and led the way up a broad stairway of marble, and, in the most pleasing manner imaginable, showed me the several unoccupied rooms of the hotel. With a delicacy of politeness peculiar to the French, she did not assign me a rank of style which was natural, by the humble manner that I entered the house, by showing me only the less expensive rooms, but took me at first into the grand apartments. Some of them were indeed magnificent enough to satisfy a fastidious taste. Their wide dimensions disclosed a gorgeous array of Brussels carpetings, sumptuous ottomans, and sofas richly carved, and gilded ceiling, and magnificently rich damask and silk hangings. I made choice of a humble and cozy room — a niche merely, compared to some of the apartments — for thirty francs per month, with light, fuel, and attendance extra. I was to take it for a month, provided I found the situation of the hotel in a favorable part of the city for my studies. After purchasing a guide-book for three and a half francs, which the concierge of the house told me was at least twice as much as it was worth, I spent the remainder of the evening in its perusal.

The morning broke upon my expectant thoughts, with inspiring effect. My first thoughts were turned, of course, towards the post-office, where, I fondly anticipated, were awaiting me letters from home. By consulting duly the intelligible plan of Paris, which I had purchased and examined carefully the evening before, I found the place readily, and without inquiring even for once. But, O how bitter the disappointment!

I now perceived that my lodgings were in an unfavorable part of the city for my purpose, and that I should do well to remove my *locale* to the south of the *Seine*, in the students' quarter. Passing from Rue J. J. Jacques, I entered the magnificent square of the Louvre, the sumptuous and varied architecture of which, nearly bewildered me with delight. In a moment, the grand and beautiful view along the quays of the Seine, was revealed. Passing down *Rue de Seine*, I found a comfortable room, on moderate terms, at Madam David's, No. 57 bis. I was quite delighted at the appearance and manner of my new landlady. She was a fine specimen of the class termed *grisettes*, who combine an assembled charm, as difficult to describe, as it would be to paint the hues of the rainbow. Her fascinating manners were the perfection of delicacy and grace. While contemplating her in animated conversation with another, it was less difficult to imagine the wonderful spell of the famed Cleopatra.

Arrangements completed with Madame D., I returned to *Hotel du Havre*, in order to remove to my new quarters. On ringing my bell, a maid appeared, and politely requested me to descend, and arrange my account with Madame of the hotel. I was ushered into a spacious and elegantly furnished room, on the story below. A lady of genteel figure and dress, was reclining upon a sofa. She immediately arose, and awaited my commands without speaking. She was tall, clad in full black, and bore a sedate and thoughtful expression. On asking for my bill, she promptly replied in a subdued tone, but with a business-like precision and air, that it would be sixteen and a-half francs. I observed, in reply, that Madame was doubtless unaware that I had occupied the room but one night. She immediately answered in a tone and manner of independence of feeling, shaded, indeed, by her inimitable grace of manner, that by a rule of the establishment, gentlemen, on securing a room for a month, and then leaving it after one or a few days, were expected to pay the hire of half a month. I remarked again, that my engagement was conditional. She promptly showed me the book in which my name was registered, against the number of my room, for a month. I called her attention to the fact, that the writing was done by another person, and not by myself, and requested that she would call the concierge with whom I stipulated for the hire of the room, to verify the accuracy of my original statement. The woman appeared, and, amid some embarrassment of manner, and the serpentine language of duplicity, gave evidence that she could not fully remember just how it was, but it was clearly her opinion, that *Monsieur* had engaged the room for one month, as she could never have made so egregious a mistake in registering his name; whereupon, Madame turned toward me with a triumphant air, and perceiving my resolution unshaken, called a male *concierge*, and in an imperious tone, ordered him to take possession of my luggage, until I should see fit to come to terms. I thrust the fellow away, who was making a little too free with me, and walking up to Madame, tendered her five francs for my lodging, — distinctly intimating to her, that on receiving further indignity in her house, I would call in a police officer. This had the desired effect. She promptly handed me my passport, took the piece of money, and allowed me to depart, graciously bidding me adieu, as if nothing had happened. The record of the incident may be serviceable to other travellers.

In respect to the passport mentioned in the above paragraph, it may be well to add further, that on engaging rooms in an interior city or town, in France, you deliver your passport to the landlord of the house, who deposits it in a public office, where a transcript synopsis is taken of it, and the original returned to you. As this passport contains, besides a certificate of citizenship, some description of your person, this arrangement is not only very convenient in enabling a stranger to trace out the domicile of a friend or countryman happening to be in the city at the same time, — which he can easily do, by applying to the proper authorities; but it affords ready means to the government of knowing always how many strangers are in the city, and furnishes efficient means of ferreting out the authors or perpetrators of crime. It is a little annoying to travellers; but there is no doubt that it contributes essentially to the order and tranquillity of European society.

On arriving at the hotel, I found my room in a pleasant state of readiness, with a glowing coal fire in the grate to cheer me, while Madame David with her amenities of manner, contributed to the hospitable feeling of home.

CHAPTER XI.

SHOPPING IN PARIS — FASCINATING MANNERS OF THE SHOP-WOMEN — BEAUTIFUL APPEARANCE OF THE STREETS — FASHIONS DIFFERENT IN PARIS, LONDON, AND NEW YORK — NAPOLEON COLUMN — GARDEN OF THE TUILLIERIES — LIBRARY OF ST. GENEVIEVE — THE IMPORTANCE OF SOME DEFINITE PLAN OF OBSERVATION.

THE first business on the morrow was, to replenish my wardrobe, now the worse for the journey thither. Madame was pleased to offer me cards of address to clothing stores, with useful advice in regard to purchasing to advantage; but although I felt obliged to her for the favor, I waived it, preferring to trust to chance for any good fortune I might meet with in the line of purchase. I purposely spent the entire day in selecting the required habiliments, in order to get a clearer view of the features of Parisian shopping. The keepers were all extremely civil and obliging, ever betraying a delicate charm of manner perfectly delightful. As you enter the store, you gracefully raise the hat, and salute the lady or gentleman within, which is returned in a polite, but not obsequious manner. The goods are shown you without stint or reserve, but you are not directly urged to purchase, — although the qualities of the articles, their newness, fitness, and such like other points, become very naturally the theme of an easy conversation, in which not rarely a suggestion is elicited that is fully calculated gently to draw you in for the purchase. The whole thing is managed with infinite tact. You feel yourself perfectly at liberty to leave without buying, and yet you are conscious of touching a golden woof whose delicate threads draw you to the interests of the seller. You are not held fast by the powers of persuasion, nor are you made to feel, that failing to purchase, you would violate any rule of propriety; and yet an eloquent tongue within, pleads for the claims of so much politeness. These remarks apply without abatement in their force, to the Paris shopkeepers in general; but they have a special application to the fair *shopwomen*, who, indeed, form the larger part in the trade. Whether these are selected for their greater personal attractions and superiority of address, I cannot say; but certain it is, that they appear the more effulgent gems in that sparkling brilliant, Parisian woman. It would be difficult, I fancy, for an American to enter a shop kept by one of these latter, and engage in a purchase, without feeling at once his purse-strings loose, under the force of her inimitable charms of manner. Her perfect neatness of person, the exquisite mode and taste of her entire dress, the blandness and grace of her manner, prepossess you at once; but when her liquid, silvery tones, modulated in soft, graceful cadences, with an accent at once harmonious and inspiring, glide upon your ear, you are taken captive, and make your purchases, without a very clear perception of the relation of your finances to the absolute need you have of the articles you are purchasing. But what if the female in question chance to be a fine specimen of one of those exquisites of the sex, termed *grisettes?* In that case, you may as well remain at home, if you are fully determined on not purchasing; for any attempt to control your will in the premises, would most certainly prove abortive. It were a futile effort to paint exactly this exotic species of woman in France. The most subtle genius might well despair of the attempt. To image forth a picture possessing truly the cognizable features of the original, would require more than the immortal pencil of a Raphael, dipped in the sublimated hues of nature. Simplicity, apparent artlessness, grace, and a certain tenderness, heightened by a tone and accent sweet and liquid, are so happily blended, as to remind you of the facile harmony of the spheres, and of a freshness, to bring to mind the carolling of the matin songster, as he pours forth his mellow, gushing notes, on the dewy spray, while all nature breathes incense to the depth and melody of the artless song.

The shops in Paris, as I have already said, are, in general, kept by females; but I observed that the clothing-stores, or those for male attire, were most commonly attended by gentlemen, or at least you are waited on by such, when making fits to your person. This struck me as being worthy of note, in a city where the struggle for pecuniary existence is so intense, as continually to threaten to ingulf in the vortex of human strife all the primary elements of innate propriety,—and where society is on so easy footing as to leave the utmost freedom to female demeanor. It only serves to add, however, further proof of the modesty of French women, of all classes, which, in their dress and manner, has been admiringly spoken of by travellers.

On leaving, you politely bow to madame, bidding her a pleasant day, which she returns with perfect grace and good-nature, and this, too, on her part, whether you have purchased articles of her, or not. This admirable trait of the Parisian shopwomen is not a little remarkable. I cannot imagine that their imperturbable blandness is always heartfelt, but it is ever, nevertheless, pleasingly admirable, and it serves to show to what point the social elements of character may be disciplined. I must confess, that I rarely left a shop myself without buying something, however small the purchase; but I often witnessed the French themselves, after occasioning a deal of lost time and inconvenience to madame in showing them the different articles in her shop, leave — receiving the same sweet and courteous adieu from the woman, as if they had purchased half the goods in her shop. Indeed, I have one case in point, fresh in my mind. While standing one day at the counter of one of those little open shops, frequently to be met with in the cross-streets of the city, and arranging for a purchase, a gentleman stepped up, and as he seemed somewhat in haste, I made a movement aside, yielding him the exclusive attention of the charming shopwoman. He was dressed superbly, and bore an air and style of manners that bespoke him one of the *exquisites* of the city. He handled over the different articles, finding fault with every object he examined, — one being too small, another too large, this too dear, that of inferior quality, — until the unwearied woman had shown him half the things in her store, which she did with the greatest readiness and patience, — when the rather pompous Parisian went away without deigning to leave a single sou of his money with the woman, to console her for the infinite pains she had been put to. He had the courtesy, however, on going away, to bestow a fine bow, and a most classically moulded valediction, while the woman returned an apparently cordial and graceful pleasant-day, her countenance and manner betraying not the slightest indication of the chagrin, not to say smothered indignation, which she must have inwardly felt at such annoying treatment.

The graceful attractions and winning manner of the Parisian shopkeepers, render *shopping* in Paris most delightful; and the effect of such amenity of manners, must be favorable to the social character of the city.

It is quite needless to add, that the various articles in the shops are arranged with infinite taste, and so presented as to show to the best advantage; for all this we should expect in a city in which style is carried to so high a point as in Paris;—but in some of the streets, the shop-windows display a degree of luxury, costliness, and magnificence, scarcely to be conceived of by those who have not looked in upon them; and the articles are exhibited in so sumptuous and alluring a shape as quite to captivate the most fastidious taste.

To a person possessing but a moderate degree of the sense of the beautiful in art, a stroll through some of the wide and clean streets of the city, with leisure to gaze in upon the magnificent array of costliness, could not but prove a luxury in its way. He would seem to realize the golden days of Persian splendor, and half fancy that the entire wealth and taste of the broad earth were concentrated within the limits of the queen-city.

The quality of style in the dress of the Parisians is beyond praise. In combining grace, lightness, and warmth, their garments are unrivalled. To be sure, Paris sets the fashions for the world; and the various other great capitals are in the monthly, I might say, weekly receipt of the latest Parisian mode, which is obsequiously copied and immediately transmitted to the smaller cities, towns and villages throughout the length and breadth of the entire civilized world; so that the grand city becomes the emporium of fashion for all civilized nations,—the fountain-head of the infinity of the streams of fashion that extend through the varied fabric of universal society. Still, the Parisian mode is quite different in London or New-York, from what it is in Paris itself. The reason for this is obvious. There is a philosophy about it. The genius of a nation may sometimes be seen even in what is commonly termed so trivial an affair as the cut of a coat. The form of a garment, aside from the standard mode, must be adapted to the style of the wearer, to have any pretensions to beauty

This principle is continually kept in view by the leading modists, who are not unfrequently persons of high intelligence and great purity of taste, in such matters. Thus a garment fashioned so as to be in perfect harmony with the light, graceful, and facile Parisian, would appear incongruously odd upon the person of an unwieldy and sturdy Londoner. Before being in keeping with the latter, it must undergo, so to speak, a process of naturalization. In a word, it must be Anglicised. Hence, you never see the true Parisian fashion out of the capital. It is an indigenous plant, and cannot be transplanted without losing some of the distinctive features of the original.

Jan. 12th. I set off early in the morning with the view of calling upon the American minister, both to pay my respects to the honored representative of our nation, in Paris, and to report myself as an American traveller, designing to tarry a few weeks in the city. Strangers, on their arrival, are expected thus to make themselves known to the resident minister of their respective countries, and it may prove of advantage for them so to do.

I took my directions from my guide-book. On my way thither, I passed the celebrated column of Napoleon, in the Place Vendôme. From the summit of the grand pillar, a comprehensive panoramic view of the city and its environs may be had, and I could not resist the temptation to tarry here a moment, and gratify my intense curiosity to look down upon the world, in miniature, below. An old soldier, — in the wars of the Emperor, — gave me a lantern, and I ascended the column, by an interior winding staircase of one hundred and seventy-six steps. The view from the top is fine, although the monuments in the proximity are seen upon a line too horizontal to appear to the best advantage. As the eye sweeps the horizon, it embraces the numerous striking edifices, towers, and palaces, which adorn the capital, rising above a confused ocean of roofs and houses of all forms and sizes, with all possible varieties of chimneys, pipes, and flues. In the distance, the eye rests upon the village of Vincennes, with its chateau and forest; and then, a little to the left, on a green-wooded hill, sloping towards the city, appear the tombs and monuments of *Père Lachaise*, while to the north, you catch a view of the hills, which crowd upon the city in that direction.

The reader may be more interested in learning the design of this splendid monument, and in attending to its description, though the account be meagre and imperfect. It was erected to commemorate the unparalleled victories of Napoleon, in the campaign of 1805, from the raising of the camp at Boulogne, to the battle of Austerlitz. Upon the capitol is inscribed, *Monument erected to the Glory of the Grand Army, by Napoleon the Great,* — and his series of heroic feats is sculptured in two hundred and seventy-six *bass-reliefs*, of which the subjects are engraved underneath, upon the cordon, rising in a spiral direction to the summit of the column. The column itself is of the Tuscan order, copied from Trajan's pillar at Rome, but of larger dimensions. It has an elevation of one hundred and thirty-five feet, and is surmounted by a colossal bronze statue of the emperor. The figure rests in an easy posture upon the right foot, with the left free, and a little advanced. The costume is his ordinary military surtout and cocked hat. There is an air of dignity and decision in the attitude, and the countenance is steady and benignant, looking calmly down upon the capital, reminding you that Napoleon is still the master-spirit of France. The *bass-reliefs*, in bronze, with which it is covered, were made out of twelve hundred pieces of cannon taken from the Russians and Austrians; and the ministers of these powerful nations, as they drive past in their splendid equipages, may well feel a momentary abasement, as they glance at the emblems which so forcibly remind them of the disgrace of their arms and humiliation of their power, by a series of victories unparalleled in the history of the world.

On reaching the place designated in my guide as the residence of the American minister, I made further inquiries, and following the directions given, entered the office of the English ambassador. I was there politely told that I should find the American minister's hôtel on the south side of the Seine, near my own quarters.

On my way home, I passed through the garden of the *Tuileries*. It would require many pages to give a detailed description of this beautiful enclosure; and then the picture thus made would be pale, indeed, compared with the original,—so entirely inadequate is language to convey any just notion to others of what corresponds to nothing in their experience with which to form a comparison. The garden is in the form of a parallelogram, and comprises an enclosed space of sixty-seven acres. It was projected by Louis IV, and laid out by the celebrated Le Notre, whose genius is strikingly displayed in the wonderful harmony with which he combined the varied elements and details of this delectable spot. The ground is laid out in broad and neat walks, and angular beds, of different size and pattern, variegated with trees, shrubbery and flowers of the choicest varieties. Beautiful circular basins, of different sizes, are pleasingly interspersed. They are ornamented with elaborate fountains, from which leap forth the waters of the Seine, gleaming ever and anon in the soft sunshine, and then falling in subdued spray upon the placid bosom of the water below. Fishes from China lazily part the limpid water beneath; while upon its mirrored surface float, majestically, cygnets of the color of alabaster, and as tame as the visitors that view them. The whole space is profusely ornamented with antiques, statues, and vases, thus adding to the other delightful features of the place the very grateful and elevating charm of classical association. The whole space is completely filled; every point being actually appropriated, — and yet amid the immense number and variety of objects almost crowding the entire enclosure, there is such a simplicity of arrangement, and symmetry of proportion, as to relieve all monotony. Every object is so precisely in its place, and such exquisite harmony pervades the entire effect, that the eye is entirely satisfied, and can desire nothing more beautiful, majestic, or perfect, either in the whole, or in any of its details. The garden is open to the public, and is the favorite resort of the Parisian, as well as of strangers. It adjoins the palace on the north, and must appear delightfully pleasing from the windows of the Chateau. Even the fastidious taste of royalty could but be gratified in embracing its infinite beauties.

Spent the evening most satisfactorily in the room of the venerable library of *St. Genevieve*. It is not so large as some other public libraries in Paris, containing only about one hundred and ten thousand volumes, and two thousand manuscripts; but on account of its convenient proximity to the rooms in which are given the lectures comprising the public course, it is much frequented, especially by the students attending these lectures. The library is open, and entirely free to the public, on every day, I think, except Sunday, from ten to three during the day, and in the evening from six to ten. So great is the eagerness, by the habitual students to this library-resort, to improve to the utmost the golden moments, that there was usually a throng before the entrance, at least fifteen minutes before the time of opening the doors. To prevent annoyance, they were required to stand in file, in a narrow passage formed by the wall of the building and a wooden railing. This, the French significantly term, making the *queue*. While waiting with half impatience, and an uneasiness of body arising from the cold, an occasional pleasant *jeu d'esprit* would be let off by some mirthful fellow, in whom the mercury had fallen so low as to disengage a latent spark from his mental crucible. The vivid scintillation would be sure to ignite the closely-pressed train of embodied spiritualities, by the keenly susceptible force of sympathy, — when the vivid flashes of wit and humor, passing rapidly from one to another, acting with suffused glow of effect upon all minds, would, for the moment at least, completely dissipate the tediousness of the delay. The French students are certainly pointedly and wittily keen. The ammonia of their volatile spirits falls with a peculiar pungency, when vehicled by their precise, clear, and dulcet language.

Students have a tendency to the witty. The drill and discipline they are undergoing, sharpen the mind, and impart to it a clearness and vividness for comparison, which render some little innocent indulgence in that way, almost indispensable. Thus, while standing *en queue*, I was more than once irresistibly provoked to a laugh, by a sure-directed pun, perpetrated against some passer-by of the humbler sort. Occasionally there would be a retort so keen, as to show that in all such encounters, there are blows to receive, as well as blows to give.

The door opens. Instantly the head of the column disappears, you find yourself in movement, and soon pass through the wide entrance leading into the library-room. As you pass the portly *huissier*, or door-keeper, who stands gaily decked with the insignia of his office, you bestow in turn your deferential salute, which he receives with the pompous dignity of a grand seigneur. The long hall comprising the interior of the library-room, has a table running its entire length, around which the company hastily but noiselessly seat themselves. In a moment, all is profound silence, as if the mortal spirits present had been borne off by those of the departed dead, into realms of pure abstraction. The room is well lighted; and, on the table before you, which is covered with green baize, are writing materials amply provided for your convenience. A number of librarians, whose business it is to keep the immense number of volumes conveniently arranged, and to assist you to any book you may be pleased to call for, may be observed with a sedate and thoughtful air, gliding noiselessly around in the different parts of the room, pleasurably intent in their grateful duties. These gentlemen are always approachable, give you prompt and explicit attention, and in their whole intercourse with you, evince a classic ease of manner, and a polished tone of mental expression, in pleasing harmony with the spiritual grandeur of the place. The collection in this library is so judiciously made, that you would rarely be disappointed in finding a book to aid you in the investigation of a particular theme, although there might be several other persons present, reading in different volumes upon the same subject. It was easy to observe that the entire company present were no listless readers, seeking to while away the time in mental relaxation. They appeared rather greedily to devour the rich and abounding mental feast before them, and to cling to the passing moments, as if each came laden with the momentous interest of success in life's career. Many were law and medical students, who were reading in connection with the public course of lectures they were attending, — and this previous investigation of the subject, could not but prove an excellent preparation to appreciate more fully the lecture of the professor, — while the subject, clearly and fully illustrated in the lecture-room, through the inspiring tones of the living teacher, must needs awaken a strong and durable interest in the student, for thorough investigation on collateral subjects. Added to this, the wringing examination at the close of the course, which decides whether the candidate is to receive the approbation of the University, and be sent out into the world with the commendatory honors of the highest authority in the world, or be rejected, to pass a life of private mortification, or to make a renewed struggle for the diploma, by a year or two of intense application, must lend additional motives for the highest effort in the power of man.

At an early hour in the evening, a door leading to a room in the second story was thrown open, when there would be something of a rush to share the privilege of the books in the reserved department; but I did not learn the particular advantage of the arrangement.

I spent much of my time, the first week in Paris, in this delightful place. The wilderness of engrossing objects which breaks upon the mind of the traveller, with almost bewildering effect, when he first takes up his abode in the magnificent city, makes some definite plan of observation absolutely indispensable, if he would use the time to the best advantage. I accordingly spent much of the first week in Paris in studying the plan of the city, in tracing its history, in making a mental survey of the various institutions and objects of prominent interest, and in settling upon a scheme for the examination of these, that would use the limited time of my stay to the best advantage. Nor was the week thus spent misappropriated. It rendered fruitful the remaining time in a high degree, and had the effect to crowd hours into minutes. It is, perhaps, not too much to say, that if a stranger in Paris has but four weeks to tarry there, and would learn the most that it is possible to do in that time, that he might profitably spend the first week in reconnoitring the ground, and laying the plan of arrangement.

CHAPTER XII.

LETTERS FROM HOME — THE EFFECT OF CONTEMPLATING ARIGHT NOBLE PUBLIC EDIFICES — BOARDING SCHOOL — PUPILS OUT ON PROMENADE — ARC DE TRIOMPH DE L'ETOILE — MINISTER OF PUBLIC INSTRUCTION IN PARIS — CIMETIERE DU PERE LACHAISE, THE PARIS OF CEMETERIES — VICE RECTOR AT THE SARBONNE — PANTHEON — DESCRIPTION.

Jan. 16*th.* It being the Sabbath, I determined to spend a portion of the day in a stroll through parts of the city, to view some of the public edifices and works of art. Not finding it convenient to attend religious worship, this course for the employment of my time very naturally suggested itself, as being somewhat akin to the spirit of religious adoration, and by no means a very indifferent substitute for ritual ceremonies. I felt, with how much truth I know not, that it would be no sacrilege of the day, leisurely to contemplate these sublime creations of man's genius, and yield to the elevation of thought and depth of sentiment which they are sure to inspire. From such high thoughts, it was natural to turn to loftier, and to be solemnly impressed with the Infinite Power that could thus breathe into humble mortals conceptions so grand, and powers of execution so wonderful, as these monuments imply.

My first course was to the post-office, where, with a longing heart, I hoped to find letters from home. Intelligence from absent friends, and dear ones, is among the sweetest joys of life. But when the endeared notes are conveyed in the tender missive, freshly breathing the holy incense of the heart's purest affection, the joy is greatly heightened. Nor is the delight less, when the happy recipient is a traveller, separated from the world of his heart's affections by many miles of dreary, pathless ocean, and the human beings by which he is surrounded can claim no relation to his sympathies, either from the past or the future. Letters from home are to the traveller in Europe the golden chain which binds him to what of life is most dear. They keep vivid the flame upon the heart's altar, and quicken the susceptibilities for the enjoyment of the beautiful around. Their power is tri-fold, — first, he glows in fond anticipation; then, he devours the sentences which unseal the fountain-spring of affection; afterwards, he lives upon the placid sea of pleasant memories.

But it is with emotions of painful solicitude that you approach the letter-office. The chances of your fate balance in the mind. Hope, fear, intensely glowing anticipation, and a shrinking dread of ill-news, by turns take possession of your soul, and subject it to the agitation of a tempest-tost sea. Does a letter await you, or are you destined to meet a disappointment so bitter as to enkindle within you feelings almost of ill-will at the cruel neglect of your friends? If a letter, what tidings will it bring? — cheering news, and balmy sympathy, or intelligence to rive your heart, and shroud the mind in the gloom of utter dejection?

I turned away from the office with feelings that may be imagined by the reader, at the disappointment of not finding a letter. Strolling along, until reaching the north-western limit of the city, I then crossed the Seine at that point, and returned home quite fatigued with the pedestrian tour. The promenade formed a circuit of several miles. In the course, I took a glimpse of the Palais du Louvre, Palais Royal, Chateau de Tuileries, Place de la Concord, Champs Elyseés, Champ de Mars, and Arc de Triomphe de l'Etoile. The contemplation of these grand and magnificent edifices cannot but exalt the sentiments. They appeal with force to the reflection, to the imagination. Erected by the genius of man, they are surviving and durable monuments at once of his power and his weakness; of his transitory stay upon earth, and his power to reproduce and perpetuate himself through endless time. The millions that were employed in producing these splendid works of art, are now, it is true, mingled with the dust which compose the earth upon which the edifices stand; still, their spirits live, as truly and effectually in these monuments as if now moving in their clayey tenements, amid the vast waves of humanity that ceaselessly surge the bosom of this great city. When we consider the large amount of human energy which these costly buildings must have absorbed, and the toil and deprivation they must have wrung from the depressed masses, the question may naturally arise, whether this large expenditure of the sinew of life can be justified. They are noble and beautiful objects, it will be admitted; but has the highest good of the greatest number been advanced by their erection? Judged by the elevated standard of humanity, have they really furthered the sum of human happiness? This question, I may not attempt to answer; but a thought or two in the connection may not be inappropriate. If the good of human life consists solely in what a man eats and drinks, then the motives which led to the construction of these edifices cannot be justified; for it is easy to perceive that the vast amount of labor required in their erection, might have been otherwise employed to augment, not a little, the sum of the comforts or luxuries of animal existence. But if life is spiritual, — if the highest form of existence is in the most elevated and noble thoughts, — if grandeur of soul, purity of taste, and depth of sentiment, constitute the essential of human enjoyment here below, then the question assumes a somewhat different aspect. Taking this view, it would be really difficult to measure their influence for good. No one possessing the least susceptibility to the appreciation of the noble and beautiful, can gaze upon them in a right disposition of mind, without feeling conscious of their influence in exalting and ennobling his being. They open his soul to impressions of the grand and lovely, and he leaves with a cast of thought that will tinge his character in all the future. As ho mingles in the ocean of human life, his each act, however slightly exalted by an enlarged soul, multiplied by the acts of a lifetime, will make an aggregate of salutary influence quite incalculable. Let the increased power thus derived for a nobler life, of one individual, be multiplied by the thousands of travellers who daily contemplate these buildings, and who bear away their impressions to be diffused like genial sunshine over the remote corners of the world, and we have a still further view of their usefulness. It cannot be doubted that these edifices constitute one of several means which continually operate, silently it is true, but effectually, to elevate the Parisian to that spirituality of mind, and polish of style, which compensate much for the grosser aliment of life. The power, too, of these edifices is continual. They act like the ceaseless hand of time. Not only will millions of the present generation of men catch inspirations from the fervor of their mute eloquence, but the uncounted millions of mankind in all future time, will successively look up to these magnificent monuments, and thereby receive an exaltation of soul that shall purify, and bless, for good.

In the day's walk, I met several times, schools issuing from their half-prison walls, for an airing. They were pupils of private boarding establishments, of which there are numbers in Paris. Some that I encountered, were schools of boys, others of girls. The boys were uniformly attired in a rather stiff costume, prescribed by the rules of their respective establishments. They marched in file, under the direction of their teachers, with a precision of gait and primness of manner, that would remind you of soldiers on drill, rather than bounding schoolboys, letting off in wild and irregular explosions the pent-up gasses of a week's confinement. The schools of misses that I met, were less stiffly decked, but they were paraded in the same lifeless style. There was none of the excess of youthful life and joyousness, brimming the eye, radiating the cheek, and giving an elasticity of movement so natural and lovely in persons of their age. None of the merry, ringing laugh, the artless, playful manner, the free gushing from the pure heart's fountain, which so gladdens the beholder, and quickens his sentiment of existence.

The advantages in Paris for pursuing a course of study, are preëminently superior; and the private schools, surrounded as they are by the vast and magnificent collections in the several departments of science, natural history, and art, and all entirely free to the students, must present strong attractions to pupils from the provinces; still I could not but regard all these glorious privileges — and most certainly they are so — as being purchased at a price by no means trivial, when losing the free and invigorating air, and the animating sports of country freedom.

I tarried also a brief hour, to contemplate the splendid monument of the *Arc de Triomphe de l'Etoile*, and to revel in the magnificent view afforded from its summit. The situation of this grand edifice could not have been better chosen. It stands upon the highest ground within the Paris basin, and can be seen from all quarters within and without, by the long avenues that terminate upon it. Its effect is the most imposing, perhaps, on approaching it from the garden of the *Tuileries*. You emerge from the grove of the garden into the magnificent *Place de la Concorde*, and through which your way is uninterrupted to the *Avenue des Champs Elysées*, along which you proceed between its stately forests of a mile in length, to the Triumphal Arch at its extremity. The ground gradually rises towards the edifice; and when first seen through the vista of the long and wide avenue, it springs upon the mind in a startling but pleasing manner. Indeed, Art and Nature have conspired to give it a happy location, and it is conceded to be far the most stupendous structure of the kind ever erected, either in ancient or modern times. Its cost exceeded the enormous sum of nine millions of francs.

The Arch was originally projected by Napoleon, after the brilliant campaign of 1805, in which at the head of one hundred and sixty thousand men, in the short space of three months, he vanquished the splendid armies of Austria and Russia, and humbled the pride of those imperious powers; and it is designed to commemorate those gigantic achievements. Suspended at the Restoration, the work was resumed in 1823, but with an entirely different destination from its original. Charles X. would finish none of the monuments and public works commenced by Napoleon. Indeed he preferred rather the destruction of those already existing; so that this monument was to be finished in honor of the victories of the Duc d' Angoulême in Spain. The revolution of 1830, when Charles was driven from the throne, frustrated this design, and Louis Phillippe, who succeeded him, animated by his love of the fine arts, and with his usual sagacity, caused the edifice to be completed after the original plan, and to be made a grand national work — a work worthy of the genius and glory of its founder. It was finished in 1836. It consists of a single arch ninety-six feet in height, forty-eight feet in width, and seventy-three feet in depth, and of two small transverse arches. The whole structure is one hundred and sixty-two feet in height, one hundred and forty-seven in length, and seventy-three feet in depth. It has numerous colossal groups of sculpture, depicting most of the grand battles gained by the French in the revolutionary war. It stands quite separate from the other buildings, affording an opportunity to be seen to the best advantage.

The monument is a fit emblem of the grand and magnificent character of its founder. It will serve to keep alive in the national heart the profound sentiment felt for the genius, splendid talents, and unparalleled achievements of the great captain. It will serve continually to encircle his name with a halo of light so resplendent and enduring, as to shine with undiminished brilliancy through succeeding generations of men. The peasant, as he looks up to this monument, will have revived in his breast the history of the glorious acts of the national prowess; his soul will expand with glowing recollections, and his sentiment of life, his love of nationality, his pride of country will be keener, fuller. I would not be thought to encourage a spirit of war, and if Napoleon had no further claims to our admiration than as having been a warrior of transcendent genius, little might be said in favor of a monument to perpetuate the glory of his name; but he stands before us as a scholar, statesman, legislator, of consummate ability; as a man who was ever alive to whatever there was of the beautiful, noble, sublime, either in nature or art, and whose profound genius was ever active, in the intervals of the engrossing duties of the eminent station in which fortune had placed him, to increase the greatness and glory of his country. This edifice will stand then to kindle animating recollections whose influence will develop much of the great and generous in human character.

In the evening, I received a letter from the Minister of Public Instruction in Paris, in which I was made welcome to visit the public schools and institutions of the city and Versailles. The letter advised me to address myself to the Vice-Rector of the University of Paris at the Sorbonne, to whom the minister had given orders to facilitate my entrance into such institutions as I might desire to visit. I had called a few days before at the office of the public minister, but not finding him within, I left my request with his secretary, who received me with due politeness, inspected my letters, and promised me, with the utmost cordiality, all necessary assistance. Perceiving that I hesitated a little in speaking, he, either to relieve my embarrassment or to try his ability at speaking English, commenced attempting to converse with me in my own language; but with all due humility, I must say that I did not conceive that he mended the matter a great deal. Although it was evident he possessed a fine education, yet he succeeded quite indifferently to express himself in the English. The minister of public instruction ranks equal with the ministers of state, and takes the title of *Grand Master of the University*. He has in his department the University, the Institute, the Academies, and learned societies, the establishment of public instruction, the libraries, the museums, and scientific collections. The University of France is composed of twenty-seven Academies, governed each by a rector.

Jan. 22d. It being the Christian Sabbath, after attending Divine worship in the morning, I made a visit to the famous cemetery, *Père Lachaise*;— no spot could have been better fitted to awaken feelings in harmony with the religious character of the day.

The wide avenue leading to the entrance of this city of tombs, was lined, on either side, with undertakers' shops, sadly displaying ready-made coffins, wreaths of evergreens, and other lugubrious emblems of the departed. This introductory scene was indeed striking; but it was by no means congenial to the feelings. It constituted a ghastly portal to the beautiful edifice within.

Proceeding along before me was a hearse, with a small train of attendants and mourners. The humble procession, with slow and saddened movement, entered the spacious enclosure of the cemetery, and halted before a narrow and unpretending grave, in that part of the vast enclosure appropriated to the burial of the poor. The space thus set off is situated at the foot of the slope, upon which are the adorned grounds for the more fortunate classes, and comprises a large area, as it needs must, to hold the million poor. It furnishes room for interment, however, only to the citizens of five, out of the twelve municipal arrondissements of Paris. The ground here is flat, unadorned, and unvariegated. Not a slab marks the limits of the graves, which are ranged in rows as if the object were to crowd into the space as many bodies as possible. This bare and desolate aspect serves, however, to render more marked the beauty of the grounds further on.

The undertaker and his assistant now pulled with a rude hand the unpainted coffin out of the rough vehicle, — thrust it unceremoniously into the shallow grave, then tumbled upon it the frozen dirt in a manner as devoid of feeling as of sentiment. They were evidently fully accustomed to the thing. The repetition of the act had completely effaced from their souls whatever of awe or sympathy such scenes naturally inspire. What induration of the human heart, that can be so easily deprived of those susceptibilities glowingly implanted there by the hand of nature! How sad, that the stern duties of life should ever blunt the tender sensibilities of the soul!

Quite a different scene was presented by the little group of mourners standing by the grave. A man bowed with years, a woman of nearly the same age, and a young man and girl who resembled each other enough to be a brother and a sister, stood wringing their hands in mute agony. The bitterness of their spirit was but too clearly depicted on their thin features. They were meagrely clad, and their dwindled forms, wasted with penury and protracted toil, showed plainly that they belonged to the humblest class, and that their lot in life was, in consequence, surrounded with unremitting dreariness. But nothing had been able to dim the fires of their affection for the departed. These had evidently burned as intensely under the dampening influences of their depressed condition, as if fanned by the genial gales of easy life. Indeed, cast off from the distracting and weakening influences of a luxurious state, the natural tie of sympathy had been drawn all the closer, and deprived of the consolations of philosophy which education brings, their anguish was thus rendered the more intense.

I now pursued my way slowly up the hill, between rows of tombs, beautifully shaded with trees, while the turf, green even at this season, addressed the eye most gratefully. From the little chapel on its summit, my eye rested for a moment on the dim spires and domes of the city, whose roar of life dwindled to a murmur. Forty thousand tombs and mausoleums, with their pyramids, obelisks, and urns, rising far and wide above the cypresses and cedars, revealed the extent of this splendid cemetery, — the finest of the Paris cemeteries, and perhaps of the world. No site near the city presents aspects more picturesque or varied; no points of view more extensive, rich, or diversified. It is situated on the flank and summit of the most eastern of the hills overlooking Paris towards *Charonne*, formerly called *Mont-Louis*. A sad feature in the picture, was the slope of the hill allotted to the poor, where countless numbers of black crosses came up in dismal array to embitter the sentiment of sweet melancholy that seizes one here.

The grounds formerly belonged to a community of Jesuits, of whom *Père Lachaise*, confessor of Louis XIV, was superior. It was converted into a cemetery by an order of Napoleon. Brongniart, to whom the arrangement of the grounds was intrusted, accomplished his task with remarkable taste and skill. No one can wander through *Père Lachaise* without being impressed with the truth, that no ordinary artist presided over its arrangements. The natural features that could be made subservient to the main design, were retained. Cypresses are thickly interspersed amid the shrubbery, winding paths laid out in every direction; and along their borders, and among the shrubbery, are endless varieties of flowers. These varied features of beauty and grandeur, so extensive and magnificent, while they breathe into the soul a solemn calm, elevate the sentiments and induce a frame of mind rather pleasurable than otherwise.

The tombs and monuments display a great variety of taste and style. Many of them are pure, chaste, and appropriate; while, of many others, not much can be said in their favor. Many of the tombs are miniature chapels, in which the survivors often worship. These may be often found furnished with chairs, crucifixes, lamps, tapers, etc. Flowers are generally kept planted around the tombs, or kept in vases and pots upon them, and regularly watered by persons employed for the purpose. Wreaths of evergreens, or *immortelles*, as the French call them, may be seen upon the tombs, placed there by the hand of affection; and the number of these, and their freshness, afford indication of how the memory of the slumbering dead is cherished by their surviving friends. An interesting feature were the epitaphs and inscriptions upon the tombs. They were generally brief and appropriate, revealing some quality of the deceased, and many of them were exceedingly tender and beautiful.

But the chief interest of *Père Lachaise* is found in the great names that are inscribed on its monuments, — names that have agitated the world, and which the world will ever remember. There repose in the severe dignity of death the remains of such immortal spirits as La Place, La Fontaine, Moliere, Talma, Delille, Rolland, and a host of spirits equally distinguished, though perhaps not so well known to most American readers. There are, also, Lefebvre, Massena, Kellerman, Davoust, and Suchet, illustrious marshals of France, and also — the spot enclosed with iron railing — of Ney, the "bravest of the brave."

One of the most striking monuments is that of Abelard and Heloise, the ill-fated lovers, whose genius and misfortune have handed down their names to posterity. Its arched roof is supported by fourteen columns, and under it is the figure of Abelard, in a recumbent posture, with the hands joined upon the breast, — and by his side, that of Heloise. The grass around the tomb was worn by the tread of pilgrims, and devoted hands had kept fresh the garlands above their marble effigies.

The magnificent mausoleum of Madame Demidoff, is justly admired, but not more so than the little tombstone of Madame Cottin, the spiritual author of Matilda.

The tomb of La Place is an obelisk of white marble, surmounted by an urn, with the inscriptions, *Mécanique Céleste — Système du Monde — Probabilités*. There is also a scroll sculptured with the sun and planets.

Selecting an elevated site, I remained some time in a reclined posture, enrapt with the solemn beauty of the scene. Before me is the densely thronged city, stretching to illimitable view, and throbbing with intense life and animation; while around me repose in solemn grandeur, the ashes of an innumerable company of departed spirits, who, but a little while ago, were moving in all the pride and glory of life. There, the rays of the setting sun, softened by the smoky atmosphere which rises from the bosom of the city, gleam from a thousand domes, spires and turrets; here, the sighing zephyrs, as they pass along the dark foliage, imprint a saddened melancholy upon the rising emotions. I stand upon the border of two worlds, and the present real, and the future unknown, rise before the mind, — the one to the sense, in distinct outline, the other to the imagination, in shadowy, but pleasing form. Du Père Lachaise is truly the Paris of Cemeteries. It partakes of the genius, the taste, and, I might say, of the vanity of the great Parisian world.

I left the cemetery, as might be supposed, in a pensive mood; and, after crossing the boulevard, which was thronged with people apparently in the happiest disposition, and the Barrière du Trône, a spot memorable for its affecting associations with other interesting parts of the city, I reached my room, not a little fatigued, where the evening was spent in meditative reading.

Monday, Jan. 24th. Proceeded to the Sorbonne, the head quarters of the schools, to present my letter from the Minister of Public Instruction, to the Vice-Rector, and to receive from the latter further instructions to facilitate my visit to the schools. After some inquiry, I found the place, and was shown into the reception-room for strangers. Remaining here for some time, and the gentleman not appearing, I was invited to proceed further, — when, in traversing a hall, we accidentally encountered Monsieur the Vice-Rector, accompanied by another gentleman. He was passing hurriedly along, with both hands full of papers. After a word of explanation, he remembered the object of my visit, from the orders received of the Minister, and at once comprehended the scope of my design. Leading the way, he conducted me to a room, begged me to be seated, and then asked some further questions, to get precisely at what I wanted. Promising to send me at my lodgings a programme comprising a few of every grade of the schools, and such as would present the most interest to a stranger, I took my leave, well satisfied with the interview. Indeed, nothing could be more simple and affable than were his manner and conversation, — and they were such as to put you at once perfectly at your ease. There was nothing of the imperious dignity which is often met with in officials, so appalling to a stranger, — and which, instead of conferring lustre on character, are only the index of a vain and narrow mind. He did not evince even the air and grace common to the French, and might as easily have been taken for an American as a Frenchman, — so thorough a leveller of character are science and literature. Scientific and literary men of all countries, resemble each other. The common world of thought, of sentiment, of feeling, in which they move, dissipates local differences, and assimilates them in character and manners. They each, by turns, attempted to speak in English; but, it must be said, that they succeeded but poorly, — and yet I was assured that they were both distinguished scholars, and were, in the common acceptation of that term, familiar with the modern languages. But the truth is, that, with some exceptions, it is no easy matter for an adult to learn to speak a foreign language with idiomatic ease and accuracy, and it is particularly difficult in the case of the English in the mouth of a Frenchman.

On my return, I looked into the splendid edifice of the Pantheon. I had visited it more than once before, and went to see it many times after. There are some works of art of which a single view or examination will not satisfy the mind. The feeling which their presence awakens, is so ennobling and mild, as to beget a desire for the repetition of the pleasure. Of this kind, is the noble Pantheon. It is doubtless less rich and magnificent than several other public edifices in Paris, and has fewer historical associations, and contains less works of art, to recommend it; still, there were none that I visited oftener, or received more real pleasure in beholding. As you gaze upon it, the mind is at once elevated, and an inspiration seizes you, that imparts a glowing existence. The English critics observe that the structure is inferior in size and composition to St. Paul's in London, which is all very true; still, to my uncultivated taste, the edifice is more pleasing and admirable. It is conceded to be a work of great merit, — the general proportions being fine, and possessing a rare degree of grace and elegance in the outline, as well as grandeur and simplicity in the design. It stands on elevated ground, clear of other buildings, so as to be seen to good advantage; and as you emerge from one of the narrow lanes of the twelfth arrondissement, the majestic portico breaks suddenly upon the view with splendid effect. It is composed of twenty-two fluted columns, each sixty feet in height, supporting a triangular pediment one hundred and twenty feet broad by twenty-four in width, in which is a sculptured composition, by David, representing the genius of France (a colossal figure fourteen feet in height), surrounded by the great men of the nation. On the frieze beneath is inscribed in gold letters: *Au grands hommes, la patrie reconnaissante.* The plan of the church is a Greek, or equilateral cross, the exterior having no windows, and being ornamented only by a frieze and cornice. In the interior a gallery and colonnade line the nave and transepts on both sides, forming so many smaller naves and aisles. Semicircular windows rise above the colonnades, throwing a strong light into all parts of the building. From the centre of the cross rises a dome two hundred and eighty-two feet in height, the lower part of which is encircled by a Corinthian peristyle of thirty-two columns, each thirty-six feet in height. The total length of the Pantheon, including the portico, is three hundred and fifty-two feet; interior length, from east to west, two hundred and ninety-five feet; length of transept, two hundred and sixty-five feet; uniform breadth, one hundred and four feet. The edifice is in imitation of the Pantheon at Rome. As you enter, the mind is instantly impressed with the air of boldness, lightness, and grace, which appears to pervade the entire interior. From this remark must be abated the slight defect arising from the substitution of four grouped columns at the angles of the meeting of the transepts to support better the immense weight of the dome, instead of separate graceful ones; and also for the substitution of four enormous pillars for twelve columns, in the second cupola; but, by this means, the artist has succeeded in imparting to the edifice perfect solidity. Over the centre of the pavement of the church, rise three concentric domes, built one within the other. Through an opening in the lower one, perhaps twenty feet in diameter, may be seen a magnificent fresco-painting on the concave ceiling of the second, quite two hundred feet above the pavement. In the centre of the dome, the sun himself seemed to send forth living pencils of light, illumining the entire pavilion. In the fullest blaze of light appears the name of God in Hebrew characters; while in the midst of the rays, strongly illuminated, appears vividly the painting designed to represent the apotheosis of St. Genevieve, the patron saint of Paris, who was buried here in 512, in a church built on the spot by Clovis. This grand painting was executed by M. Gros, — and the genius of the artist has seized admirably the appropriate character for each personage of the group, which he has united in the immense painting. The Saint is placed in the most elevated spot of the composition, and is represented as a shepherdess dressed in white. Everything breathes a spirit of happiness and immortality. It is no longer a simple human being that you see, but an air of celestial existence pervades. By his side are small angels scattering flowers. The images of Louis XVI, of the queen of Louis XVII, break forth, surrounded with celestial glory. Underneath, the most illustrious princes of each dynasty are represented before the Saint. Clovis may be recognized as a savage hero, by traits fit for such a personage. The beauty of St. Clotilda is greatly to be admired. She is a queen whose holy aspect commands admiration and respect. The altars of paganism are falling before them. Charlemagne bears a lofty, heroic mien, and in his eyes, and even in his carriage, shines forth a genius which places him far in advance of his century. Angels are presenting the cross to the Saxons, who received the light of faith under his reign. Louis and queen Margaret of Florence are upon their knees, from whom beams forth a gentle piety. Near the king, are two standards of the cross, symbolizing the two crusades. Louis XVIII, and St. Genevieve complete the picture. This splendid work of art cannot be seen to advantage from the pavement of the church, but from the balcony around the superior edge of the first cupola, a distinct and beautiful view may be had.

Besides the above painting, there are four allegorical paintings, on the pendentives of the dome, in the form of spherical triangles, over the corner of the nave. They represent France, Death, Justice, and Glory, embracing Napoleon. The effect of these is very impressive, but I shall attempt no description of them.

There were, also, on exhibition in the Pantheon, copies of the distinguished paintings seen in the Vatican at Rome, entitled the *Loges* and *Stanzas*. As Time was making sad inroads upon these splendid paintings, in 1835 M. Thiers, then Prime Minister of France, conceived the noble idea of wresting the Loges from oblivion, and having them to ornament the Pantheon. The work was confided to Messrs. Paul and Raymond Balze, under the direction of their master, M. Ingres. Later, in 1840, M. the Count du Châtel, Minister of the Interior, employed the same artists to make copies of the *Stanzas*. The artists completed their work, after twelve years of assiduous application.

The Stanzas comprise eight large pictures. They are styled the frescos of Raphael, and were originally painted in the halls of the Vatican, under the direction of Pope Julius II.

Some idea of these grand paintings may be obtained by an enumeration of their subjects. They are entitled respectively: — Theology, or the Dispute of the Holy Sacrament; Philosophy, or the School of Athens; Poetry, or Parnassus; The Mass of Balsena; The Burning of Bourg; St. Peter in Prison; Héliodore driven from the Temple; and, Attila repulsed by St. Leo. A full description of them cannot, of course, be attempted in this work. As a specimen, however, I will subjoin a brief account of the second in the series, viz: Philosophy, or the School of Athens. The place of the scene is upon the steps of a magnificent temple, whose beautiful proportions would alone suffice to prove that Raphael was an admirable architect, as well as a sublime painter Towards the top of the stairs, in the centre of the composition, are Aristotle and Plato, teaching philosophy in the midst of their disciples. Lower down, at the left, is Diogenes the cynic, carelessly reclining upon the steps. On the other side, still lower down, is Archimedes, under the traits of Bramante, tracing a geometrical figure. Near Archimedes, in a kneeling posture, is the duke of Manton, the friend of Raphael. In other parts of the composition are, Zoroaster standing, holding in his hand a globe; Raphael himself, with a black cap; and *le Perugin*, his master. On the other side of the picture, towards the centre, is Euclid, in meditation, seated, and leaning upon his elbow. Higher up, Socrates explaining to Alcibiades the theory of numbers. Below this group, Pythagoras, surrounded by his disciples. Behind, leaning against a pilaster, Epicurus, with his head crowned with leaves.

The Loges, which form a continuation of fifty-two pictures, represent the principal episodes of the Old Testament, since the creation of the world. The Birth of Jesus Christ, The Baptism, and The Lord's Supper, complete this series of composition. The originals of these, in fresco, are placed in the vaults of the galleries in the Vatican at Rome.

The Pantheon is intended to be the Westminster Abbey of France; and in the vaults beneath the edifice, are the remains of the mighty dead. This will, indeed, be a fit resting-place. It is divided into small apartments, with arched roofs; and so numerous are they, as to be quite labyrinthian. Without a guide, one would find it difficult to make his way to them all, — and when fairly in, not easy to thread his way out. I passed down, in company with several others; but we were hurried along so hastily, and the explanations made by the guide with such monotonous rapidity, as to convey little edification or delight. There were the sarcophagi of Rousseau and Voltaire, whose memory is cherished by the French, next to that of Napoleon. Over the tomb of Voltaire was his marble statue, bearing the same facetious expression as the one seen in Rouen. As I have observed before, there is something in the expression of this face, so spiritually sarcastic, and withal possessing an air of so much mockery, as to cause the beholder to shrink back with awe. Here, too, is the tomb of Soufflot, the architect of the church, who is said to have committed suicide on learning the possibility that the edifice which stands over the catacombs, might fall in. The distinguished Lagrange also reposes here in the majesty of death. The bodies of some are interred with their friends, while their hearts are deposited here in sculptured urns.

In the afternoon, called at the office of the American consul. His secretary treated me with all due kindness, and stated that letters had been received for me; but Mr. Balch, not knowing of me, after having detained them some time, and no one calling, had sent them back to the post-office. There is nothing gained, in general, in addressing letters to the care of the American consul, in Paris, — and it is a source of some annoyance to him. As the postage cannot be paid in advance, the letters which are sent to him, and are not called for, burden him with the expense of postage, which is quite an item in France. Besides, letters would be just as safe in the post-office, and can be had at any time by calling for them. It is only necessary to say, *post restante*, when they will remain until called for; otherwise, they may be sent to you rooms, and, by mistake, lost.

CHAPTER XIII.

PUBLIC SCHOOLS — MONSIEUR LEFEBVRE — ORDER AND PRECISION OF THE SCHOOL — CORPORAL PUNISHMENT PROHIBITED — MODE OF TEACHING THE ALPHABET — DRAWING — SINGING — ADVANTAGE OF THE SYSTEM — ITS DEFECTS — MUNICIPAL SCHOOL FRANCAIS — THE PRINCIPAL AND HIS PROFESSOR — PLAN OF THE SCHOOL — PREPARATORY DEPARTMENT — NOTRE DAME DE LORETTE.

HAVING received the promised credentials from Mons. C——, Vice-rector à la Sorbonne, consisting of a list of such schools as it was thought would be most interesting to me, — with a letter of recommendation to the several directors and principals, and a general order for my free admission to such establishments as I might wish to inspect, I set off for the nearest school, indicated on my programme, that of Monsieur Léfebvre, situated in *Rue du Bac*. It is one of the Communal Schools of Mutual Instruction, for boys, and the tuition is free. It is composed of two hundred and forty pupils, between the ages of six and twelve, who are of the poorer classes of the Parisian population. They are taught here the elements of reading, writing, grammar, arithmetic, singing, and drawing. One master presides, assisted by a monitor, and ten sub-monitors. The sub-monitors are selected from the advanced classes of the school, and officiate by turns, serving, often, not longer than one day at a time. The business of these latter is to drill the classes over whom they are placed; in doing which they pursue a set and undeviating mode of procedure, as they had previously been taught by the principal, or director, as he is called. For this purpose the class of pupils that are to officiate as monitors for the day, meet with the principal in the morning, from eight to ten o'clock, before the assembling of the school.

The room, which is on the second story, is of convenient size, and quite comfortable, being high in the walls, well open to the light, and amply provided with means of ventilation, although possessing no claim to superior beauty or elegance. It is duly furnished with black-boards, and the walls are hung with maps and cards, on which are traced geometrical diagrams. Plates, on which are engraved brief, but appropriate maxims and moral sentiments, are also suspended from the walls. I noticed several, quoted from the writings of our own Washington and Franklin, — names scarcely less revered in France than in the United States. The seats and forms were of a length to admit some dozen pupils at each, with room to pass behind. They are graduated in height to the size of the pupils, who are seated in them in strict conformity to this condition. The school, when thus seated, presents a beautifully uniform aspect.

The principal gives no particular instruction, himself, in the school-room; his business being rather to superintend the general government of the school, and give direction to the changes of the classes. Sitting in his chair, with a tin whistle he directs the movement of the school with as much ease and precision as an engineer would a steam-engine. The discipline in respect to order, was wellnigh perfect; the pupils passing through their school evolutions and changes with a promptness, precision, and concert of movement, really inspiring to the visitor, and which would remind you of the mechanical exactness of the drill of Prussian soldiery. To show with what ease Mr. Léfebvre ruled his little world, I might mention, that during the entire day that I spent at his school, he sat by my side, conversing freely, while not the least embarrassment could be observed in the exercises of the school.

The spacious room, occupying the entire dimension of the edifice, upon the ground-floor, directly underneath the school-room, is very appropriately assigned as a baggage and store-room, where the pupils, on arriving at school in the morning, deposit their outdoor clothing and noon-luncheon, and, also, as a comfortable resort for shelter and recreation at noon or during intermissions. Two long seats were arranged quite around the room, next to the wall, for the children to sit on while partaking of their collation, while the remainder of the space was left entire for free movement. Hooks were fastened in the walls, and numbered with mechanical exactness, for clothing and dinner *paniers.*

Corporal punishment was never resorted to, it being, in fact, prohibited by the government, in all the schools under its control. Not only is the rod and ferule, as instruments of punishment, banished entirely from the school-room, but all other modes of physical suffering are forbidden, — such as cuffing, pinching, unnatural and painful postures of the body, imprisoning, and whatever else would tend to deform the body, excite the passions, or sour the disposition. Incorrigible pupils, as a last resort, are expelled from the school by the local committee. Among other modes of punishment practised, to secure order and obedience, as a penalty, the pupil is made to stand face to the wall, with hands behind, and suspended around his neck a badge, marked *naughty*, or some such term of reproach. He is sometimes required to remain after school, or lose a merit-mark, or subjected to such kinds of penalties, which, according to circumstances, would be suggested to the ingenuity of any teacher.

Rewards are resorted to, to inspire emulation. The pupil who misses in his recitation, is put down; and the one who is found at the head, at the close of the exercise, receives the reward, — which consists, for the time, of a small piece of pasteboard marked "*prize.*" After having received a certain number of these, they are exchanged for a certificate; and a certain number of these other, are exchanged for a book, or some other appropriate and valuable token of merit.

To secure punctuality, recourse is had to a system of demerits, and petty deprivations; and if this gentle means is not sufficient to correct the evil, a printed note of inquiry is sent to the parent, asking an explanation of the delinquency; but parents are not imprisoned, as it is stated they are in Prussia, for non-attendance of their children.

Mr. Léfebvre informed me that there is a difference of opinion among practical educators, in regard to the point so long mooted with us, — whether, in teaching the alphabet, the letters should be learned separately, and then combined in syllables and words; or, whether whole words should be first taught, and afterwards analyzed, or resolved into their elements. Many teachers practise both methods simultaneously; and all educators concur in the opinion, that the sounds or powers of the letters should either be taught before their names, or in connection with them. It should be observed, by way of explanation, that the orthoëpy of the French, as well as that of the modern languages of Europe generally, is much more regular than that of the English, — so that spelling words by the sounds of the letters, instead of their names, would be more natural and successful with those languages, than with ours. In this school, the names of the letters were first given to the pupil, and afterwards their different powers or sounds. Arithmetic was taught much in the same manner as with us. In teaching reading, cards, on which were printed in large, plain type, the several elements of discourse, from a letter to a paragraph, were made use of. The monitor points to the letter, or word, and the class, either separately, or in concert, give the element or combination, and then it is analyzed.

Pupils practise the first rudiments of writing, by means of slate and pencil. The scholars remain in their seats, each with a slate and pencil in hand, and eyes fixed upon the card before the class, upon which has been written, by the monitor, the lesson to be imitated by the pupils. When all is ready, the monitor commences by reading to the class, in an audible manner, and with distinct utterance, the word to be copied. Then, at a signal, the first division make the copy, in a deliberate manner, and with all due pains-taking. The other divisions follow the same mode. The exercise is of an hour's length.

Drawing is here taught principally by means of the blackboard. The teacher, or monitor, who is of course a proficient in the branch himself, makes the copy to be imitated, adapting it in character to the average capacity and stage of advancement of the class. The pupils then set themselves earnestly to work, animated, evidently, by a healthy emulation, each to make a more perfect copy than his neighbor. Before commencing the exercise, the teacher gives some general description of the picture, both to impart a clearer visual conception of its character to the class, and to interest them in its subject,— while during the continuance of the exercise, he frequently calls attention to particular features, sometimes giving explicit directions to be faithfully observed. I noticed, however, a class composed of older pupils, practising from cards on the forms before them.

The principal is required by law, to impart to the school moral and religious instruction. For this purpose, the Bible is used in the school, although the Old Testament part of it is excluded. In the first exercise in the morning, the whole school go through with prayers, which consists of a brief form which they repeat mechanically, and in a monotonous manner, each division in concert, after their several monitors; and, at the closing exercise in the afternoon, they make some signs connected with the mysteries of their religion, which is followed by singing in Latin a verse,— of the meaning of which, the teacher told me they were completely ignorant. Besides these exercises, they repair in company to the church, two or three times a week, where they receive from a priest instruction in the Catholic catechism, with such moral instruction in addition, as is thought befitting.

The order of the school was admirable, although I observed several pupils cry during the day. There was no whispering, clandestine communication, nor unnecessary movement, nor noise. Everything in this line moved with the utmost precision, promptitude, and regularity. A sentiment of mutual respect, and reverence for the teacher, seemed to pervade the school, very grateful to the feelings of the cursory visitor. Industry and assiduity were visible among all the pupils. The calisthenics, with which the exercises were interspersed, had the happy effect of relieving the monotony of the school exercises, and imparting animation to the pupils. The singing was really inspiring. Every pupil joined the exercise with readiest ease, and engaged in it with evident enthusiasm; and it is by no means easy to judge of the effect of two hundred and forty juvenile voices in a single room, bursting upon the ear with their sweet, silvery, joyful melody, with the most exact movement of time, in excellent tune, and with wonderful blending of voices. The charm was really magic-like, and for the moment you are carried away into a region of blissful emotions.

The compensation of teachers for this class of schools, in the city of Paris, is from three hundred to four hundred dollars per annum. They have, besides, opportunity to increase this sum, by teaching evening schools, or in engaging in any other pursuit for which their talents qualify them.

Mr. Léfebvre had been engaged in teaching, twenty years; and in the present school, eight years; and yet he evinced all the vivacity and enthusiasm of youth. This is the more surprising, as he was engaged in teaching from six in the morning till eleven in the evening, — having private classes, and being employed to teach in one of the evening schools for adults. It should be observed, however, that his duties in school are much less arduous than with those teachers who, in addition to government, have to instruct classes.

He received me with the utmost politeness of manner, and with true cordiality and frankness, — spared no pains to show me all around, and give me such information as he had in his power.

This school was pointed out to me by Monsieur le Vice-Rector à la Sorbonne, as the best of the eleven schools of mutual instruction in the city, which were established in 1815 by Messrs. Martin and Froissard. The plan is copied after the Lancastrian schools in England, and their success is spoken of in high terms of praise by the authorities in charge of the matter. Undoubtedly, this system of mutual instruction is carried in these schools to a good degree of perfection, — and in the matter of pecuniary economy, there is much to recommend it. Only one master of moderate attainments is required for a school of from two hundred to three hundred pupils. Besides, so perfect is the system, and so exactly is it followed, even in its minutest details, aside from obtaining considerable elementary knowledge in the branches, they necessarily contract valuable habits of order, economy, punctuality, obedience, and respect for superiors. Still, no philosophical educator will fail to perceive that the system is incapable of affording the highest form of instruction, or imparting the fullest development to mind. Education can never fulfil its high mission, unless the teacher can command time to become familiar with each individual mind under his care, and to adapt his mode of teaching to its peculiarities. This idea is fully carried out in the more liberal and enlightened institutions of Europe, in many of which there is a teacher for every eight or ten pupils.

Jan. 27th. Made a visit to the *Municipal School Français 1, Rue de Blanche.* On presenting myself at the gate, which opens into the court, the porter took my letters to Mr. *Goubeau,* the Director of the establishment. The latter gentleman, handsomely dressed, rather portly in person, and with a business air, received me with perfect courtesy and cordiality, and at once entered into lively conversation, communicating in the most rapid manner imaginable, items of information concerning the school. His enunciation was so distinct, and the tones of his voice so clear, that I understood readily nearly all he uttered; but in a few moments, he begged to take the liberty to introduce to me his professor in the English language, who would be most happy to give me such information as I might desire, and to show me over the establishment. The latter gentleman soon appeared, and went on in the same hurried manner, detailing the plan and arrangements of the institution, comparing it with similar institutions in Germany and England, in which countries he had himself journeyed, — and, in fine, developing to my mental view the comprehensive and complicated system of schools in Paris. But his pronunciation was so indistinct, and his utterance so hurried, that I but partially understood him, and more than once reminded him of his being the teacher of English, and that I was able to understand that language somewhat better than the French. At last he plainly told me, that although professor of the English language, and having travelled in England, still he never attempted to speak the language. I could hardly make myself believe that a professor of one of the best and most distinguished schools of Paris, could be wanting in the very branch to which his entire time was devoted. But, perhaps, the eminence even of his position made him fearful of attempting to express himself in a language, which he could hardly have done without making some mistakes.

It being Thursday, there was no afternoon session of the school, so that I was not able to witness recitations, — but an inspection of the rooms, premises, apparatus, with full and minute explanations, in regard to everything there, enabled me to get a tolerably good idea of the institution.

The school was founded by the city, in 1844, and is under the supervision of a board of six distinguished literary or scientific gentlemen. The professors and associate masters are chosen by the administration of the school. The institution is designed to occupy a medium rank, between the more common private seminaries, and the University of France. It affords superior facilities for acquiring a very thorough and extensive practical education, for the various avocations of life, including the pursuit of teaching. Indeed, in regard to the latter point, the professor of English very deliberately informed me, that the school had been more successful, even than the best Normal schools, in sending out accomplished and efficient teachers of public and private schools, and even Academies.

The institution corresponds to those schools which have been in existence for fifteen years in almost all the German states, and which are there styled *Real Schools*. The course occupies six years, one class graduating every year, and the instruction, except in those branches based upon the ancient languages, is considered complete. The student is advanced to a higher class only after a most rigid examination, and his qualifications having been confirmed by the board.

The examination for admission to the freshman class, requires the applicant to be tolerably familiar with reading, writing, the elements of orthography, the first notions of geography, Sacred history, and the ground-rules of arithmetic in whole numbers and decimals. The pupil must also be able to write with sufficient ability to take notes without hesitation, and to follow readily a dictation.

The course of instruction comprises the study of the French grammar, the French language and its writers; the English, German, Italian, and Spanish languages; history and geography in all their branches; computation; arithmetic, with its applications; geometry, algebra, accounts, cosmography, zoölogy, husbandry, botany, geology, mineralogy, natural philosophy, chemistry, industrial mechanics; the study of first materials; technology, linear-drawing, ornamental drawing, carpentry, architecture, laying of plans, perspective, drafting, construction, and singing. At the request of parents, languages not comprised in the course are taught their children by private instructors. This course will appear the more extensive, when it is considered that many of the branches are taught by professors who have made a distinct branch an exclusive subject of investigation for many years, and who thus having a most thorough and extensive knowledge of the subject, have facilities for illustrating the details of the study.

The studies are so arranged, that the pupil who should be compelled to leave before having completed the course, will have received a knowledge of the fundamental principles, around which it will be comparatively easy to gather dependent acquisition.

SCHOOL REGULATIONS.

For the benefit of such applicants, as are not able to pass an examination for admission to the freshman class, there is established a preparatory department.

Both boarders and day-scholars are admitted. The school is formed into two divisions; the smaller college with pupils thirteen years and upwards; and the larger college, with those who have not attained the age of thirteen.

The dormitories and study-rooms of the divisions are entirely separate, as well as meals and recreations.

The religious direction of the school is confined to *M. L' Abbé Duncel*, curate, or vicar of *Notre Dame de Lorette;* while M., the pastor Coquerel, gives instruction every week to the protestant pupils.

The medical counsel of the schools is composed of four distinguished physicians.

Every three months the parent of the student receives a certificate of the conduct and progress of the latter, with remarks from each member of the faculty. Besides this, each pupil is required to transcribe into his journal the register of his standing, in regard to scholarship, conduct and moral character, as given him by the professors, which is to be inspected and signed by his parents or guardians, on their days of visit to the school.

Pupils who have not applied themselves satisfactorily to their studies during the term, are required to study during the vacation.

The pupil before being admitted must present a certificate, first, of his birth; second, of his vaccination; third, of his good conduct, if he has ever attended another school.

Pupils are required to be in their rooms as early as nine o'clock in the evening. They are permitted to receive visits only from their parents, correspondents, and persons allowed by their parents or by the faculty of the school.

Parents are requested to leave in the hands of their children no valuable trinket, or spending-money. The pupil must bring no book to school without submitting it to the director for his approbation.

The terms are, two hundred dollars per annum, for boarders and forty dollars, for day-scholars.

I have been the more particular to enumerate several of the more prominent features and regulations of this school, as it is esteemed one of the best appointed in Paris.

On my return, I looked into the church of *Notre-Dame-de-Lorette*. Although this is not usually spoken of in the descriptions of Paris, as one of the most notable religious edifices, yet I must confess that it presented points of interest and beauty that I have not found surpassed.

It is completely isolated on all sides, and forms a basilica, uniting the Grecian style of architecture, and ornament, of the fifteenth and sixteenth centuries, mingled with the Byzantine. The interior is of the greatest richness. The numerous paintings with which its chapel is filled, were executed upon the spot, and were designed for the places they occupy, giving to the *tout ensemble* of the view a unity and agreeableness of effect that could not otherwise have been obtained. Aside from the places reserved for Divine worship, the church is capable of accommodating about three thousand persons.

CHAPTER XIV.

COMMUNAL SCHOOL — CHARACTER OF THE SCHOOL — PRIVATE DAY AND BOARDING-SCHOOL BY THE FRERES — PLAN OF THE SCHOOL — SINGING — MUNICIPAL SCHOOL SUPERIOR — ARRANGEMENT OF THE BUILDING — DRAWING — CHURCH ST. EUSTACHE — CATHEDRAL DE NOTRE DAME, COMPARED WITH THE ROUEN CATHEDRAL — BELL — SPLENDID INTERIOR — HISTORICAL ASSOCIATIONS — CORONATION OF NAPOLEON — ENGLISH EPISCOPAL CHURCH — MUDDY STREETS — PRACTICE OF THE LADIES — HOTEL DES INVALIDS — EXTERIOR — INTERIOR — BRILLIANT REMINISCENCE OF THE OLD SOLDIER — MILITARY SCHOOL — WOMAN AMONG THE LOWER ORDERS.

Jan. 28th. Visited one of the Communal Schools, kept by the Freres rue Montgolfiere. The director received me with great delicacy and politeness, mingled with a goodness of manner that was really delightful. With the utmost willingness, and apparent pleasure, he conducted me through the different apartments of the school, explaining everything on his way, and answering my numerous questions with the utmost readiness.

The school is composed of about six hundred pupils, and is conducted by six teachers, — a single teacher having the management and principal instruction of one hundred pupils. The director informed me that it was not at all difficult for a teacher to manage successfully so large a number; but I was inclined to differ from him in opinion on that point, and my observations upon the school fully corroborated my view. The order in the different rooms was by no means satisfactory. The pupils were not only noisy, but they had listless habits, and were not prompt in obeying the teacher's commands.

The exercises in arithmetic were indifferent. Although the pupils showed considerable readiness in performing examples, and especially in applying the principle of cancellation, yet they were unusually ignorant in regard to the principles of the rules, and were unable to give a reason for some of the simplest steps in the process of a solution. The reading, too, in my humble judgment, was the poorest that I ever listened to in a school. The pupils called the words with sufficient fluency, but their enunciation was sadly indistinct, the pronunciation faulty, while there was nothing in their reading that could, with a shadow of justice, be termed expression; but on the contrary, the most disagreeable monotony pervaded the whole style, robbing the pieces of whatever of pleasure the sentiments were calculated to inspire.

The drawing and writing, to which much attention is given here as in all the schools, were, however, superior; and some specimens shown me, executed by comparatively young pupils, were surprisingly excellent, and would have done credit to artists of greater pretensions.

Here, as in several other schools that I visited, the teacher most cordially assented to my request for permission to address the school. The announcement of this intention by the teacher, produced, with good reason, a lively sensation among the pupils, and every eye beamed with expectancy. To hear their own language from the mouth of a foreigner, kindled their juvenile curiosity so high that they leaned forward, as if they would press out of their seats; and when I asked who would perform a few simple questions for me, every hand was up, and many of them trembling with a nervous ment, indicating intense eagerness. The questions I put, were such as these: "Can you begin at the left hand to add?" "The explanation for multiplying by the factors of a number?" and their almost total ignorance of the principles, gave further proof that it is quite impossible for one teacher to instruct well so large a number as one hundred pupils.

They learn here, Reading, Writing, Arithmetic, the French language, Drawing, and the elements of some of the higher branches.

The principal informed me, that there are some thirty schools taught in Paris by the Frères. The compensation of teachers of this class of schools, is about three hundred and twenty dollars per annum. Such as are successful receive, besides, medals of honor, and a gratuity in case of being disabled; and in case of decease, something for their families.

After looking in upon several schools, I was conducted by one of the Frères to a private institution which received both boarders and day-scholars. This was of a more elevated character than those just named, and its members were from families in easy circumstances in life. I did not, however, see that neatness and elegance, either in the rooms or in the dress and persons of the pupils, which I expected. This was styled one of the Christian schools of the Frères, and is established with the idea of rearing a solid education upon a religious basis. Although private, it is authorized by the University of France, and its plan is after those which have been for some time in successful operation in Rouen, Rheims, Lyons, Nantes, Sainte-Etienne, and in other large places in France. The school is divided into two sections; the first includes youth between the ages of fourteen and eighteen, who design to follow a mercantile or industrial life. They are carefully instructed in the tenets and forms of religion, and are taught grammar, and the principles connected with it, — such, for instance, as grammatical analysis, logic, and some idea of style. Also, Arithmetic, Book-Keeping, Geometry, with its applications, such as drawing plans, carpentry, etc.; Drawing, including perspective, linear, ornamental, and figure; Geography, including commercial and historical; History, including Ecclesiastical, Ancient and French; Vocal Music; the elements of the Natural Sciences.

Ornamental branches not included in the above lists, — such as instrumental music, and the study of the living languages, such as English, German, etc., are extra.

What is termed the second section of the school, composed of young children, who design at a later period to pursue the study of the Latin language, in an establishment of secondary instruction, are carefully taught the elements of such branches as are appropriate to their age and designs.

Pupils enter school at eight o'clock in the morning, and leave at half past five o'clock in the afternoon, taking their dinners at the establishment, for which no extra charge is made. The expense to this class of pupils is about one dollar per week. A slight additional charge is made for use of furnishings at the table, library, and philosophical and chemical apparatus.

Pupils are accompanied in a promenade every fortnight, or Thursday afternoon; and parents are required to furnish their children who are members of the school, a uniform-coat, after the style adopted by the institute, for Sundays, fête-days, and for promenade.

The several branches comprised in the course are efficiently taught here, by six or eight competent professors. The time for each recitation is ample, the classes conveniently small, and there is an appearance of the work being well done. English is taught by a professor from London, who divides his time among several schools in the city. The director spoke English very distinctly, and with tolerable ease, although he assured me that he had attended to learning the language but a short time, and could get but little opportunity for practice. It is really surprising with what difference of facility different minds acquire a foreign language; some gaining enough to be able to express themselves intelligibly, and with ease, in a short time; while others, with equally good intellectual capacity, never arrive to any fluency or correctness of expression, however much study or practice they may have given to it.

No corporal punishment was allowed in this school; and the order was by no means good. Several regulations I have omitted here, being the same as in the school described under the head *Français 1.*

The exercise in music to which I listened, was highly interesting and satisfactory. It was conducted with a degree of spirit, energy and thoroughness, that could not fail to impart to a stranger a high opinion of the efficiency of this department of instruction in Paris. The professor, himself familiar with the subject, conducted the exercise in an easy, animated and enthusiastic manner. His habits of mind, as evinced in his instruction, were evidently reduced to the strictest method, and to great simplicity of arrangement and gradation in the steps of mental effort, and were well adapted to the minds of his class. There was, moreover, a philosophical character pervading the whole, which revealed the true master; and from the moment of commencing, to the close of the exercise, he moved rapidly and boldly on, without the slightest hesitation or unnecessary repetition. The pupils, catching the inspiration of the teacher, were all ear, eye and mouth, completely thrilled with emotion, and almost bounding with interest.

Instead of the ordinary staff with lines and spaces, the tones were indicated by means of figures, arranged in a horizontal line. This new method of representing musical characters, though not generally adopted, has an advantage over the old, of greater simplicity; and the professor informed me, that although he instructed his class in the old method, he was more successful with the latter, and that he hoped ere long to see it generally introduced.

He spent about half the hour in drilling his class on the different scales, and the remainder of the time in executing combinations as a drill, and some of these were difficult in a high degree.

Jan. 29th. Visited the *Municipal School Superior*, kept by *M. Pompé, rue St. L'Orient*. The building, which is quadrangular in form, encloses a small square or open court, which affords a delightful retreat to the scholars at recess and noons. The interior front of the edifice is ornamented by a portico supported by fluted columns extending quite around the square, presenting not only a pleasing aspect to the eye, but a most agreeable promenade, protected alike from the rays of the sun in midsummer, and the rain in inclement seasons. The rooms through which the director escorted me, with an air a little dignified and condescending, were by no means elegant, though they were spacious and conveniently arranged. The walls of the *salle à manger*, or dining-room, were covered with fine drawings, made by those who either were at the time, or had previously been, pupils of the school. One of these was a map of Paris and its environs. It was on a surface of not less than ten feet square, and was most elaborately and beautifully done. Much attention here, as in all the schools, was given to drawing. In the *Salle à Dessin* were several exquisite models for moulding in plaster, while the walls were hung with elegant patterns. The chemical laboratory was well appointed, and the philosophical and other apparatus quite complete.

The school is composed of about three hundred and twenty pupils, — eighty occupying a single room. The order was good among all the divisions; and there was an appearance of industry and care with the pupils, which spoke well for the school. They are received here at the age of thirteen, and remain three years. The pupils are mostly from the middling classes of the Parisian population, and pay tuition. A few indigent pupils, however, are admitted, whose expenses are defrayed by the city. The highest sum paid any teacher in this school, is six hundred dollars per annum. Much use was made of the Black-Board. No reading taught here. No corporal punishment. Emulation encouraged. For prizes, medals and books are given. Pupils expelled, as a last resort.

On my return, I looked into the beautiful church of *St. Eustache*, in the Third Arrondissement of the city. A detailed description of it could not be given here, even if it were certain that the account would prove entertaining to the general reader. This vast edifice, commenced in 1532, and only finished in 1642, was at first only a small chapel dedicated to *St. Agnes*. The great length of time occupied in its building, fails to astonish the mind, when the immense pile, with its decorations and sculpture, are once fairly contemplated. The church is rich in pictures, and the traveller would be well repaid with a visit to them.

CATHEDRAL DE NOTRE DAME.

There are very many religious edifices in Paris, all of them more or less instructive and interesting; but there is no other, perhaps, that impresses the mind so strongly, and awakens so many and diverse emotions in the breast of the beholder, as the church of *Notre Dame*. Its antiquity, its immense size, the style of its architecture, its interior decorations, and especially its historical associations, all combine to render it a pile of thrilling interest. In external appearance, majestic as it is, it does not equal the Cathedral at Rouen; but its decorations, both within and without, are more curious and elaborate; the former being chiefly paintings, the latter sculptured ornaments. It would require volumes to give a description of these compositions. There is scarcely a prominent person or event in scriptural or ecclesiastical history, that is not here illustrated, with many fanciful inventions besides.

Its façade is grand and imposing beyond expression. A high, and deeply cut, arched door-way, massively rich in sculptured ornaments, opens to the main entrance. On either side is a smaller door-way, and above this, in solemn grandeur, an elevated and massive tower, evidently intended for the bases of steeples. The general architecture is pure, pointed gothic, and though its effect is grandly impressive, its beauty is somewhat marred by the absence of steeples, pinnacles, etc. It is a cruciform edifice. Its length externally is four hundred and forty-two feet; breadth, one hundred and sixty-two feet; length of transepts, three hundred and fifty-two feet. The towers are two hundred and thirty-five feet high.

You reach the summit by a stairway of three hundred and eighty-nine steps, situated in the western tower, from which a splendid view is spread out to the eye, displaying, in picturesque beauty the chief points of interest in the capital, the winding course of the Seine, and the magnificent country views with which Paris is surrounded.

In the western tower is the bell, whose deep and heavy tones are only heard on occasions of great solemnity. Its dimensions are so huge as to require the utmost exertions of sixteen able-bodied men to give it motion.

The vastness and religious gloom of the interior of the church impresses strongly, from the first, the mind of the beholder. After contemplating the exterior of the grand edifice, you experience on entering it no feeling of surprise or disappointment. There is a correspondence and harmony of effect, which do not destroy nor weaken the first emotion, but only elevate and strengthen it. The mind is almost staggered with delight, as the brilliant sanctuary, resplendent gildings, costly marbles, and master-pieces of statuary, burst upon the view. The perspective from the front entrance to the depth of the sanctuary is surpassingly fine, and, as you gaze upon the lofty vaults, the numerous pillars that sustain them, the happy disposition of the masses, the harmony of the whole, the perfection in the details, you can hardly realize that it is all the work of three centuries.

Upon the identical spot now occupied by Notre Dame, there existed, it is said, in the reign of Tiberius, a temple dedicated to Jupiter, Vulcan, and Castor and Pollux. As early as A. D. 365, after the Parisians had become Christians, they threw down these idols, and replaced them by a Christian church. This edifice becoming insufficient to accommodate the increase of the population, in 1161, Maurice de Sully commenced the erection of the present noble structure, and Alexander III. placed the first stone, in the year 1163. Successive additions were made to it up to the sixteenth century.

The historical associations of Notre Dame invest the gloomy pile with intense interest. Here, in November, 1793, was enacted that blasphemous scene which astonished all Europe. A courtezan, by the name of Maillard, was installed as the " Goddess of Reason," upon the high altar of the cathedral, by Herbert and his associates, surrounded by immense throngs of infatuated men. Here, too, in April, 1802, less than nine years after, was celebrated the reëstablishment of the Catholic religion, with great pomp. But the most gorgeous and magnificent ceremony, which the venerable walls of Notre Dame have ever witnessed, was the coronation of Napoleon and Josephine, in 1804, as emperor and empress of the French. The display of splendor and riches on that occasion, dazzled the eyes of even the Parisians. The pope came from Rome to place the crown upon his lofty brow. Such an honor had not been conferred on any monarch for ten centuries. Charlemagne was crowned by a former pope, but the Emperor of the West had to go to Rome for the honor. The precise spot of the coronation is indicated by a star wrought in the marble floor, in front of the great altar; and the robes worn on the occasion by the different high functionaries, are still shown the stranger. They are all splendid; Napoleon's, surpassingly so.

Sunday, Jan. 30th. Attended Divine service to-day at the English episcopal church, rue d' Agguessiau. It is a small, but beautiful church, having been recently fitted up in the English-Gothic style, for the English ambassador, and the English residents in Paris.

As I entered the vestibule of the church, I was the occasion of a trivial incident, which I hardly knew whether to receive, or not, in a complimentary light. The sexton, to whom I addressed myself, in English, for the favor of a seat, replied to me in very indifferent French, thus leading me to conclude that my poor English, and what my friends are often pleased to call un-American features, had very naturally betrayed the too credulous Englishman into an egregious error as to my nationality.

The company assembled was not large, but the air of manners, and quality and style of dress, showed it to be very select in character. I observed here a similar feature in the mode of conducting the worship as prevails in the French protestant church, in the city. It is in having two officiating clergymen;

one, to conduct the preliminary exercises, such as the opening prayer, reading the hymn, etc., and affording to the other, who is the preacher proper, entire freshness of powers for the effort of the sermon. I would not say that this mode is not preferable to that in our own country generally, requiring all the services, excepting singing, of the preacher. It was certainly in conformity with the practice of the extreme division of labor, so fully carried out in Europe, in all departments of life; a principle which contributed, no doubt, to the superior character of those sermons which I listened to in Paris. They gave evidence of high talent united with research and care in writing.

The subject of the text was, the miracle of Christ on the occasion of casting out evil spirits from men, and causing them to enter a herd of swine. The preacher contended that these were really evil spirits, or demons, and not a state of lunacy. He refuted the objection often made, that this miracle seemed an exception to the general benevolent tenor of Christ's work. The style of the preacher was clear, argumentative, and elegant, and highly impressive.

Jan. 21st. The weather, which had been so severe as to freeze over the Seine, was now as mild as a day of Spring. The softening of the air, and some falling weather, had rendered the streets, as a matter of course, uncomfortably muddy. This annoyance was, however, in a good measure remedied by the efficient means used, by men employed by the government, to remove the dirt. Troops of them might have been seen in all the principal streets, some with huge brooms, which they used with admirable dexterity; others with teams, to remove the muddy excrescence; while others still, with engines ready to apply a moderate shower-bath to such parts as the public convenience seemed most to require. Muddy streets are ever a sore grievance to the foot-passer in the city; but the Parisian manages to let this, as well as most others of the petty miseries of life, disturb but little his equanimity. Especially is the remark true of the women. As carriage conveyance is exceedingly cheap, perfectly convenient, and safe, most well-dressed ladies would, of course, choose that mode of transit, especially in foul weather; yet there may always be seen ladies elegantly attired promenading and crossing the streets at every possible angle. When it is the fashion, as is most generally the case, for the robe of a lady's dress to fall so low as to sweep the pavement, muddy streets would be to some females a matter of real embarrassment; but not so with the fair Parisians. They resolve the matter at once, by gathering up with the utmost *sang froid*, their gown, and not unfrequently skirts and all, completely away from all contact of the envious element below, — displaying to the more curious, the perfect contour of the lower nether limbs far more than would meet the approval of the fastidious. This practice cannot but strike very oddly an American, accustomed as he is at home to a degree of fastidiousness in the manners of the fair sex, approaching to squeamishness. Accordingly, it is with them a subject of general and lively remark, and not unfrequently of severe animadversion. The American lady in Paris is, of course, at first a little shocked; but the repetition of the sight, and the perfect indifference with which it is regarded by the Parisians themselves, gradually efface the feeling of indelicacy which first arises. I would not speak positively upon a subject so much a matter of taste, but laying prejudices aside, and viewing the thing in a rational and candid light, it may be fairly doubted whether, after all, the custom is so very reprehensible. The question will arise to an impartial mind, why it may be regarded more immodest to reveal a neatly-laced ankle, enveloped in nice silk hose, when demanded by necessity, than to display ostentatiously the arms and breast. The truth may be, that we are wont to decide upon forms of propriety, by some standard in our own mind, and this standard may be the result of little else than certain accidental conventionalisms. Nothing is more common for us, when abroad, than to decide upon things as they square with our preconceived notions. Thus, whether we judge aright or not, will depend upon the justness of our standard, and not upon the thing itself. Perhaps it would be a better rule to follow nature and common sense. Again, let us look through the medium of pure intention. An evil imagination will lend a coloring of debasement to the most simple act. *Honni soit qui mal y pense*, is a good motto. The lady of elevated taste, will be simple and natural, — avoiding on the one hand unnecessary display, and on the other, prudery.

I made to-day an unsuccessful effort to gain admittance to the Chamber of Deputies, during a session of its members. The proper officers to whom I applied in person at the *Palais Bourbon* (which is the name of the edifice where the chamber is held), for a ticket of admission, informed me that I should address them in writing. On leaving, I noticed a long file of some fifty persons, making what the French term the *queue*, before the closed door at the east wing of the building. They were waiting with the hope of getting admittance to the free gallery of the chamber; but as this accommodates but about twenty-five persons, it is not easy to see what rational hope the hindermost could have entertained of success, unless, indeed, they expected that some before them, weary of waiting, would leave before the hour for opening the door. The powerfully excited and deeply interesting state of the discussion upon the subject of foreign affairs, having fully aroused the highest talent of the Chamber, had lent great intensity to the desire, always strong, to witness the eloquent and thrilling debates.

The doors were to be opened at twelve o'clock, M., yet it was now only ten A. M.; and some had been there, I was told, since eight in the morning,—so eager was the general desire for admission.

The Chamber of Deputies, the popular branch of the Legislature, was about the only public place difficult of access to a respectable foreigner, in the French capital. The narrow gallery was always filled, when the debates were at all interesting, by a class of idlers who could afford to wait outside in the street some two or three hours. A few more persons were admitted by ticket, which was obtained on application to Messrs. the Questeurs at the Palais; but the limited number thus favored, bore no proportion to the pressing applications. The Minister from your government had no power in the premises, except to loan you his own ticket to his private box. Hence, many who tarried but a short time in Paris, had to go away without having their desires in this particular gratified.

On my way, I looked into the *Hôtel des Invalids*. Paris is munificent in establishments of a benevolent character,—of asylums devoted to the support of the aged and infirm; but by far the most important, both on account of the grandeur of its buildings, and the benefits which it confers upon its inmates, is the *Hôtel des Invalids*. It is intended for the support of disabled officers and soldiers, or such as have been in active service upwards of thirty years. The institution supports, at present, upwards of five thousand of these scarred and disabled veterans,—fading mementos of the military glory of France.

The edifice was erected in 1670, by that magnificent monarch, Louis XIV, who sought a building and institution worthy of his services, and the grandeur he wished to impress upon his reign. Napoleon, whose mortal remains sleep beneath its gilded dome, changed, if I remember rightly, its original destination, and converted it into a hallowed home for the noble and brave whom Mars had spared the envious stroke of death in the gory field of war. The luminous sagacity of the great captain could not but see how much of inspiration it would lend to the military genius of the country, as well as aid to embalm his own memory in the gratitude of his soldiers, thus in providing for them a grand retreat to surround their declining years with a mellow halo of mild and awakening associations.

It is a vast and splendid establishment, and is a conspicuous object from a distance, on account of its gilded dome, lantern, and spire, rising to the height of three hundred and twenty-three feet above the floor. It is situated on the south bank of the Seine, opposite the Champs Elysées, and the enclosure occupies some sixteen acres of ground. The immense esplanade in front of the Hospital, extending down to the Seine, is laid out with much taste with gravelled walks, trees, and shrubbery. The trees are so arranged, that while they afford a most grateful promenade and shelter to the old soldiers, open a beautiful vista, through which is heightened the majesty of the edifice, — the whole façade of which is thus uncovered, and may be seen at a great distance. Boulevards planted with trees surround the monument, where terminate in a focus four grand streets. A fountain of simple, but elegant construction, sports into the air several beautiful jets, in the midst of the esplanade, which is crossed by three streets leading to the military school, and to the *Champs de Mars.* The esplanade is separated from the first court by a fossé furnished with twelve pieces of cannon, in the midst of which a bridge, closed by a beautiful gate, gives entrance to the noble asylum of valor. The edifice is composed of five courts of equal form and size, surrounded by buildings five stories in height, and covers a space of nearly seven acres.

The church of the establishment is indebted for its noble appearance, principally to its magnificent dome, supported by twenty pairs of composite pillars. It is considered the master-piece of French architecture, and is thought to rival in beauty — though of inferior proportions — the celebrated domes of St. Paul's in London, and St. Peter's at Rome. As it was undergoing repairs, I did not gain access to the interior of the dome. I could perceive, however, that it is undoubtedly very rich in architectural ornament, sculpture, painting, carving, and gilding; yet, to my untutored eye, the dome appeared too elongated, and to have too much elevation, for the proportionate height of the main buildings.

The interior halls are named after the great battles of the emperor, Austerlitz, Wagram, etc. The library is in the first stage of the pavilion, and commands a handsome view of the Champs Elysées and the Avenue de Neuilly. The interior of the buildings is everywhere ornamented with statues, groups, antiques, bass-reliefs, paintings, — most of them having significant allusion to ideas of martial glory, or to the distinguished actors in the military history of the empire and the republic. The walls of the interior of the church were festooned with national flags wrested from the enemy in the astounding victories of the empire and the republic. Almost all the nations of Europe were represented by these fading testimonials of the national prowess. Many of them were tattered, thus faintly showing how desperate had been the struggle on the one part to retain, and on the other to bear off, as trophies of victory, these banners — not of love, good-will, and peace on earth, but of hatred, revenge, and direful carnage.

The crowning-interest of this grand establishment is the tomb of Napoleon, in the chapel of St. Jerome. I was not permitted to visit the spot, where repose in the calm and severe dignity of death, — investing the immediate presence with a sublime awe, — the man who had broken up the despotic institutions of a thousand years, and changed the face of Europe and the world.

Besides pensioned officers, there are sub-officers and privates who are boarded, lodged and clothed, and receive a monthly stipend, varying according to rank. The dormitories contain each from fifty to sixty beds; besides which, there are large infirmaries for the sick. All, except field-officers, mess at the public tables, and wear the same uniform. Dinner is served at twelve o'clock, M., a departure from the French custom. The dining-room was ample, the walls of which were handsomely painted in fresco; but I was not permitted to inspect the *cusine,* on account of the inconvenience of the hour.

The Hôtel des Invalids is under the especial surveillance of the minister of war. A marshal of France commonly officiates as governor. The council of administration is composed of military officers of the highest grade, with eminent statesmen. The most skilful physicians of the army prescribe for such as may be sick, who are tended by the gentle and humane hand of the Sisters of Charity.

The different inmates whom I met, in traversing the building, dispensed the usual civilities of courtesy, with a respectful but lofty bearing. They seemed impressed with a profound sentiment of the grandeur of that brilliant period in French history, of which they were the sad remaining vestiges. How could it have been otherwise? For how full had been their experience of what lends intense force to the energy of the soul? What scenes of sublime and awful reality had passed before their eyes to fill the page of reminiscences in the book of life! And now, what visions of Austerlitz, Marengo, Borodino, etc., sifted with fiery vividness through their fading memories! They had many of them witnessed the rising majesty, the noon-day splendor, and the setting rays of that splendid meteor, which had intoxicated France with its glory, and flooded Europe with its dazzling beams. And now they were guarding, with a sentiment of deep and pious reverence, the ashes of the sublime spirit who had been removed from his sea-girt prison to repose in the bosom of his own French people.

From the Hotel des Invalids, I went to the Military School. It was founded in 1751, by Louis XV, as an establishment of education, for the gratuitous instruction of five hundred poor gentlemen, the sons of deceased officers. They receive here, of course, a military education, and are especially trained in the spirited and graceful accomplishment of horsemanship. Its form is that of a parallelogram, occupying an area of fifteen hundred feet in length, and eight hundred in width, and comprises six buildings, and fifteen courts and gardens. In the dome, crowning the edifice, is a clock supported by two figures, Time and Astronomy. There is also, in the establishment, an observatory.

The Champ de Mars is a vast parallelogram of two thousand eight hundred and fifty feet in length, or more than half a mile; and nine hundred and sixty-nine feet in width; extending from the Military School to the banks of the Seine. The level surface is broken by no trees or shrubbery. It has served various purposes, and the spot brings up to the mind familiar with the history of Paris, some thrilling incidents in its eventful periods. It has not only been employed for the exercise and review of the pupils of the school, and the National Guards of the city, but it has served, at different times, for public fêtes, and political gatherings. In the stormy days of the old revolution, it was the scene of many midnight orgies, as well as the rendezvous of many a foul plot, or demoniac machination. Here the first mayor of Paris lost his head, and other dark deeds of blood shade the memory of the place.

It is now used by the pupils of the school as a race-course, and for grand reviews.

On my return, becoming embarrassed as to my route, I made inquiries of a woman tending a fruit-stand, at the corner of two streets. The good-hearted creature, not satisfied with pointing out to me my way, left her little bazaar with a lad, and actually accompanied me at least a quarter of a mile, that I might be the more sure of finding my place of destination. The pleasure of conferring a favor seemed to lend a glow and vivacity to her nature, and she chatted upon all subjects with the utmost simplicity and animation, evincing not unfrequently a degree of intelligence and discrimination far above her condition in life. Her kindness, natural manner, and spirituality of expression quite charmed me, but her familiarity, in any other than a French woman, might have been misconstrued. While referring to the great number of strangers in Paris, she suddenly turned the question by saying, "But, sir, of what country are you, may I ask?" You can, of course, very easily divine, replied I. Fixing a full, but placid look upon me for a moment, she suddenly burst out in a kind of good-natured petulance, declaring with emphasis, that I was really inexplicable, — that I certainly had the accent of an Englishman, but the unmistakable features of an Italian.

This woman was not at all singular in her manner, for a Parisian. The traits of character she displayed were such as are common among the female populace. The stranger does not meet here with that affectation and reserve often found elsewhere; on the contrary, all is simple, natural, and cordial. All the women among the lower orders of Paris, whom my business furnished a pretext to address (and I took particular pains to get the greatest possible number of examples), evinced, without a single exception, the same easy and unaffected style in their intercourse. They would always enter into the very spirit of my demand with promptness, ardor, and apparent disinterestedness, and would even take special pains not only to furnish me with all the information in their power, about what I wished, but to render me such further aid as was possible. And this complaisance did not seem to arise from a calculated habit, or even from formal politeness, but appeared to spring from a natural spontaneity of goodness. If the conversation became discursive, she would roam with me, with great naturalness and vivacity of manner, broaching any subject, treating it with perfect freedom, and never failing to impart to it a peculiarly lively interest from the brilliant hues of her own mind. The different postures and movements of the body, and the expression of the countenance, were all free, open, and in keeping with the intellectual character. An American, accustomed to the staid, and almost prudish, deportment of his own fair countrywomen, is at first confounded at a style of manners so different; but he cannot help but be in the main highly pleased with the change, and the new feature will be sure to improve upon acquaintance. The truth is, we cannot but love even the semblance of truthfulness and simplicity; and nowhere are these traits so fascinating as in woman. I am not certain, however, but that this freedom of manner would not more easily expose the female to rudeness with the unmannerly of the rougher sex, and that it would not tend to weaken the barriers which surround what is most lovely in woman. Modesty is, indeed, the priceless gem in the brilliants of woman's character, and we are wont to show the estimation in which we hold the valuable pearl, by hedging it in with what we call by different names, — such as prudent reserve, becoming dignity, unobtrusiveness, etc.; but whether what is thus saved can compensate for what is lost by the degenerating of these qualities into a stiff, prim, and cold manner, lending a most uninteresting trait to the female character, I do not know; but every one will agree, who has been favored with some observation in this matter, that perfect delicacy of modesty is often seen blended with simplicity, grace, and vivacity — each heightening and beautifying the other.

CHAPTER XV.

PALACE OF THE LOUVRE — FORMER RICHNESS IN ART — THE COMMON MIND A JUDGE OF ART — CHARACTERISTICS OF THE SEVERAL SCHOOLS OF PAINTERS — SUNDAY AT THE LOUVRE — INFLUENCE OF THE ART UPON THE MASSES — SCULPTURE, PETRIFIED BEAUTY — MARINE MUSEUM — ROYAL INSTITUTION FOR THE BLIND — BENEFITS OF THE NOBLE SCHOOL — PROFESSOR-LECTURER OF CHEMISTRY — GARDEN OF PLANTS — DESCRIPTION — ADULT AND JUVENILE EVENING SCHOOLS.

The Palace of the Louvre, a magnificent edifice, the origin of which is unknown, was rebuilt from the ruins upon the spot, in 1528, by Francis I, who ordered Peter Lescot to construct for him a palace worthy of a king of France, and of the century in which he lived. It was enlarged and improved by subsequent sovereigns, when Louis XIV, wishing to unite it with the Tuileries, invited the most skilful architects of Europe to furnish him with plans. None of the foreign nor the French architects who had accepted the invitation, were able to satisfy the luxurious monarch. The cavalier Bernin, the most famous architect of Italy, was then called to Paris, but he was not more successful. At length, the physician Claude Pernault proposed the present magnificent perystile, which is justly esteemed one of the most beautiful pieces of modern architecture. Its construction commenced in 1666, and ended in 1670.

The building is quadrangular, enclosing a court of some four hundred by five hundred feet, which is entered from the east by a noble portal. This front, five hundred and twenty-five feet long, is adorned with twenty-eight double Corinthian columns, and is indeed a fine specimen of architecture. The other sides of the quadrangle, both within and without, though less elegant, are very striking, both from their extent and their style. In the middle of the court, rises upon a pedestal of white marble, ornamented with two bass-reliefs, the equestrian statue in bronze, of the Duke of Orleans, eldest son of the late king Louis Phillippe. The prince holds his sword in the attitude of command, and the general air is lofty and imposing.

The Louvre was formerly a kingly residence, but is now devoted to the royal museum of painting and sculpture, forming one of the most extensive collections in Europe. During the latter years of the reign of Napoleon, this gallery was the richest and most magnificent by far of any that has ever existed. It could then boast of the *chefs-d'œuvres* of Rome, Florence, and, in fact, of the greater part of continental Europe, carried off by the conquering legions of France; but victory having deserted the eagles of Napoleon, these treasures were restored to their former possessors, and the Louvre has now no longer to glory in the Apollo Belvidere, the Venus di Medici, and other matchless productions. Still, the collection is a very extensive and noble one, and will richly reward the lover of art, in a visit thither. Eighteen large halls on the ground-floor, are filled with pieces of sculpture, including the choicest treasures of the Villa-Borghese, and many works that once embellished ancient Rome. Many of them are esteemed of great value. Five other rooms in the basement story, are devoted to the reception of works by modern artists. In 1830, a large apartment was filled with a collection of Egyptian antiquities; and there is now a large gallery called the *Musée de la Marine*, or the Marine Museum, comprising models and sections of vessels, plans of forts, and other curiosities. The great picture gallery, which is on the first floor, is approached by a grand staircase, painted by native artists, and comprises a suit of nine apartments, — the walls of which are lined with upwards of fifteen hundred pictures belonging to the French, Flemish, Dutch, Italian and Spanish schools of painting. The stranger at first saunters through these spacious and lofty rooms, with their richly frescoed ceiling, and amid such a profusion of the gems of art, in an entranced and bewildered state of mind. Intense anticipation now suddenly merged into the reality, the glowing associations of the place, the inspiring agencies by which he is everywhere so thickly surrounded, hurry away the soul to a region beyond the confines of earth, while the vast multitude of subjects which burst upon the mind, completely distract the attention. It is thus only after repeated visits to this world of paintings, and a degree of familiarity with its entrancing scenery, that the mind becomes sufficiently composed to study advantageously the individual works of great artists, or to compare faithfully their distinctive merits. It would, of course, be presumptuous in any but artists, or professed amateurs, to speak with lengthened criticism of master-paintings, especially such as are met with in the noble collection of the Louvre. Yet, a novice in the sublime art, under the influence of natural emotions, and exercising the principles of common sense and common observation, may venture to give the impressions which works of art make upon his mind, or indicate the emotions they give rise to in his breast.

If the end of painting is to move, to vivify thought, to excite emotion ; and if the success of a production is measured by the force and felicity with which it seizes and excites the mind of the beholder, then may not even the uneducated in art, venture to pass an opinion upon the more obvious and striking features of a picture? To be sure there will always be much about a painting beyond his powers of appreciation, — nice principles of science, exquisite touches of art, etc.; still, if the subject be within his understanding, and the thoughts it is calculated to awaken, such as find a response in his breast, may he not conclude with some assurance in regard to the success of the artist, by the agreeable effect of the painting upon the mind? The observer may not be able to analyze his sensations, or trace them to the spring of movement; yet conscious of their possession, he will not doubt the power of the hand that gave them rise. This view may be illustrated by the peculiar nature of oratory. Here the speaker is deemed successful, in proportion as he carries conviction to the minds of his hearers, or moves their feelings ; while the latter judge of the power of the former by their emotions, without asking the cause. The auditors may not be able to enter into the minutiæ of technical grammar, rhetoric, figures of speech, or even analyze the discourse; still he judges, and at least with some general grounds of safety, of the merits of effort, by his own consciousness.

It would be a futile effort to give a detailed account of the immense collection of the Louvre. A description, comprising the briefest account of each painting, would fill a large volume. Without attempting, therefore, to enumerate the great works which are there to be met with, let me aim at only a delineation of the *general character*, by which the different schools of painting are distinguished.

The first hall of the Louvre, in the picture gallery, is filled with paintings of the French school. The principal artists, whose works are here exhibited, are Nicholas Poussin, Claude Lorrain, Vernet, Le Brun, Gaspar, — and the modern painters, Gerard, David, Gros, Paul de Laroche, and Eugene Delacroix. The general character of the school of French historical painting, is the expression of *passion* and *violent emotion.* The coloring is for the most part brilliant; the canvas crowded with figures, and the incident selected, such as would enable the painter to display, to the best advantage, his knowledge of the human frame, or the varied expression of the human countenance. The moment seized is uniformly that of the strongest and most violent passion; the principal actors in the piece are represented in a state of phrenzied exertion, and the whole anatomical knowledge of the artist is displayed in the endless contortions into which the human frame is thrown. The French paintings, therefore, although they may produce a striking or dazzling effect, at first, upon the mind, and may excite a degree of admiration; still, they do not possess in the same degree as the master-pieces of some of the other schools, qualities which move deeply the feelings.

The paintings of Poussin are distinguished for a classical elegance of style; and those of Claude, for a perfection of coloring, which leaves nothing to be desired. Le Brun was the most distinguished painter of the seventeenth century. His works were characterized by ease and breadth of composition, and for remarkable grace and sweetness. Vernet stands high among French artists. His sea-pieces are truly admirable, both for the drawing, and for the feeling with which they are painted. The room which contains his " Sea Ports of France," is not one of the least attractive of the Louvre. He painted from nature, and though the subjects he chose were not of a lofty kind, he has treated them with great simplicity and truth. His two pictures, Le Depart and Le Retour are full of pathos and beauty; but for grace, and charm of coloring, what can rival that, known as the " Broken Pitcher?" The fresh, rosy, and beaming countenance of that young girl can never be recalled without pleasure; nor is it possible to pass, however hurriedly, through the great gallery of the

Louvre, without pausing for a moment, to smile back upon that lovely and ingenuous face, as it smiles upon you from the canvas. The paintings of Vernet, in this collection, are perhaps the finest specimens of that beautiful master. There is a delicacy of coloring, a unity of design, and a harmony of expression in his works, which accord well with the simplicity of the subjects which his taste has selected, and the general effect which it was his object to produce.

David was a distinguished painter, and the founder of a new school. Napoleon encouraged and liberally rewarded him. It was with the heroes of Greece and Rome that he covered his canvas; and the severe subjects he chose, he treated with characteristic sternness. To touch the softer emotions of the beholder, he never attempted.

Gérard possessed, in a high degree, the art of coloring. His drawing, too, was generally correct and pure. His Cupid and Psyche are among his best pieces. The expression of the heads is charming; the coloring fresh, and agreeable,—and the attitudes extremely graceful.

Gros is esteemed the greatest of the scholars of David. His portrait of Napoleon is much admired. The finest of his large paintings is the battle of Eylau. But the most important work of Gros, — because upon the largest scale, and in a public edifice, — is the Dome of the Pantheon, already mentioned in the description of that splendid edifice. The death of this eminent artist, in 1835, was a most melancholy one. Overwhelmed with disappointment and chagrin, he put an end to his existence by throwing himself into the Seine. With him died the last painter of the time of the empire.

Paul Delaroche was the son-in-law of Horace Vernet. His works are numerous. All the subjects have been taken from modern, and many from English history. Among the latter, are the Death Scene of Queen Elizabeth, — a forcible illustration of vanity and royalty struggling with old age and death; the terrible and touching scene of the Murder of the Princes in the Tower; Charles I. insulted by the Guards; Strafford on his way to the scaffold; and the truly pathetic scene of Lady Jane Grey upon the scaffold. But of all his works, the one the most admired, is his Saint Cecilia playing on an organ held before her by an angel. This was made after his return from Italy, where he had been sent by the government of Paris to execute some paintings for the Madeline, — and the painting partakes much of the character of the Florentine school. The calm and heavenly beauty of the saint, with the simplicity and grace of her drapery, throws around the work exceeding beauty. It shows, too, that the French are capable of expressing high delicacy of sentiment.

Eugene Delacroix is a painter of great originality and powerful imagination; his coloring is vigorous and effective. An admirable specimen of his talent may be seen in the gallery of the Luxembourg. It is his " Dante and Virgil, conducted by Flegias, crossing the lake which surrounds the infernal city of Dite." Another is Cleopatra, the fair Egyptian queen. But his most important work is at the Chamber of Peers, where he painted the Cupola of the Library.

You come next to the Dutch and Flemish school, which is distinguished by a character of a different description. The well known object of this school was to present an exact and faithful *imitation of Nature*. They did not pretend to aim at the exhibition of passion, or powerful emotion; nor was it their object to represent deep scenes of sorrow or suffering which accord with profound feelings. They selected as subjects the ordinary scenes and occurrences of life; and the power of the painter was seen in the exactness of the imitation, and the minuteness of finishing. Of this class of painters, in particular, were Teniers, Ostade, and Gerard Dow. There is a very great collection here preserved of the justly celebrated Rembrandt.

There are forty pieces of the Wouvermans here, all in a fine state of preservation. The works of this artist are generally crowded with figures; his subjects are commonly battle-pieces, or spectacles of military pomp, or the animated scenes of the chase; and he seems to have exhausted all the efforts of his genius in the variety of incident and richness of execution which these subjects are fitted to afford. These paintings are certainly beautiful; and it is almost impossible, without having seen them, to get an idea of the variety of design, the accuracy of drawing, or delicacy of finishing which distinguish his works from those of any other painter whatever.

There is a large number of the paintings of Vandyke and Reubens. There are sixty pictures of the latter of these masters, in the Louvre; and, combined with the celebrated gallery in the Luxembourg, they form the finest assemblage of them to be met with in the world. The character of his works differs essentially from that of both the French and Dutch school. He was employed, for the most part, in designing great altar pieces for splendid churches, or commemorating the glory of sovereigns in imperial galleries. The greatness of his genius rendered him fit to attempt the representation of the most complicated and difficult subjects. But in aiming to tell a whole story in the expression of a single picture, he attempts what it is impossible for painting to accomplish. The endless power of creation which this splendid genius possessed, is seen in the multiplicity of figures which crowd the canvas.

It is in the Italian school, however, that the collection of the

Louvre stands most unrivalled. The general object of this school appears to be the expression of passion. Their pieces are mostly of a religious character, in which are touchingly portrayed the sufferings and death of our Saviour,— the varied misfortunes to which his disciples were exposed, or the multiplied persecutions which the early fathers had to sustain. They aim to awaken pity or sympathy in the spectator.

There are a great many of the works of Dominichino, and of the Caraccis, in the collection. They bear a dark and gloomy character, and are designed to express deep and profound sorrow

Guido Reni, Carlo Maritti, and Murillo, have a general character, but somewhat different from Dominichino and the Caraccis. They have limited themselves, in general, to the delineation of a single figure, or a small group, in which, by a subdued tone of coloring, are expressed emotions of a softer and more permanent kind.

The distinctive feature in the small number of the paintings by Salvator Rosa, is a wild and original expression. In some of his pieces there is a sullen magnificence combined with splendid ideality, which mark the profound poetical genius.

But the softer expression of Correggio is quite different. Tenderness and delicacy are his prevailing qualities, and there is a softness in his shading of the human form, which is entirely unrivalled. He has represented nature in its most pleasing aspect, and enrobed individual figures with all the charms of ideal beauty.

The single picture by Carlo Dolci, in the Louvre, is in itself a gem, and alone is sufficient to mark the genius of its author. It represents the Holy Family, with the Saviour asleep. The delicacy and softness of shading exceeds even Correggio himself, while there is a deep, spiritual beauty pervading the whole, beyond the power of language to describe. The sleep of the infant is perfection itself; it is the deep and tranquil sleep of youth and innocence, subdued by a holy and angelic calm, unspeakably beautiful.

The works of Raphael aim at the expression of a sublime feeling, and they possess a high tone of spirituality rarely reached by the efforts of other artists. In his larger pieces, as in the Transfiguration, the effect is often injured by the confused expression of varied figures; but in his smaller pictures, the genuine character of his transcendent genius fully appears.

The Louvre is free to the public on Sundays, from ten A. M. till four P. M. It is likewise open to artists on week-days, between the same hours, and to strangers, on the presentation of their passports.

On Sundays, the halls never fail of being thronged with visitors. All classes may then be seen promiscuously sauntering through the splendid rooms. You will be jostled on one side by a fine lady, and on the other by a dusty workman in his dingy *blouse* and wooden shoes. The remark applies equally to other like places. Here, the humblest may have free access to the public gardens, palaces, buildings, repositories of art and science, — and the humblest make use of the munificent privilege. This having the grand and beautiful continually before them, has the sensible effect to elevate and refine their taste and manners, and to spiritualize their whole nature. Its influence upon their character may be seen in the elegance of the dress of the Parisian, and in his polished and graceful manners. Its deeper influence lays the foundation for that ardent attachment to the institutions and glory of France, which is the vital part of a Frenchman's character.

On week-days, as I have already intimated, there were in the gallery of paintings, artists, either making complete copies of some of the pictures upon the walls before them, or sketching off rough drafts, to be filled up at a future time, thousands of miles, perhaps, away. It was interesting to watch the expressive countenances of these young aspirants, in the difficult path of their art. On their faces varied emotions were, by turns, legible, according as, by a happy touch of their pencil, they had embodied a beautiful conception, or when the stubborn material refused to give forth the thought.

The halls of sculpture are on the ground-floor. You experience a sudden elevation of feeling, as you contemplate these gems of heathen eloquence. Here remain in a fixed and eternal repose, the sublimest expression of human character. Petrified beauty perpetually beams from those divine forms, to animate and delight. You cannot but reverence the geniuses that could breathe so much life and grace into the inanimate marble; that could give such expression to inert material, that nothing but breath seems wanting. The fleshy roundness of those limbs, the ease and flow of that dress, with its delicate waving, partly clinging to the body, partly fluttering in the wind; that delicate balance which alarms with the expectation of movement; those inimitable features stripped of everything gross and earthly, and beaming with the most celestial beauty, entrance the soul in a feeling of wonder and delight. In gazing upon these symbols of purified thought, we are reminded of the Spartan prayer, "Give us what is good and what is beautiful." Indeed, beauty ever excites religious emotions.

A marked difference between painting and sculpture is, that the latter, with the exception of a few pieces — such as the Dying Gladiator and the Laöcoon, exclude all passion and even emotion, and represent the human mind in a state of tranquillity and repose. The figures seem to be more than mortals, and to indicate a state in which the unruffled repose of mind has moulded the features into the perfect expression of the mental character

They seemed possessed of that permanent inward joy and loveliness which cast an everlasting sunshine and beauty around,—that radiance of immortal life which breathes an eternal happiness.

Another difference between painting and sculpture, consists in the universality of the latter. It is completely divested of the peculiarity of the schools. The statues of antiquity were addressed to the multitude of the people, and were intended to awaken devotion in all classes. They possess, in consequence, a general character, and speak directly to the common heart. Hence the admiration for this kind of art, which has survived the lapse of time.

To communicate thought and emotion, the art of printing has long since ·taken the place, in a great measure, of painting and sculpture; still, so long as a love of the beautiful exists in the human breast, these divine arts will continue to be cherished. They serve to embody thoughts which language has not power to utter; they convey lessons of wisdom and virtue to the ignorant; and without their aid, many a noble deed or heroic act would hardly have reached posterity.

I was much interested in the collection in the *Musée de la Marine*. You there see drawings of ships, sails, masts, and everything connected with naval affairs. Besides, there are exquisite models of all forms of vessels, French and foreign, from the full-rigged ship down to the smallest craft, exhibiting the different kinds of naval architecture in every stage of the process of constructing the vessel. The different improvements or changes that have been made from time to time, were here all curiously exhibited to view. Here, too, are models of the principal towns containing maritime arsenals; and one can see L'Orient, Rochefort, and Brest, without the trouble of going there. There is in this museum, a fine series of busts of French naval commanders.

The Louvre is the grand central point of art in France, and is, indeed, rich beyond conception. It stands out in relief from the numerous other collections in Paris and other parts of France, and, indeed, Continental Europe, like a sun, diffusing light and radiance. The numerous grand historical facts, the many touching incidents, and the abundance of thoughts and ideas which are here displayed, and which may be daily read, constitute the Louvre a grand and splendid book, unexpressively rich in whatever elevates and refines the soul; and its freedom of access to the masses of the people, cannot but render it an ever-acting and powerful means in forming the taste and giving complexion to the thought of the Parisian.

On Wednesday, Feb. 2d, I visited some of the Primary Schools of the city. The *Frère* who conducted the first at which I called, received me with the kind and polite manner invariable with that remarkable religious community; but as it was the day for religious instruction, he pointed out to me another school near, of a similar grade, and sent one of his pupils to accompany me thither. There I remained the half day, unusually interested. The reading here was much better than in most of the other schools of this class, but still, enough defective. They went through a spelling exercise somewhat novel to me. The lesson consisted of printed sentences, which were dictated by the teacher, then written by the pupil, and afterwards spelled orally by the latter. In each lesson, some one principle of grammar was exemplified, and the word in which it occurred, was printed in italics. The pupil was required to state the reason for his choice of writing the word as he spelled it. The exercise struck me favorably, as being well calculated to lead the pupil gradually into the grammar and philosophy of the language, while he was gaining a practical knowledge of the form of words. The order in neither school was remarkably good. The former consisted of two hund.ed pupils, with two teachers; and the same in the latter. They were not conducted on the mutual-principle system.

In the afternoon, I visited for the second time the Royal Institution for the Blind. I was immediately admitted into the reception-room, in which were several strangers in waiting,— and among them, an intelligent German traveller. The director of the establishment soon made his appearance, and immediately took us over the entire institution, explaining only when called upon, and then in a manner so quiet and taciturn, as to show that the exercise to him was a duty rather than a pleasure. He was not, however, permitted the indulgence of his disposition to silence, — for our German companion, who seemed to be particularly in quest of information, and pertinaciously bent on learning everything to be known about the school, with pencil and note-book in hand, plied the director so rapidly and constantly with questions, as to leave the latter barely time to take a long breath. All well-educated Germans speak the French language fluently,— and I was forcibly struck with the greater ease with which I understood the German than the Frenchman, owing, doubtless, to the more distinct utterance of the former, and to his native accent corresponding more nearly to the English than that of the French.

Institutions had long existed for the *employment* of the blind; but no effort seems to have been made for their *instruction*, until Hauy, of Paris attempted it, in 1781. The effort was crowned with complete success, and this unfortunate class of people are now taught reading, writing, and ciphering; the mathematics, various languages, geography, and music. In the last branch, they are particularly successful.

The present edifice was recently put up, and is a noble and beautiful one, comprising the improvements in school-house architecture and appointments. It contains two hundred pupils, of both sexes, who are permitted to remain eight years. Besides the branches, they are taught various mechanical employments, as a means of pecuniary support. We were interested in examining the different articles of handicraft, in the exhibition-room, made by the pupils, — and particularly, to witness them at work in the fabrication of articles, both useful and ornamental, in which they showed a degree of cleverness and skill really surprising to any one not aware how one sense may be made to take upon itself the natural use of another. Many of the more curious and elaborate of the finished pieces, that we examined, bore the most scrutinizing test that we could apply, and were, in every way, so far as we could judge, as neatly and perfectly finished as if made by the most accomplished artisans. We each, of course, purchased some little article to take away, as a memento of the noble and interesting school.

We were shown the neat and beautiful chapel in which they are wont to assemble to express their feeble adoration and gratitude to the Author of so many and tender mercies. We passed, also, into the *Salle à manger* or dining-room. It was ample, and displayed almost perfect neatness. The tables were of marble, and everything else was in the same costly, and substantial style. Many, if not most of the teachers are graduates of the institution, thus proving that, in the opinion of the intelligent faculty which has the care of this eminent institution, the more gifted of the blind, when well instructed, are equally competent and successful teachers as the seeing.

In the workshops, several laborers occupied the same room, and were permitted, in a moderate degree, the interchange of thought and sentiment; but such as were practising their lessons in music were confined, each in a separate apartment; an arrangement favorable to acquiring that concentration of mental power, and delicacy of perception so indispensable to reaching great excellence in the sublime art of music. We were permitted to peep into these narrow and imperfectly lighted practising rooms through a little glass window in the upper part of the door; and we could not but be struck with the energy and apparent devotion with which they were practising upon the parts which had been assigned them as lessons. Apparently they could not have been more earnest if stimulated with the hope of winning, one day, the applause of the great world. Did such an idea enkindle their ardor? or was it the more natural and immediate influence of that glorious principle of the human mind, which loves to overcome difficulties,— heightened by the inspiring tones of the breathing instruments? As we passed along by the rooms arranged consecutively on either side, the sounds from the different instruments, such as pianos, violins, flutes, etc., came rolling down the long and narrow aisle, in mingled and confused movement, it is true,—but they fell upon my own ear most gratefully, both as awakening pleasing recollections of delightful friends at home, of the same unfortunate class as the inmates of this school; and as giving rise in my breast to thoughts of noble and generous pride at the splendid triumphs of human art, and the exhibition of God-like benevolence of which this institution is so grand and beautiful an illustration. Those tones, drawn from humble instruments of mere mechanical contrivance, seemed to issue directly from the deep and living recesses of an inward world, — from a world of thought, of sentiment, of emotion, where gladsome spirits, cut off from the distracting beauties of external nature, were revelling in the ambrosial fields of a purely spiritual existence. And who shall confidently assert that the touching deprivation of the inmates of this school will, after all, prove to them a state of comparative greater unhappiness? Their case, viewed in connection with the grand principle of compensation which evidently runs through nature,— equalizing the real condition of mankind,— assumes an aspect more favorable to them. They are, indeed, separated from very many delightful sources of enjoyment from the world without, but may they not be compensated for this loss, at least in a great measure, by keener inner susceptibilities. They are certainly spared many scenes, which, while they rend with anguish the spirit, blunt the finer susceptibilities, as well as removed from much of low and obscene, to tarnish the purity of the soul; and when with a duly cultivated moral and intellectual nature, they possess that source of light and beauty within,— that everlasting sunshine which can be thrown on everything around, till it reflects on them what has beamed from their own serene heart, and without which the gorgeous beauties of glorious nature are a meaningless picture, and life, a plattitude of insipidities,— their condition may certainly be favorably compared with the generality of the human race. It is a point of opinion that hardly admits of doubt, that many a clear-sighted man would have his mental vision improved by spending some portion of his time in a retirement, in which the soul is driven back to observe its own operations, and seek improvement and enjoyment from its own resources. It would serve, like Crusoe's desolate island, to develop powers and elicit feelings of which he was not before conscious.

The pupils whom we saw, were clean in person and neat in dress, and appeared cheerful and happy, showing that that agreeable state of the mind which philosophers call happiness, does not depend upon circumstances of life.

I passed down into the basement-story under the edifice, in company with the German companion, conducted by the fireman of the gloomy precincts, to see how the grand establishment was heated, and supplied with warm water. Seven large furnaces were in constant and active operation, and the entire apparatus, which was minutely explained to us, seemed admirably adapted to the end for which it was arranged. Indeed, there seemed to have been spared no expense to impart to the entire establishment all the advantages which science, art, and benevolence could bestow; and I felt on leaving, an involuntary admiration for the enlarged benevolence of a people who could have first put in successful operation, and have ever since sustained so completely, so eminently a wise and humane institution.

Feb. 3d. I made a visit to the school of Medicine, at the Sarbonne. The lecture was on chemistry. I found the room,—which was circular, with seats gradually rising in an amphitheatrical form,—filled with students, a little impatient for the commencement of the lecture. There might have been an audience of six hundred. The professor, a middle-aged man, presently entered, with a brisk gait, and immediately commenced speaking. On his appearance, there was a momentary suppressed applause, when all was perfect stillness, which continued during the entire lecture, excepting when the professor indulged in a *saillie d'humeur*, when there would be a slight relaxation for a moment only, as all seemed disposed not to lose a word. The students remained covered, and with their port-folios upon their knees, before them, were busily taking notes. A long counter before the lecturer was filled with glasses and various pieces of chemical apparatus, and elements for combination, while behind him stood a large frame in which slid up and down in grooves, and by means of pullies, black-boards arranged behind each other, upon which the eminent professor wrote his theory by means of symbols. He spoke without notes, in a fluent, easy, and graceful manner, and was evidently perfectly master of his subject. A slight stepping to and fro, with moderate gesticulation, gave a pleasing animation to his manner. He was attended with several assistants, who, disposed on either side of him, performed all the experiments. It was remarkable with what adroitness these manipulators performed their parts, managing to have the experiment come off invariably, just in the nick of time. The professor would talk rapidly on, apparently without the slightest thought of the experimenter, and at the time he would say "There, gentlemen, you perceive," and on the last word, the phenomenon would burst to view, just as if connected with it by the law of affinity. There was not a mistake; no repeating, no blundering, and never a moment's hesitation. If it all had been guided by the most systematic mechanism, it could not have been more exact and sure. Several gentlemen accompanied the professor, and remained seated by the side of him uncovered, — friends or acquaintances present, doubtless by invitation. The lecture I listened to, was one of a course of public lectures which come off here every winter, and which are entirely free to everybody. It is a single department of the school of Medicine, a branch of the University of Paris, the great central establishment of education in France. The number of regularly-entered students in medicine is upwards of two thousand, besides such as do not choose to be put upon the list. Examinations are publicly held four times a year, under four professors appointed by the Academic Council. The examination of each candidate must last at least one and a half hours, but may be protracted at the pleasure of the professors. All the higher degrees are granted only after severe trials, and numerous candidates are annually rejected.

GARDEN OF PLANTS.

I left for the last time this noble enclosure. One at all gifted with an appreciation of Nature, and imbued in the least with the spirit of revelling amid its endless varieties and matchless perfections, would wish to linger here forever. It is not only an extensive volume of animated nature, but it is a world of nature in miniature. It embraces a condensed view of the three kingdoms, Animal, Vegetable, and Mineral; and so extensive is the collection, that there is scarcely an individual species known in the three grand compartments of creation but that may not here be found; and all so exactly classified and beautifully arranged, as to present almost at a single glance the wonderful and endless riches of the entire domain of fruitful Nature.

It would be tedious to recount the history of this grand institution, from its foundation by Louis XIII, in 1626, up to the present summit of perfection. The history of the men whose labors have enriched it, and whose names and statues adorn it, is the history of the natural sciences for the last two hundred years. Little did the monarch imagine when he doled out a few acres of useless land for a museum with only three professors, that he was preparing a magnificent temple for the wonders of nature, — a temple destined to become not only one of the principal ornaments of the capital, but an honor to France and even the entire world.

The garden, consisting of thirty-three hectares of ground, lies on the south side of the river, near the bridge of Austerlitz. As you enter by the northeastern gate, the splendid enclosure presents you the view of a large grove divided into four parts by three avenues running its whole length. The space contains a Menagerie, a Botanical Garden, with hot-houses, a Museum and Library of Natural History, a Museum of Comparative Anatomy, a Museum of Mineralogy and Geology, and an Amphitheatre with laboratories and apparatus of every possible description for public lectures. The lectures are delivered by an attached corps of thirteen professors, comprising the most distinguished men in the kingdom, and are perfectly open and gratuitous. The whole establishment is maintained at the expense of the government, at an annual cost of about sixty thousand dollars; and it gives employment to one hundred and sixty persons.

The Menagerie is avowedly the largest in Europe, and the most complete in its arrangements. It alone requires the space of about twenty-four acres; and the surface, which is perfectly level by the side of the amphitheatre, varied pleasingly in the middle by inequalities, and terminating upon the quay in an embankment, communicates with the garden by three fine entrances. The tame animals are kept in fourteen parts, — six at the east of the building, called the Rotunda, and eight at the east towards the Seine. Each of these is again subdivided into as many smaller compartments as the establishment contains different species. To each park is annexed a building conformable to the instinct and mode of life of the animal, into which it may retire at pleasure. Nothing can be more picturesque than this site; a movement of surface ever varying, heightened by the unique and fanciful cottage homes which adorn and variegate the entire enclosure. It would be impossible to enumerate all the species of tame animals and reptiles; but suffice it to say, that you can scarcely realize that you have directly before you all the various animals, and more, about which you have read, or seen in pictures, which you may now scan, and whose very habits you may now observe at leisure. Here you see an alpaca, remarkable for the length and fineness of his wool; and a little further, an African sheep, with a long tail; again, you meet with the goat of Tartary, India, and Upper Egypt, besides different species of Europe. Near them is a Mexican lama. Besides these already enumerated, are giraffes, elephants, camels, zebras, deer, antelopes, ostriches, cassowaries, etc.

Towards the Seine, is a Menagerie for wild beasts, composed of twenty-one enclosures. There may be seen several species of bears, a jaguar, lions, hyenas; but the most curious is the black panther.

The palace of the lions forms a range of strong cabins, divided longitudinally into two sets of apartments, — the inner being appropriated for the feeding and rest of the beasts; and the outer being strong cages, defended by iron bars in front, where the animals sun themselves. The large family of *monkeys* are appropriately provided for in a stone edifice, which has in front a circular cage of some fifty feet in diameter, where these mischievous and tricky animals can remain during night or day, in cold or rainy weather. It is warmed in the winter, and being provided with galleries, ropes, and ladders, affords opportunity for these singular creatures to exhibit themselves much to the amusement of the crowd. In the palace of the Birds of Prey are specimens of every variety of eagles, hawks, and vultures, with some others. In other enclosures may be seen the gallinaceous birds, the aquatic birds, and a great variety of other families. There are enclosures for the various species of reptiles. You almost tremble to see several species of serpents, coiling around each other in loving embrace, with their fiery forked tongues in quick and menacing movement, or, peradventure, the great anaconda or boa-constrictor, with a slow and majestic movement, basking his huge body in the sun.

The *Museum of Natural History* is contained in a long range of buildings three stories high. A detailed acccunt of this vast collection, in which almost every class of living beings has its representative preserved, would fill volumes. The interior of the building is divided into six halls in the first stage, five in the second. In the first are the reptiles and fish; in the second, the quadrupeds, insects, and shell-fish.

The collection of fish comprises about five thousand individuals, and about half that number of species. They are preserved with an art so exquisite, as to leave in perfection their exterior form, thus revealing how well the Creating Hand knew to vary his gifts. In the midst of this world of wonders, is the statue of Buffon, the great French naturalist. It is draped in an ordinary loose dress, standing, in the act of writing on a tablet resting upon a terrestrial globe. His head is turned away from the tablet, and he seems intently examining the objects around. Under and about his feet are the head of a lion, a dog asleep, a serpent, some marine productions, and a large group of rock crystals. The observer is at once favorably struck with the happy conception of the artist, in combining with the individual traits of the eminent naturalist, the noble thought of representing the minister and interpreter of nature; and he reads upon the pedestal the fitting memorial of Buffon: *Majestati Naturæ par Ingenium*. Pajon, the sculptor, is considered as eminently fortunate in delineating the features and portraying the expression of the great man, to be transmitted to future generetions; but Buffon was as great a writer as naturalist, and he who felt that *the style is the man*, will survive in his immortal writings, the mouldering atoms of tablet or marble. He lives there, and will live, so long as shall exist the French language, and the works of nature which lent inspiration to his thoughts. His works themselves are a much fitter eulogy than the inscription upon the pedestal of his effigy.

The most brilliant part of the Museum is in the second story.

Five thousand mammalia, forming as many species, appear under their natural colors; in their distinctive features are revealed their natural instincts; upon their varied mien are imprinted their qualities or powers; their forms, even, are admirably adapted to the circumstances of the country which produced them, and to their dispositions, whether mild or malevolent. The soul involuntarily bows in humble adoration to the energy and creative power of such wonders. It experiences the same sentiment, in a more lively degree perhaps, in viewing a variety not less astonishing, both in configuration and color, of six thousand individuals and two thousand three hundred species of birds. What exquisite richness of plumage have they! Every color,— the purest gold, silver, azure, rouge, and green, is reflected from their glossy feathers with a brilliancy and lustre inimitable.

The museum of mineralogy and geology is beyond all question the richest in the world. In the middle of the gallery extends throughout its entire length a series of glass cases, in which are admirably arranged all the minerals which form the crust of the earth, classed according to their age and formation. These cases form, thus to speak, so many archives, in which are inscribed the series of all the revolutions of the terrestrial globe. Here was a crystal of quartz three feet in diameter; beryls, ten inches; ammonites, eighteen to twenty inches; and many beautiful specimens of fossil fish, from one to three feet long, in some of which, not only the size and shape, but also the color of the scales, was distinctly discernible.

In the intervals may be seen magnificent marble tables in mosaic, comprising specimens of the various kinds of marble any where found. Upon one of them is a huge stone which fell at some time, from the upper regions; also an enormous mass of iron-ore of the same origin.

In the middle of the hall is a noble statue of the illustrious *Cuvier*. It will be remembered that at an early age, the eminent man was called to Paris to fill the professorship of Comparative Anatomy, and soon attained the highest distinction as a naturalist. The Cabinet of Comparative Anatomy formed wholly by him, and his various other works on natural history, form an imperishable monument of his genius. Cuvier was a protestant and Christian, and it was delightful to see in the labors which constituted the basis of his fame, none of those elements of fragility which mark the conclusion of science when opposed to the works of God. The statue stands on a base about five feet high, in his ordinary dress as lecturer, his left hand resting on a globe, the forefinger pointing into the interior, as if directing attention to some internal phenomenon, while the right hand is raised up nearly in a line with the face, as if in the act of explaining it. On one side of the pedestal is his name; and on another in a unique inscription, a list of his different publications. It is highly appropriate. His works do indeed praise him.

The *Museum of Comparative Anatomy* is in a building to the west of the enclosure. It was commenced in 1775, by Daubenton; guided by the profound genius of Cuvier, who knew equally well to discover truth, or perceive her intimate relations, or give embodiment to her hidden mysteries in the noble form of speech. The specimens are grouped so as to present the common resemblances on which the divisions into genera are founded, and the particular differences of species at one view, affording great facilities for study and comparison. The specimens are preserved with infinite art by the injection of fluid into their minutest arteries; and not only is the human organization compared with that of diverse animals, but the different races are compared with each other; such as the European, Tartar, Chinese, New Holland,

Negro, Hottentot, several savage tribes of America, and ancient Egyptian mummies. You are struck with the resemblances and diversities. There is also a large collection of monsters and *lusus naturæ*. The wax preparations are numerous. There is a room expressly devoted to craniology, in which plaster models of skulls are arranged with such taste and skill as would delight a phrenologist. You proceed from surprise to surprise through the fifteen halls of which the cabinet is composed, which contains more than fifteen thousand anatomical specimens, and the collection is rapidly increasing.

The collection in the vegetable kingdom is immense, and the classification and arrangement into orders, genera and species are astonishing and beautiful. Near the library building is a large square filled with trees, that burst their foliage in the spring, separated from others merely ornamental in the summer. A second walk, bordered by maple trees, separates a rich group of autumnal fruit-trees, and these, in turn, are separated from a grove of evergreens. Further on, is a space appropriated for the culture of culinary vegetables; then comes the school for plants of domestic economy, such as are used for the subsistence of man, animals, or employed in the arts. In the first parterre, situated in the interval of the broad walks, extending opposite the galleries, are first, flowers, and perennial plants; then, in an enclosure accessible by means of iron gates, exotic trees, and especially such as are resinous, which are undergoing a process of acclimation. In the middle of this is a beehive, and then a school for the cultivation of flowers. Several square plots, in the vicinity, are used for the cultivation of medicinal flowers. The entire interval extending to the right of the broad walk, bordered with lindens to the Swiss valley, is devoted to the study of six thousand species or varieties of fruit-trees growing on the French soil. A little further on is the Botanic school, or seven thousand plants arranged according to the natural method of Jussieu. Each is labelled according to its name, family, and class.

Besides these are extensive hot-houses, in which are beautifully arranged every species of exotic plant that requires a warmer climate than that of Paris. The array here presented is actually overpowering, and the mind is staggered under such a wilderness of vegetable wonder and beauty.

All the ground not actually appropriated for a specific scientific purpose, is delightfully embellished with trees, shrubs, plants, flowers, or broad and well gravelled walks, to charm and delight you at every step. The natural inequalities of the ground are preserved, in order to present the greatest possible variety, and it is so adorned as to exhibit the wildness and luxuriance of nature, heightened by the gilding hand of art.

You pass on to the upper garden, through enclosures of fruit-trees and hot-beds, towards the rising grounds, on which are erected the magnificent conservatories. Between these, is a path leading to a little elevation, called the Labyrinth, on the ascent of which is a noble Cedar of Lebanon, four feet in diameter at the base, which was planted here more than a century ago by the celebrated Bernard de Jussieu, who brought it from England. It is a beautiful tree, and appears not unworthy to be the emblem of the majesty of Israel. Not far from the cedar is the tomb of Daubenton, who devoted more than fifty years of his calm and laborious life to the study of nature in this museum. You reach the summit of the hill by a spiral path bordered with evergreen. Upon the summit is a kiosk, or iron turret, from which a good view of the city may be had.

Such is a brief and necessarily imperfect sketch of this miniature world of nature. No description, however elaborate or colored, can convey a faithful picture of the original. To get an adequate idea of its wonderful extent, riches and beauty, one must actually visit it, and linger amid its munificence.

One evening I was called on by a gentleman, whose acquaintance I had previously formed, and who very kindly offered to accompany me on a visit to some of the adult and juvenile evening schools. It was Monsieur the Director of the School of Frères. On descending from my room, I found him in the private saloon with Madame David, engaged in lively conversation, chatting and occasionally joking as familiarly as if they had been old acquaintances, although this was their first meeting. We were soon joined by two or three others of the Frères, when our little party set off in lively mood, in one of the omnibuses which may be found at all times in any part of the city. Monsieur le Directeur was in excellent spirits, and actually poured forth his capacious and generous soul for my peculiar edification and amusement. He was beyond middle age, above the medium stature, and rather corpulent. His massive face, beaming eyes, and open and radiant expression, betokened the voluminous and versatile nature of his spirit. He permitted not a moment of the time in our passage or return, to pass unfilled. He was at times instructive, caustic, humorous, sentimental, but always kind, gracious, and animating. In spite of his religious garb, it was easily seen, that the world and its cares sat lightly upon him. He had a smile for its follies, a tear for its miseries, but a willing heart and a ready hand to advance the good and noble wherever found. Of an observing cast of mind, possessed of a well-digested fund of thought and information, with an easy and appropriate flow of language, he was eminently entertaining. He was one of those men rarely to be met with, in whose society you feel a continual glow of agreeable excitement.

These schools were recently established by the city, for the benefit of the laboring poor. Only a portion of this class avail themselves of their liberal provisions; yet the institution attests the humane and munificent spirit of the government, and refutes the charge sometimes made, that monarchical governments are neglectful of the improvement and welfare of the people. The school that we were visiting, was one of the largest and most successfully conducted of this class, in the city; and I was necessarily deeply interested in inspecting the mode of its operation, and learning of its character and success. My friend the conducteur, who seemed perfectly known to every one we met, took me through all the rooms, introducing me to the teachers, and sometimes to the scholars, and explaining explicitly everything worthy of note. His very presence diffused around a genial and gladsome feeling wherever he went. The scholars seemed to regard him with a paternal and reverential sentiment akin to adoration. I was struck with the spirit of willingness, and the habits cf strict assiduity which prevailed entire among the learners, and the kindly and earnest disposition expressed in the affectionate tones of voice, and the benignant regard of the teachers. The one party seemed imbued with profound gratitude for so grand and munificent a privilege, and appeared determined to improve the moments as if each came laden with golden opportunities; the other showed that they felt the humane nature of their mission, and would ameliorate by hearty kindness the task rendered doubly difficult by early omissions. The spirit which prevailed was delightful — charming; it bordered on enthusiasm; and, carried away by its sympathetic influence, and the crowd of animating associations which the scene and occasion gave forth, I was filled with deep emotion. It was certainly unique and profoundly interesting to see men bowed with age, struggling with a manly heart but with a child's perception, to master the mere elements of their vernacular tongue. Here were persons forty and even fifty years of age, who had come up to the place fatigued with the day's labor, cheerfully yielding the small fragments of time left them amid the incessant and depressing toil for the narrowest physical subsistence, in order to gain the keys of knowledge, which were to unlock the portal, revealing to their eager gaze the world of thought and sentiment. The muscular working of their manly countenances betrayed their intensity of soul, — and as they brushed from their brow the sweat and dust, which in their earnest desire for mental acquisition, they had not removed before leaving their toil, I could not but feel abashed and humiliated in view of my own delinquencies, — at the thought of hours misspent, and opportunities misimproved. It is impossible for us who have learned some of the elements of knowledge in our youth, to estimate their value, or appreciate the want of them felt by those who were so unfortunate as to be deprived of the glorious blessing. These early privileges were brightened into our youthful mind imperceptibly, like the gradual opening of the noon of day; while their possession and noble results flowing in upon our being in broad and intermitting streams, are like the gladsome and genial sunshine and dew, whose very universality, life-breathing fragrance, and perennial beauty, render us indifferent to their value and loveliness.

A feature of this school, not unworthy of mention, was the prominence given to Drawing. I had observed the large share of attention devoted to this branch, in the other schools I visited, and I thought to comprehend the reasons for the course pursued; but here, where the learners, from the nature of the case, could not be expected to be taken farther than the mere elements of reading, writing, and spelling, it seemed an injudicious appropriation of time, to spend any of it in the acquisition of any branch of learning, but such as constitute, in common opinion, with us, the simplest ground-studies of an education. A moment's reflection, however, rectified this view. The truth is, that the notions of the French, and those generally prevailing, in this country, in regard to the comparative value of certain branches of education, and particularly that of drawing, are different. We are accustomed to look upon drawing, in a course of study, as ornamental only, — calculated, at the most, but to cultivate the taste and elevate and refine the sentiments; but the French, in addition to this influence of the beautiful art, connect it directly with the common pursuits of life, and make it an indispensable acquisition in every artisan who would expect to excel in his trade. And it cannot for a moment be questioned, that the superiority of the French in the grace and beauty of their fabrications, can be traced directly to the great attention given by them to the art of drawing. In this school a considerable proportion of the scanty time was devoted to this exercise by all; the walls of the room were covered with patterns, illustrating every stage in the progress of the learner, from the first rough lines, to the most perfect and beautiful picture; and the readiness and evident pleasure with which the teacher showed you the more successful efforts of the learners, commenting, at the same time, upon his enviable talents, — while other branches were omitted, — clearly evinced the value attached to the attainment by the French, merely in its ordinary relations to practical life. And the exercise was engaged in here, by the scholars, not as it is too frequently among us, merely to while away the time, or as a relief from more irksome studies, but with a spirit of deep and earnest enthusiasm, — and the improvement made was correspondingly good. Indeed, I was shown some specimens, executed on the spot, which for perfection and grace of outline, delicacy and charm of shading, and life-glowing and spiritual beauty breathed into them, would have done credit to any artist, — but when considered as the productions of beginners, mere tyros, in the art, they were really wonderful. Our first astonishment, however, at such superior acquisition, will be diminished when we consider that the Frenchman seems endowed by nature with a peculiar talent for the appreciation of the nice and beautiful in form; and were it not so, the influences of his external life could not but form such a quality of his being. The great attention given to art throughout the country, the vast gardens in which every form of nature is admiringly displayed, the numerous public monuments adorned with the riches of ancient sculpture, the vast piles of architecture everywhere offering to view their grandeur and magnificence, the immense collections of paintings glowing with beauty, with which Paris and all the important towns of France are filled, and all entirely free and accessible to everybody, are so many educational influences, silently but unceasingly, forming in the soul of the native the very spiritual essence of art. The Parisian is surrounded by such influences from infancy to age. The first plaything of his nursery is, it may be, an exquisite copy of the Venus de Medici or the Apollo de Belvidere; the fountain in which he sports his tiny bauble, is filled with Naiads and Tritons; the garden whither his nurse or governess takes him for an airing is decorated with statues and antiques; indeed, he cannot cast his eyes up, or around, without meeting with some object of art. He breathes, as it were, an atmosphere of art, — and so saturated becomes his soul with the forms of beauty, that he has only to acquire the rules of outward form, and the spirit flows in, as by natural accord.

We were led from the ordinary study-rooms into a small *studii* for moulding heads and busts. A student was hard at work, all covered with dust. He was mentioned to me as possessing very superior talent, — and having passed rapidly through the several grades of drawing, crayoning, etc., was now finishing off in this department previously to his departure for Philadelphia, where he intended to pursue his vocation. He was eager and minute in his inquiries touching the United States; and when he learned that I was from Boston, he invited me to step in some day, and make him a call, when he should be installed in his new Western home, — never for a moment imagining that many people, residing in Boston and vicinity, never go to Philadelphia even for once in their life.

The school session is between seven and ten in the evening, and is held every day of the week except one. The teachers receive about one hundred and twenty dollars per annum.

We passed into the basement story, and were soon standing before a large class of juvenile, indigent, evening-scholars. They were poorly clad, covered with the dust of their labor, and had the appearance of having come direct from their toil to the school. Their countenances bore a depressed and saddened expression, but their eyes sparkled with youthful hope and vivacity. They were deeply interested, I was told, and were making rapid progress. Who knows, mused I, that here is not developing genius, one day to illumine the world? It was certainly a touching spectacle to contemplate this Spartan band of youth, who, contemning the captivating recreations of children, had nobly decided — even against the immense odds — to conquer or die in the struggle for improvement. The genius of learning ever lends a listening ear to such suitors, and never fails to dispense her favors generously when thus wooed. The example of these youth, giving the few moments of their time in the intervals of their severe toil, to intellectual culture, should put to shame many of our sons and daughters, who find study irksome even when enlivened by the pleasing and delightful circumstances of books, teachers, apparatus, and all the appointments which human ingenuity can invent, or a noble benevolence apply, to lessen the toil of the student in the declivitous path up the hill of science.

CHAPTER XVI.

PALACE OF THE LUXEMBOURG — RICH PAINTINGS — INSTITUTION FOR DEAF-MUTES — HALE AND CHEERFUL APPEARANCE OF INMATES — MODE OF TEACHING — TEACHERS OF FRENCH — PALACE OF THE FINE ARTS — A NICE PARTY OF COUNTRY BEAUX AND LASSES — CHURCH OF THE MADELINE — ITS MAGNIFICENCE — RICH TREAT AT THE PROTESTANT CHURCH — NUNS AT THE CHURCH OF ST. GERMAIN L' AUXERROIS — RURAL-RESTAURANT — MADAME DAVID — REUNION OF OUVRIERS — BISHOP OF PARIS — DEEPLY INTERESTING CHARACTER OF EXERCISES.

ON Friday I made a visit to the Palace of the Luxembourg. It is boldly situated at the head of the *rue de Tournon*, and has connected with it, on the south, an extensive garden, beautifully laid out with walks stretching through trees, shrubbery and flowers; and the whole enlivened by sheets of water, upon which I frequently saw, in my rambles in that direction, skaters in brisk and jocular exercise. The present edifice was commenced in 1616, under the direction of Marie de Medicis. In 1798, it was greatly improved and decorated. Its principal entrance presents at its extremities two large pavilions, united by a double terrace, pierced by four arcades. In the middle of the edifice, upon a quadrangular basis, rises a neat and elegant cupola. It develops three orders of architecture: first, the rez-de-chaussé, — or ground-floor, — exhibits the Tuscan; then, in the first stage, comes the Doric, and the Ionic displays itself in the second stage. The whole appearance is masculine, and singular. There are many paintings, and some of great value, in this palace. Among them are gems, from the pencils of Reubens, Raphael, and Benjamin West. How indefatigable must have been the industry, as well as profound the genius of these sublime spirits, especially the two former, whose works may be found in nearly every gallery of consequence in Europe! How is it, that great genius is so often found united to great industry and perseverance? May it not be, that the latter serves to give birth to the former? Some of these paintings are more than two hundred years old, and yet they retain, in a good degree, their spirit and freshness. . The art is indeed noble, that can arrest the varying expression,— the faithful index of the fugitive emotions of the soul,—and transmit it thus, through successive generations.

The library is two hundred and twelve feet in length, by twenty-three in width. It is decorated with many choice pieces of paintings and sculpture. The central cupola of the gallery, painted by Eugene Delacroix, represents the Elysium of great men, as described by Dante.

The chapel, which is on the ground-floor, is beautiful, and near it is a magnificent hall, painted by Reubens, called the sleeping chamber of Marie de Medicis. There are many other things here of deep interest, but space would fail me to enumerate them. The paintings struck me as being larger, more highly colored, and to represent action and violent emotion in a higher degree than those in general in the Louvre. Perhaps it was because more of them were of the French school. My guide, whom I did not fancy, took me hastily through the building, reciting his story in a monotonous manner, to which I gave little attention. Here, in the gallery of paintings, as in that of the Louvre, were artists assiduously engaged in making copies of some of the smaller works.

After spending much less time than I could have wished in this interesting palace, a few moments' walk brought me to that nobly humane asylum, the Royal Institution for the Deaf and Dumb, situated in the *Rue de St. Jacques*. The building is by no means imposing in appearance; but an inspection of its interior shows it to be sufficiently ample and conveniently disposed. The superintendent showed me over the edifice with a delicacy of politeness which in Paris extends even to the government, and which here seemed tempered with a suavity and kindness inspired by the benevolent influences of the spot. The males whom I saw, were scattered in the different rooms, intently occupied in various mechanical employments. They were garbed in blouse; and bore a hale and cheerful aspect, which seemed to show that no care pressed upon them, and that no thought shaded by the irrevocable misfortune of their condition, was wont to cross their minds. How fortunate the nature of man, that can thus be formed to the contingencies of any lot! The articles of fabrication shown me, were even superior to those made by the blind. If not more delicately elaborate, they exhibited more solidity and a smoother finish. Indeed, I half fancied that I discovered traces of superior care and devotion in the nicer parts, not found in the fabrications of hearing persons, distracted as they are by appeals to the external sense, and hurried by an impatience to participate in the gladsome notes of social and musical life.

The sublime and humane idea of restoring to society men whom nature would separate, is due to the Abbé de l'Epée. With a fortune greatly disproportionate to the largeness of his soul, he devoted his narrow means for the furtherance of his noble mission, compensating by talent, energy, and devotion, and by a rigid simplicity of life, for the want of greater pecuniary means. He at first assembled in his own house forty deaf and dumb persons, boarded them at his own expense, and after reserving the merest pittance for his own sustenance, expended the entire of the remainder of his estate in educating them, and in founding one of the noblest institutions that has ever blessed humanity. In the Salle des Exercises, is a fine picture of this founder of the school, embracing the young deaf and dumb Count de Toulouse, whom he had educated. There is, moreover, a bust of the Abbé de l'Epée, as also one of the Abbé de Sicard, who, on the death of the Abbé de l'Epée, in 1796, undertook the management of the establishment. It has since been transferred from a convent of Celestines, to the buildings of the Séminaire de St. Magloiré, where it now exists.

The school comprises two hundred boys and sixty girls, who are admitted between the ages of ten and fourteen years, and are retained in general six years. The best two among the male pupils belonging to each class of the sixth year, are selected to receive the advantages of a superior course of education for the additional term of three years, — and from what is called the class of instruction complimentaire. They are supported by a fund left by the late physician of the institution, the benevolent Dr. Itard. Most of the pupils are supported here, at the expense of the government, but a few are kept at the school by their relatives. The expense of the government is about ninety dollars per annum, and private scholars are charged one hundred and seventy dollars. The number of instructors is, eight for the males, four of whom are deaf and dumb; and four for the females, besides four or five young persons who are preparing for situations as teachers, by attending the exercises of the school-rooms, and rendering assistance from time to time as they find the opportunity. These are called aspirants, and become subsequently teachers, if their talents and success seem to warrant the merit.

The salaries of the teachers are not large; but after thirty years service, they receive on retiring, a pension from the government of half-pay for life.

I was not permitted to see the female part of the school. The sexes are kept entirely distinct; and to my request to be shown through the department, I was told that no man was allowed there but the priest. The reason for the separation of the sexes, is founded on the belief that, deprived of articulate speech, the ordinary advantages of social intercourse would not accrue to these pupils. In this decision, it is forgotten that the communication of thought, of sentiment, of emotion, does not depend wholly upon speech. The beauty and poetry of the soul often finds a happier and more forcible medium of expression in the manner, the countenance, the eye, than could be given to it by the meagre and inadequate power of language. And imperfectly developed must ever be that character, which comes to age without the vivifying influence of intercourse with the opposite sex.

In this admirably arranged charity, the pupils of both sexes are instructed by means of three different languages, namely, by alphabet, by mimic-signs, and by dumb-articulation. The last mentioned mode, although successfully pursued in several distinguished institutions in Germany, has not yet gained much favor with the French. It has been repeatedly attempted in this school, but the system has not gained particular favor. The professors have declared, that in their opinion, the advantages to be gained by this mode, were by no means equal to the comparative time and effort necessary to reach the result.

Here, as elsewhere in the schools, all are carefully taught drawing, for the double purpose of cultivating taste, and of enabling them with facility to delineate the signs and the alphabet, by which they can mutually communicate their ideas to each other.

In taking leave of this interesting establishment, I could not but pause for a moment in the entrance-square, to contemplate an object of great curiosity. It was an enormous elm, two hundred and forty-six years of age, and ninety feet in height, which had been planted by Sully, minister of Henry IV. It shows no sign of age, and is considered the finest tree in the neighborhood of Paris. Its gigantic stature, and wide-spreading branches, are not unemblematic of the support and protection which the government of France affords to its unfortunate children.

One of the lecture-rooms at the School of Medicine, which I looked into on my way home, detained me but a few moments. The professor, a venerable-looking gentleman, apparently fifty or sixty years of age, seated in an armed-chair, was reading a lecture from a manuscript, in a dull and lifeless manner. Specimens of anatomy were promiscuously lying on the table before him, at some distance, which he sometimes referred to by leaving off his reading, taking up the part to be explained, and deliberately exemplifying the point that he had presented. His lack of animation was accompanied by its usual result, a thin attendance; for the room was no more than half filled.

I was called on, in the evening, by a young gentleman who had been sent to me by my friend Monsieur the Director, and recommended by him as a suitable person to improve me in the graces of French pronunciation. He was a very young man, perhaps no more than twenty years of age, yet full of spirit, vivacity, and grace, and possessed of a smooth and fluent utterance. As he could not speak English, he offered his services to me for four francs a lesson, — five being the usual price. I struck a bargain with him for a lesson a day, of an hour's length; and I had no reason afterwards to regret the choice I made in him, for he proved a faithful and excellent instructor, and he aided me in other respects. I had previously called, for purposes of mere inquiry, however, on several of these *conveniences* to strangers in Paris. They are quite a numerous tribe in this well arranged city; and their cards, ostensibly posted, frequently meet the eye in certain quarters. These gentlemen-teachers are entirely complaisant, enter readily into conversation with you, — and by the perfect coincidence of opinion and congeniality of feeling between you, they will be very likely to touch your sympathies at once. It may, perchance, appear a little singular at first, that they happen always to have just time to teach one more pupil, and that although they have before them several applications for this hour, you would most assuredly receive the preference. After learning that I was from Massachusetts, they would enumerate the distinguished men from my own State, whom they had had the honor to instruct; and I really began to feel a kind of social elevation, in being so near such eminent society.

Feb. 5th. I attended in the morning, two lectures at the Sarbonne. The rooms were not filled. The professors spoke with notes before them. In one room each student had with him a book, to which I noticed he was frequently cited by the speaker.

In the afternoon, I passed through the Palace of Fine Arts. In company, was a small number of persons belonging to the rural population. My attention was as much engrossed with the interesting company, as with the remarkable objects to be seen in the museum. They were evidently in Paris for the first time, and as they would probably never see it again, they could not but be highly impressed with the value of time. Every traveller feels that a day in Paris is equal to weeks or months elsewhere; then how concentrated must be the feelings of the inhabitant of the country or smaller town, who has been accustomed to look up to Paris as the sum of artificial creation, and the end of travelling life, — as a world of beauty in miniature, and the grand centre of opinion and style for the world, and to which he must make one visit in his life, as would a Mohammedan to the city of Mecca. So strong is this feeling among the rural class in France, that sometimes the surplus earnings of many years, if not an entire life, are freely consecrated to this one long-nurtured purpose. " Who has not seen Paris, has seen nothing," is a common saying in the country towns in France.

The party in question was composed of youthful persons of either sex, and by the evident agreeable state of their feelings, they were nearer to each other in sentiment, than to warrant the opinion of being merely second-cousins. They passed through the different rooms, following our guide in the most docile manner, apparently thinking more of themselves and of each other, than of the interior of the edifice. Whenever their attention was a little diverted to the objects we met with, it created only a mixture of surprise and distraction, similar to that which the boy experiences when he enters for the first time a store filled with the captivating objects of his admiration.

The buildings occupying the spot whence now rises the vast and interesting structure, called the *Palace of the Fine Arts*, was used, after the Revolution, as a general depôt for the tombs, statues, bass-reliefs, and other decorations wrested from foreign churches and private establishments by the conquering and grasping power of the French arms. These profaned relics of victory were gathered in the various halls, cloister, and garden of the establishment, classified and arranged according to their century. This collection, which must have been unique and deeply interesting, received the name of the *Museum of French Monuments*. At the Restoration, however, most of the monuments were returned to the churches whence they were taken; and the present edifice is used for a museum and school.

An ample stairway, overlaid and ceiled with marble, formed under a grand vestibule, and sustained by marble pillars, leads to the first stage of the building, which comprises several spacious compartments decorated with paintings. In one of these rooms constructed in an amphitheatrical form, is the celebrated fresco, from the pencil of Paul-de-la-Roche, representing the eight principal schools of painting: namely, the Roman, the Venetian, the Florentine, the German, the Spanish, the Holland, the Flemish, and French school. I was particularly struck with the portrait of Raphael, in the piece, bearing a more than mortal expression of beauty

Two other rooms constitute a museum of *chef d'œuvres* of antiquities. In the chapel of Medicis is a copy of the masterpiece of Michael Angelo; and in the ancient church of the *Petites-Augustines* is the splendid copy, by Singlon, of his "Last Judgment." This picture is very large, and the canvas is crowded with figures displaying, with boldness, an infinity of attitudes. The picture illustrates the powerful creative genius of the great Italian painter; but the impression which it makes upon the mind is rather confused.

In the rooms in the first stage take place the annual expositions of works of art, sent by pupils from Rome. The second stage contains the works which have obtained the prize at the Institute.

After leaving this royal museum, I made a visit, for the twentieth time, perhaps, to the justly celebrated church of the Madeline. I could have wished to visit it twenty times more; and when I did leave it for the last time, it was with a feeling of regret which one experiences on the separation from a scene enshrined in the mind with delicious emotions. Its noble and symmetrical proportions, its pure but splendid architecture, its gorgeously rich interior and decorations, the fine paintings with which its walls

CHURCH OF THE MADELINE. 211

and ceilings are adorned, combine to render it by far the most beautiful work of art I ever beheld.

The magnificent structure is in the boulevard of the same name, opposite the Rue Royale; and is after the Parthenon at Athens, but larger, being three hundred and twenty-eight feet in length, and one hundred and thirty-eight feet in width, while its archetype is only two hundred and twenty-eight by one hundred feet. It stands upon a platform twelve feet high, surrounded by a magnificent peristyle of fifty-two Corinthian columns, each sixty feet high and six feet in diameter. Nothing can be finer than the view presented by the façade, ornamented as it is with all which sculpture has produced that is rich and elegant. But in gazing upon this splendid triumph of genius, the eye first falls upon the noble fronton, upon which, in a vast composition with alto-relievo, is represented the Last Judgment. The figures have a proportion of about fifteen feet. In the middle, rises the person of Christ; and at his feet is the Madeline in a suppliant attitude; she appears to solicit pardon of the fishermen near her, while an angel, armed with a sword, repulses them.

Passing from the majestic corridor of the double range of columns, at the southern front, through the massive bronze doors, you enter the body of the edifice. What a scene bursts upon your enraptured view! The floor entirely of marble, divided into compartments of various figures and colors; the numerous chandeliers of burnished gold, gilding the vast space of the interior; the pictures of consummate execution speaking to you from the walls; the beautiful statues, adorning all the niches, representing the sublimest form of thought; the magnificent group of sculpture over the high altar of the virgin herself, of the purest white marble, guarded by two angels of extreme grace and beauty; all conspire to render it a scene of indescribable beauty.

The interior of the edifice is totally different from most great Catholic churches. It is not divided into nave and aisles, but forms a vast hall without windows, receiving its light from openings at the centres of three fine domes that form the interior roof.

The history of the church is curious. A religious edifice was ordered to be built here, by Louis XV, and the first stone was laid in 1763. The Revolution of 1789 suspended the work. In 1808, Napoleon changed entirely the plan and destination of the structure of twenty years, which had cost nearly two millions of francs, and caused to be erected on the site a *Temple of Glory* in honor of the Grand Army. But this, as well as many of Napoleon's gigantic plans, was arrested in 1813, at the restoration of the Bourbons. Louis XVIII. recommenced the building in 1816, with the design of finishing the church to receive the monuments of his family, and to be dedicated to the Magdalen. Louis Phillippe, with his unbounded liberality to the fine arts, had the unfinished work completed.

However rich and beautiful the interior of this church, its highest charm consists in its fine exterior. The profusion and variety of beauty within, overpowers and distracts the mind; but in contemplating its noble and elegant proportions from without, the soul is gradually elevated, the thought concentrated ; while the emotions, purified, become entranced in a spiritual elysium. The contemplation of this edifice, and that of the Pantheon, produces a similar effect upon the mind. The lover of the beautiful will ever feel that he cannot look upon them too often, or gaze upon them too long, — while in after years, their image will ever and anon float in his memory, awaking delightful recollections of the past.

Sunday, Feb. 6th. First, went to the post-office, but received only, as compensation for my trouble, a renewed practical illustration of the pronunciation of the French negation — *ne rien*, a sound, by the way, with which my ear was already but too familiar. Afterwards, I attended service at the great Protestant church of the city. On arriving, I found the church, which is capable of holding two thousand persons, nearly full, and numbers, besides, rushing forward in quest of seats. From this impatience of movement all around, and the glowing expectation which was depicted upon the countenances of the audience, it was easy to infer that some bright particular star, of powerful attraction, was to be the spiritual guide of the forenoon's service. Nor was I at all deceived in so natural a conclusion. The address, which was of unusual length, and very diversified in style, was remarkably well sustained in interest, and had the power to keep the vast audience enchained in almost breathless attention, throughout its entire delivery. The speaker was slightly below the medium stature, and rather inclined to corpulency. His movements, however, which were nervous, joined to his beaming countenance and eyes radiant with glow and fervency, added force to his brilliant style. He spoke without written notes, although it was evident enough from the perfection of the plan and details of the discourse, that it had at least been well engraved on the tablet of the mind. French speakers rarely or never read their addresses. Neither the genius of the language, nor the impetuosity of the French character, would admit of such a form. It is said that their speeches are often memorized, which is undoubtedly true, but they appear as spontaneous as if gushing directly from the fountain of the soul, with irrepressive force. Hence, their eloquence has the intensity of burning flame, melting with whatever it comes in contact.

On returning to my lodging, I spent a brief hour or two in the church of *St. Germain l'Auxerrois*. This edifice possesses interest on account of its antiquity, it having been erected at first, sometime in the seventh century. Standing for a long time without the walls of the city, it more than once experienced the devastating influence of civil and foreign wars. It presents now very many points of interest to the lover of art, and of the curious, but space fails to enumerate them here. It happened to be a time of service with them, and I had the enviable pleasure of listening to some excellent music, and of witnessing some curious ceremonies. The nave of the church was nearly half filled, mostly with a class resembling the common people, a large number being children, accompanied by their teachers. There were, besides, a goodly number of that humane class of females entitled Sisters of Charity, who were easily distinguished by their simple and unique garb. In this latter respect, they more nearly resemble the Quakers, or Friends, than any class that I can liken them to. I should not omit to mention another class present, which would be likely to attract the attention of a stranger. They were a band of young women, bearing a common resemblance in dress, age, and manner, and whom I took for nuns. Arranged on a long seat, they remained in a fixed attitude, presenting a demure and docile aspect. Their countenances, however, bore a bloom and redolence, reminding you of the first blush of spring. They were handsomely attired in long, flowing, silk robes, a white veil reaching below the breast, and white kid gloves of immaculate purity. Each bore in her hand a book of worship, beautifully gilded. The unique grace and elegance of their costume, and their subdued sedateness of expression, joined to the recollection of their secluded life, invested the spectacle they formed with a poetical charm which appealed with lively force to the imagination. They were in consequence, the object of a covert scrutiny by the strangers present; and one of the maidens, more lovely in appearance than the others, ever and anon sweetly nestled in her place, with a kind of pardonable vanity apparent from her frequently rearranging some portion of her dress, and making occasional side-glances at some of the spectators present. In contemplating these interesting specimens of the fairer creation, one felt to question the heart-wisdom at least of an institution that would thus pluck from social life such lovely flowers, to "waste their fragrance on the desert air."

After tea, I compounded with my conscience so far as to adopt the resolution to visit one of the many rural restaurants situated in the verge of the city, where the common people are wont to assemble on a Sunday evening, to forget for a brief moment, amid singing and dancing and convivial enjoyment, the weariness of their labors, and the pain of their hard lot. I found the place at last, with some difficulty, and after much particular inquiry; but on arriving, I found that I should lose the gratification of my curiosity in the object of my visit thither, as it was not the season for the indulgence of such amusements. I was permitted, nevertheless, to inspect the place fully, and had all my questions abundantly answered. There was a cozy and rustic cottage in the midst of a pleasing garden shaded with trees, and interspersed with delightful arbors, with seats and tables for the lovers of the sparkling cup. In the middle of the garden was a small, open square, where rustic swain and buxom lassie had often, amid tumultuous music and hilarity, gracefully circled in the seducing and merry dance.

On my return home, I spent a brief hour in agreeable conversation with Madame my graceful and kind-hearted landlady. Being the only foreigner out of the sixty young students who had rooms in her hotel, she had the politeness to grant me alone the privilege of spending with her and her maid, occasional fragments of time, for resolving my doubts on perplexing points in the days investigation, as well as receiving suggestions as to the course to be pursued to see and learn the most at the least expense of time. She was remarkably intelligent, spirited, and witty. Her little private parlor was graced with a small library, containing a choice collection of standard works in French literature. Her knowledge of the passing world was obtained from the journals, the loan of which she purchased at second hand, for a *sou* a reading. It would be rare, even in our own school-boasting country, to find a lady of similar early advantages, and the same occupation in life, to be so well versed in literature and a knowledge of the world, as was Madame David. She had been a long time engaged in the same occupation that she was now following, and which her mother pursued before her. Taking her word for it, she did not get rich — so much competition was there in the trade — although she lived very frugally. She furnished the lodgers with meals when they ordered them, but her own were obtained by her maid from the restaurants, — and it was really curious to see, as I sometimes accidentally did, how very minute quantities of the different dishes they indulged in, sufficed her simple appetite.

Before the evening was far spent, I set out for the *Réunion des Ouvriers*, held in the capacious basement of the Church of St. Sulpice, to which I had already received a printed invitation by my friend the Directeur. On arriving, I found the room crowded, and the exercises already begun. A seat had been reserved for me near the desk, to which I was immediately conducted amid marks of respect. A young man was reading an essay; but before I could well gather up the thread of his discourse, he came to an end. Having been previously informed that the bishop of Paris would honor the meeting with his presence, I was just imagining the sort of personage I should see in him, when (a slight movement announcing his entrance) the entire assembly rose simultaneously to their feet, and remained standing in a deferential attitude, till the distinguished functionary had glided along through the aisle, rapidly but noiselessly, to his seat behind the desk. While the president of the meeting — after announcing to the audience that it was the especial request of their honored visitor, that there should be shown him no applause — was offering some remarks of his own, I had a moment's leisure to survey the high clerical dignitary. My imagination had pictured a lordly personage, garbed in pontifical robes, and moving with measured dignity. But far different was the reality. He was of the medium French stature, corpulent, but showing none of the unwieldiness which usually attends obesity. He was simply attired with a small French *toque* upon his capacious head. A massive gold ring, encasing a brilliant, the badge of his office, was upon one of the gloved fingers of his hand, and constituted the only ornament he wore. On his expansive forehead was enthroned the grandeur of lofty intellect. From his genial countenance beamed intelligence and benignity, while his eyes floated in a sea of sympathy, and were radiant with the fire of genius. His manner had the simplicity of a child. He followed the president, in an extemporaneous address of considerable length; and if my astonishment was great before, it was redoubled on hearing him speak. From the commencement to the close of his remarks, every mind was riveted to the speaker, with intense interest. His vast soul seemed pouring forth in a torrent of eloquence, while the deep sea of embodied sympathy which filled the spacious room, was profoundly agitated like a tumultuous lashed ocean. Now lively or humorous, now fervid or impassioned, then flashing in sallies of wit, and again abounding in melting pathos, the entire audience hung entranced upon his moving accents. At one moment the house was convulsed with laughter; at another, tears trickled down upon manly cheeks. He painted with masterly touches the numerous haunts of folly and vice in the new Babylon, as he termed it, and forcibly showed how superior to them were such soul-elevating places as that institution. Besides, added the speaker with peculiar significance, "You have the example of Christ, of the Apostles, and of the great and good of all ages." In common with the audience, I was deeply affected, and felt refreshed and elevated by his noble strains.

He was followed by a very young man, in appearance no more than sixteen years of age,—but what a falling off was there! His style bore the faults of youth and inexperience, without the marks of genius.

Then came the report of the critic,— the reading of which produced some merriment. This, as I understood, closed the regular exercises. Then followed volunteer speeches from gentlemen invited, or accidentally present. One of the most notable speakers, was the governor of the Hotel of the Invalids. He spoke fluently, and with animation, and his remarks, happily pointed off with apt illustration and sparkling anecdote, were well received by the company. Then followed a young gentleman, whom I took for a lawyer. After some vain display of person, and an obsequious apology for lack of preparation, he commenced. He was certainly fluent, and pleasing in his style; but rambling through fields of science, art, poetry, and literature, he had scarcely come to the point, before his time expired. Then followed the report of the treasury, dry and uninteresting, as such papers usually are. We were afterwards favored with a prosaic speech from one of the Professors of History at the Sarbonne. Volumes of books were then distributed, according to a previous arrangement, whether by lottery or otherwise, I could not under stand. The exercises were closed with singing and prayer. There was singing, also, after every exercise. Twice, a single powerful and cultivated voice, accompanied by an instrument, filled the room with its deep and rich melody. At other times, the singing was performed by the audience, — every person present, except myself, I believe, taking part. It was accompanied by a fine-toned organ, and the effect was grand and inspiring. It produced upon my feelings an elevation and impressiveness, impossible to express. I could have listened to it forever. Just imagine, for a moment, the effect of perhaps a thousand or fifteen hundred cultivated voices (for all are thoroughly taught to sing in youth), in perfect harmony, and inspired by elevating exercises, pouring forth their deep melody, exquisitely blended with the artistic tones of the organ. The singing and happy hits of the speakers gave more than freshness and piquancy to the exercises, and breathed into the whole a fraternal spirit.

The character of this institution is professedly moral, religious, literary, and scientific, and is designed to furnish healthful relaxation, elevating amusement, and practical improvement, to the laboring classes; and from this meeting, and several others which I attended, I should think it admirably adapted to promote so laudable an end.

The Parisians are represented by some, as gay and frivolous, and entirely given to vain amusement; but here is a society in the heart of the city, comprising more than a thousand persons — and there are several others such in the city — the members of which, for sobriety of demeanor, earnestness of feeling, and thirst for solid improvement, will compare with any people in the world.

This institution resembles considerably our Lyceums or Institutes. They are organized, however, on a broader basis, and their exercises are of a more diversified character. All but Jesuits, who are at the bottom of this, as well as most other like moral and religious enterprises in the city, pay something for admittance.

CHAPTER XVII.

TO VERSAILLES — CHATEAU — VASTNESS — SPLENDID GROUNDS — SUMPTUOUS INTERIOR — HOTEL DE BRISSAC — CONDITION OF DOMESTICS — NORMAL SCHOOL — HEALTHFUL APPEARANCE OF STUDENTS.

Feb. 7th. I started by railroad for Versailles. A train leaves every hour, from both sides of the Seine, during the day and evening. The distance is about twelve miles, and the rates of fare are forty, thirty, and twenty-five cents, according to places. I observed well-dressed and respectable-looking people in the second grade, and even the third. Indeed, it is said that "only women and fools go in the first place;" or, with more propriety of expression, such as would purchase exclusion. The time occupied thirty-five minutes. Arriving, I called on M. le Directeur of the Norman School, to whom I had letters of recommendation from the Vice-Rector at the Sorbonne. The Director received me graciously, assuring me that I was most welcome to inspect the entire establishment at pleasure. As the Palace of Versailles would not open on the next day, I decided to make immediately my visit to this justly celebrated establishment.

CHATEAU DE VERSAILLES.

I cannot, of course, attempt anything like a full description of this celebrated Palace, which would, indeed, require a volume; but I am bound to say something about it, as well as its history.

About the middle of the seventeenth century, that magnificent monarch, Louis XIV, surnamed the great, becoming tired of St. Germain, determined to build a palace, and create a court that should attract the admiration of Europe, and become the centre of the politics, art, literature, and refinement of the civilized world. He chose for this purpose the gently elevated and undulating grounds in the hunting forests, about twelve miles southwest of the capital, where his ancestors used to pursue the chase.

Le Notre was employed to lay out the gardens and grounds, and Lebrun to paint the apartments. In order to obtain ample room, the surrounding domains were purchased, until the whole, gardens, parks, and forests, expanded to a circumference of some sixty miles, with villages and agricultural grounds interspersed. A little to the east of the elevated plateau, upon which the palace was to stand, a town was laid out; and some idea may be formed of the extent and prodigality of this court, when it is remembered that a town of one hundred thousand inhabitants sprang up, as if by magic, adorned with public squares, fine private hotels, and a number of public institutions, among which was a royal college.

But the vast expenditure which was necessary, first to create, and then to keep up such a palace and court, impoverished the nation, and contributed materially to the subsequent revolution in 1789. It is said that the actual expenditure on the buildings and grounds, was nearly two hundred millions of dollars.

The town at present contains but about thirty thousand inhabitants; but is considered one of the handsomest in France, although it now wears a dull and deserted appearance, being no longer resorted to by the *beau monde*. It consists principally of three wide streets, lined with trees, diverging from the *Place d'Armes*, an open space in front of the palace. The central and widest of these streets, is called the Avénue de Paris; and those on the north and south, the avenues of St. Cloud and Sceaux. The other streets, though of less width, are equally regular, cross each other at right angles, and are lined with handsome residences.

From the *Place d'Armes*, eight hundred feet wide, you pass into the grand court, which is three hundred and eighty feet wide As seen from the grand court, on the side next the town, the palace seems an intricate and interminable aggregation of buildings, at one point advancing, at another, receding, yet magnificent amid this apparent confusion. But it is only when viewed from the garden, that the vastness of the huge and interminable pile is fully realized. You are now perfectly overwhelmed with the extent of the mass. The centre of the façade alone is three hundred feet front, and two hundred and sixty deep; while on each side of it, a wing stretches off at right angles, to something like six hundred feet, presenting an entire façade of nearly two thousand feet, ornamented with Ionic pilasters, and with eighty statues sixteen feet in height, allegorically representing the months, seasons, arts, and sciences, and crowned by a ballustrade. This immense façade is pierced by more than three hundred windows and doors; and the impression of the vastness of the whole is heightened by remembering, that many of these windows admit light into single halls more than two hundred feet in length, thirty-five in breadth, and forty in height.

Neither is the visitor less astonished, if he turns his attention to the grounds. Not only is he struck with their extent, but his mind is enraptured with admiration, in view of their inconceivable beauty, and the profusion of their decorations. From fountains worked on a gigantic scale, leap forth silvery waters, painting to the eye, at times, every hue of the rainbow. One of these fountains, the Neptune, cost three hundred thousand dollars; and the expense of playing it, on the Sunday fêtes, for the amusement of the people, is from eight thousand to ten thousand francs, or from fifteen hundred to two thousand dollars. Within the grounds are large lakes, embowered in refreshing groves, on which glided formerly boats and even ships, for the amusement of royalty. There are, also, two minor palaces, mere summer houses compared with the Château itself; but the larger is nearly of the size of the President's house at Washington. These are called the Grand and the Petit Trianon, and were erected for the use of favorite mistresses. Disgusted with the unmeaning pomp of royalty, here the beautiful but unfortunate Marie Antoinette used to hie away from the palace, and regale in happier moments her buoyant and graceful life. To the south, is the orangery, where a whole grove of these trees bloom in winter, and are removed in summer to border the avenues and walks, and load the air with their rich fragrance. The avenues, arbors, the margins of the lakes, and the fountains which meet the visitor at every turn, are appropriately adorned with countless groups of beautiful statuary, imparting a classic air to the whole magnificent scene.

I entered the palace by the way of the town. In the court, I was immediately besieged by persons offering themselves for guides, or exposing for sale hand-books containing a succinct account of the palace and its gardens. Upon the frieze of the imposing front of the main range of buildings, you may read in large golden letters, "*A toutes les gloires de la France,*" which indicate the new destination of the palace and grounds, under the reign of Louis Phillippe. As you enter, a liveried huissier or door-keeper politely indicates to you the direction you are to take; and at the entrances of all the apartments, these persons are stationed for the same purpose. But for this arrangement, strangers would find it impossible to make their way successfully through the labyrinths of rooms of the interminable Château. In regard to the extent of the interior of the palace, I can only say, that it is judged that it would require two hours to walk through the entire establishment, without stopping a moment to examine the different objects. I was myself five hours in going through, hastily and with intense industry, tarrying only long enough to make a rapid inspection of some object particularly remarkable, or peculiarly interesting from its historical associations. The splendor of what I had before seen in the Louvre and in the Luxembourg, was lost in the magnificence of this palace. The painted ceilings, the pictured walls, the size and number of its mirrors, the highly finished floors, the tapestry, the gilding, the exquisitely wrought furniture, admit of no description which can convey an adequate idea of its sumptuousness. The *Salon d'Hercule*, and the *Salles des Marécheaux, de Venus, Diane, Mercure, Mars, Apollon, l'Abondance, de la Guerre*, etc., so named from the paintings on their ceilings, walls, or other appropriate devices, are all truly noble apartments. The *Grande Galerie* is two hundred and twenty-eight feet in length, by thirty-two feet in breadth, and forty-two feet in height. The ceiling, painted by Le Brun, represents some of the most striking events in the early part of the reign of Louis XIV.

The Museum of Versailles is the History of France in action. All the battles, all the most brilliant actions, are here represented, from the foundation of the monarchy up to the present day. Each period has its saloon or gallery. A part of the ground-floor is devoted to sculpture. The rest of the palace is filled with pictures.

The victories of the Republic, and the glorious events of the reign of Napoleon, have a large space appropriated to them. Here may be seen the grand and celebrated compositions of the Coronation, the battles of Austerlitz, d'Eylau, and many other pictures, master pieces of the modern school of painting.

The more recent events, of the Revolution of 1830, and the brilliant campaigns in Algiers, have also a place appropriated to them.

The historical portraits are numerous. First, may be seen a collection of the portraits of all the kings of France; afterwards, the constables, great admirals, and marshals. In an immense saloon are arranged, besides, the portraits of personages of all nations, and times, who have been illustrious either upon the throne, or in war, politics, literature, or in the arts and sciences.

One entire room is devoted to the views of the historical chateaux of France. In another, is a collection of paintings in watercolors, tracing the campaigns of Italy.

The busts and statues form an extensive and interesting collection of the most celebrated persons of all countries and times. There are, besides, the tombs of the kings, queens, and princesses of France.

Many of the works are from the most celebrated artists. Among them may be recognized pictures, from the pencil of Horace Vernet, Paul Delaroche, Deveria, and a host of other celebrites.

Nothing can be more imposing than the perspective of these immense galleries, and range of rooms, losing themselves in the distance. Those called after the luxurious monarch, Louis XIV, I thought magnificent, beyond even the power of imagination to conceive. They looked directly out upon the garden, and were as beautiful and gorgeous as the finest gilt, marble, and glass could be formed by the genius of man. As I stood at the entrance, memory rolled back to by-gone years, and fancy pictured many a gay and brilliant scene of the past, when the monarch, surrounded by groups of the gayest and most chivalrous gentlemen, and beautiful and elegant ladies of the realm, were gliding in the voluptuous dance. Such a living picture as could be imagined would surpass a fairy scene.

The expense of keeping up such an establishment has deterred all the sovereigns from residing there since the Revolution. At that time, it suffered greatly by the irruption of the populace into the château. Its decorations were then much mutilated. Louis Phillippe, with his grand munificence, restored, at his private expense, its ancient splendor, and gave a new destination to the whole.

I took lodging for the night at the *Hotel du Brissac*, the identical house once occupied by the duke of that name, a circumstance upon which my accommodating landlord frequently dwelt, as if it had invested his house with some strange charm. After supper, which was excellent, I sauntered out in quest of a *Cabinet de Lecture*, or reading-room, but finding there were none, I realized fully the deprivation of what constitutes, in Paris, to a reading man, so agreeable a resort. I managed, however, to spend the evening pleasantly enough, talking familiarly with the landlord, his wife, and such gentlemen as happened to come in. One of these latter told me, with all due gravity, that the Americans and English are more polite than the French, although he admitted that the French are the more *gallant* of the two. He insisted further, that the English, great numbers of whom reside in Versailles, speak French more correctly than the French residents themselves. I took this as coming from one of those ambiguous personages who may be frequently met with in Europe, hanging about hotels, and eking out a scanty subsistence from travellers, by flattery, or by means even less justifiable.

While sitting in the dining-hall, the family came in, and made their supper, consisting of soup, a scanty supply of meat, with cider instead of wine. They were followed by the domestics, who appeared in the merriest mood imaginable. They seemed not to suppose that I had ears of my own; for they chatted with unbounded freedom upon any subject that happened to come uppermost, making all manner of remarks about my humble self. It being the season of Carnival, bright anticipations floated in their merry minds, and lent a gay volubility to their irregular conversation.

Domestics at the hotels, restaurants, cafés, and other like places, rarely receive compensation for their services, of the landlord; but rely upon what they can obtain from travellers, for favors done, such as cleansing and polishing boots, removing baggage, etc. Indeed, in some establishments, the situation is so enviable as to induce the domestic to purchase his place. This being the case, it is not so surprising that domestics in these countries are somewhat importunate to travellers. It was the rule at this establishment for the domestics to retire, ordinarily, from ten to eleven o'clock; but on Sunday evenings, they were allowed to go to masquerade balls, and be out, if they chose, all night.

Accommodations and fare here, were excellent, and much cheaper than at Paris.

Feb. 8th. Proceeded early to the Normal school, where, after a slight delay, I was admitted, — conducted through the different apartments of the building, and over the grounds, by one of the sub-teachers assigned by the director, who happened himself to be engaged. The young gentleman who accompanied me, was affable in his manner, particular in his attentions to make me see all, and enthusiastic to have me duly appreciate the various excellent points of the establishment. I was also admitted to the sessions of the several classes.

This school, as its name implies, is designed to educate and fit young gentlemen for teachers of schools in the smaller towns and rural districts; although, such as graduate, may become teachers in any school, or even engage in other pursuits, if it should turn out that their peculiar talent and tastes make the departure desirable. The number of students between the ages of fourteen and eighteen, was one hundred and fifteen. They remain but two years, and do not study the languages. There is a juvenile department connected with the establishment, comprising several schools, of children of different ages, in which students of the principal department teach by turns, as a preparatory practice. Students are admitted after a satisfactory examination. Among other things, they are required to be able to pronounce Latin, without, however, understanding it. The average compensation of the Normal graduate, in a good situation, is from one hundred and seventy-five to two hundred dollars per annum, — the latter being considered excellent pay. None are admitted without boarding at the establishment. No corporal punishment is permitted, order being maintained by moral means, system of demerits, and in other such ways. Emulation is encouraged, and medals awarded to the most successful and worthy students. The school is conducted by a principal and ten professors, one for each department of instruction, namely, Ancient and Modern History and Geography, the Art of Teaching, Religion, Mathematics, Natural History, Book-keeping, Music, Designing or Drawing, Gymnastics, etc. I was shown the cabinet and library. They are doubtless ample, but by no means extensive. The students were muscular and hale, and looked as if they came from the rural districts. Indeed, many of them wore wooden shoes, and were dressed in blouse. The building is not imposing, nor the rooms superior. A small garden is assigned the students, each being allotted a separate plot; and after the first year, they are regularly instructed in the theory and practice of agriculture. In the play-ground connected with the establishment there is a meagre gymnasium for physical exercise. I must confess that I was somewhat disappointed in the school, which though evidently of an elevated character, and conducted with ability, yet appeared hardly a model school for the nation. Connected with the Principal department, there are, as I have already observed, three primary schools, over which the Director has a supervision. Two are for very small children; the other is entitled, Primary School Superior, where lads remain four years, and are prepared for the practical avocations of life. I noticed a difference between the pronunciation in Versailles and Paris.

CHAPTER XVIII.

REVOLUTION OF FEBRUARY — CAUSE, REUNIONS — ITALIAN INDEPENDENCE — JUST MILIEU OF MR. GUIZOT — MORE REMOTE CAUSES — LOUIS PHILLIPPE — STORMY SESSION OF THE CHAMBER OF DEPUTIES — EVENING SCHOOL FOR JOURNEYMEN AND APPRENTICES — PALAIS DE LA BOURSE — A STROLL IN THE ENVIRONS OF PARIS — FORTIFICATIONS OF PARIS — PLACE DE LA CONCORDE — PARISIAN CAFES — DAME DU COMPTOIR — GARCON — DANCING — MODEL OFFICE — THEATRE FRANCAIS — ORCHESTRA — EXQUISITE PLAYING — LECTURES AT THE SARBONNE — MONSIEUR FRANK.

Paris, Feb. 9th. I spent the evening in the Reading Room, near my lodging, which had become for me a frequent resort, to frugalize spare moments of time in glancing at the current of events and opinions. The journals were filled with the discussion in the Chamber of Deputies, which had become ominously animated, if not exceedingly violent. The debate was upon the last paragraph of the address of the Government to the Chamber, at the opening of its session, and particularly upon a single clause therein contained, by which such as had participated in the late Réunions, were characterized as *politically blind,* and *decidedly inimical* to the government. These *Réunions* were simply political gatherings, composed mainly of opposition members and their constituents, held at various times in different parts of the kingdom, and partook somewhat of the nature of social, convivial meetings for free interchange of opinion and sentiment upon the policy of the government, and the condition and prospects of the country. I speak now of the ostensible character of these assemblings. Undoubtedly, the real purpose among the few contrivers of the scheme, was a general plan of agitation, with no well defined aim, — but which proved a powerful lever for a change of power. At some of these *Réunions* held of late, gentlemen had indulged in sentiments well calculated to irritate or alarm the government. At one, a Polish refugee declaimed wildly against the Russian and Austrian governments, and complained bitterly of the course pursued by the French minister. On complaint being made to Louis Phillippe, by the ministers of the former governments, the noble exile was summarily punished for his temerity, by being immediately banished the kingdom. At another banquet, the customary sentiment of drinking the health of the king, was omitted. These, and other plain indications of a rapidly growing spirit of democratical audacity, joined, doubtless, with a lively conviction of its danger, unless opportunely checked, had determined the government upon measures to stay its progress. Hence the introduction of the topic in the Address, as just mentioned.

Aside from the energy of will and power for unfaltering perseverance which arbitrary opposition is always sure to impart, the agitators and the popular party had their enthusiasm aroused and sympathies ardently excited, by the struggle for freedom then going on in Italy — that land of noble and animating recollections — against the crushing and blighting tyranny of Austria. The coldhearted and unnatural attitude of the French government toward the unequal combatants, and particularly the equivocal policy of M. Guizot, its Prime Minister, as expressed by him in the notorious phrase, *Le Juste Milieu*, or *Masterly Inactivity*, as American politicians would have it, only deepened the feeling of resentment toward the government, and fanned the flame of feeling for popular rights. England had openly expressed her sympathy for bleeding Italy; and that France, the rival of England, herself the most powerful and enlightened nation in Western Europe, — a nation, too, that had already sacrificed so freely in blood and treasure, for human freedom, should now inhumanly fold her arms in a sort of stoical indifference not only to abstract justice, but to the fate of human liberty on the Continent, was not only a dereliction from the plainest principles of humanity, but would ever constitute an unpardonable national reproach. This sentiment widened and deepened, seizing the thought and sympathy even of the more conservative part of the nation. Italian propagandism spread rapidly, as on the wing of thought, to every part of the kingdom. It diffused itself and penetrated among the mass of the population with electric celerity, awaking in the national heart stirring reminiscences of past glory, modified, indeed, by a feeling of shame and indignation against the government. The Frenchman of republican tendencies recognized in every Italian patriot a suffering brother, and saw in Austrian tyranny the prelude of his own bondage. These were some of the immediate circumstances that had sprung up to widen the breach between the Government and the Opposition; and to hasten the grand crisis which was sooner or later to fall upon the nation like an avalanche. There were other causes, fundamental, of long but powerful action, gradually but surely alienating the mind of the nation from the Government, and preparing it for a grand revolt. To understand the exact posture of affairs at this time, it will be necessary to glance at these, even at the risk of becoming tedious.

The luxurious expensiveness of the reign of Louis XIV, the licentious extravagance of Louis XV, together with the popular writers of those reigns upon the grandeur and beauty of freedom of thought and political equality, had prepared the way for the Revolution of 1789. The vacillating conduct of Louis XVI, the deranged state of the finances when he was called to the throne, and the success of the American Revolution, were circumstances that precipitated that mighty event. The insane fury of the revolution itself, the all-grasping ambition of Napoleon, and the success of the allied armies, restored the monarchy, but they did not quench the spirit of political freedom and human improvement in the national breast. The reappearance of Napoleon upon the soil of France revived the national sentiment for its old prestige of liberty, and at the approach of the new luminary, Louis XVIII. fled from his throne, like a shadow chased by the sun. The second defeat of the "Man of Destiny" placed the yoke of monarchy again upon the unwilling neck of the nation. As soon as the democratic spirit of the nation had had time to rally and combine its forces, Charles X. was repulsed from the throne of his ancestors.

Lafayette, then the oracle of the free party, believing France not yet ripe for an unlimited republic, declared in favor of a constitutional monarchy, and Louis Phillippe, son of the atrocious *égalite*, was elected the "Citizen King," amid a profusion of promises to obey the spirit of the nation. The country further imagined, that from the impulse imbibed from his jacobin father, in his own political predilections as shown in his public career, in his wisdom gained in the school of experience, and in his knowledge of the fate of his predecessors, they had a sure guarantee of his devotion to liberal principles. But in this they were to be doomed to utter disappointment. Louis Phillippe has strong claims for respect and admiration upon the French nation, and upon the world; but he did not fulfil the mission for which he was chosen. He possessed vast experience, a luminous intellect, and a liberal and humane spirit. His family was a model of mental industry, moral purity, and domestic affection. He improved the system of public instruction, placing it upon a liberal basis, and generously fostered all kinds of literary and humane institutions. He was a liberal patron of the arts, spending large sums of his private fortune for their promotion. He more than once preserved the peace of Europe, when events threatened a general conflagration of war. He was magnanimous toward the fallen family of Napoleon. And the general spirit of his policy was humane, liberal, and peaceful, calculated to promote the great branches of industry and the moral and intellectual improvement of the nation. Still, he neglected the great principle which placed him upon the throne; and for this unpardonable dereliction, he was dreadfully punished. Several distinct acts of his reign may be cited to confirm this position. He usurped the elective franchise, by greatly narrowing the basis of popular representation. The Chamber of Peers became little more than a creation of the king, without independence of action, or true dignity. The Chamber of Deputies, the popular branch of the legislature, upon which the hopes of the nation relied to carry on the popular reform, lost its efficiency by the bestowment upon many of its leading members of a part of the enormous government-patronage in the hands of the king, to purchase their influence to the royal cause. He contracted a marriage between one of his sons and the sister of the Queen of Spain, in violation of a solemn treaty, thus endangering the peace of Europe. He surrounded Paris with stupendous fortifications, at an enormous cost to the nation, with the ostensible purpose of protecting the capital from foreign invasion; but doubtless with the real design to give firmness to his own power. These are some of the acts which give an idea of his policy. For some time after his accession to the throne, he flattered the hopes of the liberal party. He was wont to mingle freely with the populace, and occasionally to join in the chorus of the *Marsellaise*. He educated his sons in the public schools, to identify them with the sympathies of the people. He sympathized with the Italian and Spanish patriots; but Austria and Russia became alarmed at the danger of France becoming the centre of republican institutions in Europe, and the propagandist of liberal principles on the continent. Envoys were immediately despatched from those powers to Paris. From this moment, the " Citizen King" seems to have taken his part. He gradually turned his back upon Lafayette, and Lafitte, to whom he owed his crown. He repudiated the programme of liberal principles, acknowledged by him at the Hotel de Ville, and fell back upon the Chatre as the limitation of constitutional power. He denied the professions of political faith which he had made in conversation with Lafayette;— and he applied, continually, the untiring energies of his powerful mind, the resources of France, and his own enormous private fortune, to the consolidation of his power and the perpetuation of his dynasty. The leading powers of Europe recognized his legitimacy, and entered with him into an alliance; and with them as allies, and the vast army of four hundred thousand men in France, he hoped to secure the permanency of his throne. But it proved that the spirit of human liberty is more powerful than armies.

The disaffection in the nation had become general. The legitimists regarded him as a usurper; the liberal party looked upon him as a traitor; the press,— the more powerful in France as it is often conducted by the most eminent writers,— spread the grounds of discontent before the masses of the nation, and with that *verve* of eloquence peculiar to the French language in the hands of a skilful writer, excited all minds to revolt. Such was the posture of affairs in February, 1848, when the National Assembly were in session to deliberate upon the affairs of the nation. It is true, all was peaceful and harmonious without; but penetrating minds well foresaw the certainty of an approaching crisis. Louis Phillippe had, indeed, the body of the nation in his hands; but its spirit had eluded his grasp.

The sessions of the Chamber of Deputies had become stormy, and the debate intensely fierce. The pending question of the right to hold the banquets, had drawn forth the leading talent of the Chamber, and this question was made a pretext for discussing the foreign policy of the nation. M. Guizot, the Prime Minister, and a consummate parliamentary orator, maintained the position of the government with a coolness and ability that commanded universal admiration. The opposition orators, on their part, were by turns sarcastic and impassioned. M. Thiers charged the government with yielding up Switzerland and Italy to the rapacious grasp of Austria,—thus lending the mighty power of the nation to retard the glorious march of enlightened freedom upon the Continent. "What!" exclaimed Lamartine, in one of his noble bursts of eloquence, "shall France, the foremost country in progress and freedom in the old world, side with despotic Austria, her old rival and foe, to crush the struggling spirit of freedom which France has crossed a sea of blood to protect, and leave to England the honor of advancing the liberties of the world?" These speeches were spread rapidly over the country, and fell like firebrands among the already excited populace. Had some compromise been made at this critical juncture, the downfall of the monarchy might have been arrested; but the government seemed fated to its destruction.

Feb. 11*th.* One of the Frères kindly accompanied me to one of the evening schools for journeymen and apprentices. Here I was cordially accosted by two teachers whom I had before met. One spoke a *leetle* English, as he termed it, and seemed proud of his enviable attainment. The school is composed principally of adults, although it has a juvenile class. The apprentices number not more than one-fiftieth of this class in the city and the journeymen are as large a proportion as one-fifteenth. Most of the students whom I saw, were engaged in drawing,—and some of their specimens shown me, were fine. I inspected a model steam engine, made entirely by a boy, after his daily task. It was ingenious and beautiful, but cost two years' effort. Several other equally curious specimens of work I had the gratification to inspect. They usually make the drawing in the class at school, and then model from it at home, at their leisure. The school is supported by the government, and is entirely free. It cannot but prove a useful institution, and will doubtless be better patronized, when its merits are more fully appreciated. It had already been instrumental in calling forth native talent, which might otherwise have slumbered in the breast of its possessor. It moreover attests the paternal care of the government.

Feb. 13*th*. In my ramblings to-day, I accidentally stumbled upon the *Palais de la Bourse*, or Merchants' Exchange. It is a magnificent edifice, standing in the middle of a handsome square, surrounded by shade-trees. It is of recent construction, having been commenced only in 1808. The plan of the building presents a parallelogram two hundred and twenty-five feet in length, by one hundred and thirty-four in width, surrounded by a fine peristyle of sixty-six Corinthian columns, raised upon an elevated basement. A gallery, ornamented with *bass-reliefs*, emblematical of the operations of commerce, extends quite around the building. The interior has a single grand hall, for the free intercourse of the sons of Mammon. There is, however, a small space of a circular form, and surrounded by a railing, in the south part of the room, allotted to the salesman of stocks, to separate him from the crowd. Sales were going on at the time. A number of persons pressed closely around the enclosure just alluded to, while a man within was conducting the sale with half-frantic gestures, and with most intense and impetuous earnestness. The competition among the buyers was apparently so eager and furious, that the bids appeared simultaneous. The vaulted arch of the edifice, by some principle of acoustics, increased and reverberated the sound, which rolled along the spacious room, through the gallery into the decorated tribunes, in a commingled and deafening roar. The scene appeared to me incomprehensible and ludicrous. I could not for the life of me perceive how the salesman could distinguish between the bids, so great was the confusion and the interminable roar of sound; but the ear can become betrained to wonders.

Feb. 13th. The day was fine, and the atmosphere soft. It being the first really spring-like day since my arrival, the effect upon my feelings was such as to tempt me out for a stroll amid some of the charming environs of Paris. In passing through the garden of the Tuileries and the Champs Elysées, it became evident that my feelings were shared by many others. Those enchanting resorts were thronged with persons of different sexes and ages, eager to drink in the first incense of the early dawn of the approaching spring. In the garden of the Tuileries, my heart was gladdened by the sight of covies of rosy children prettily and tastefully dressed. They were gambolling about on the smooth walks, as happy in their fresh and sunny existence, as the most joyful nature could desire. They were attended, of course, by their nurses, tidily dressed, who with a sedate aspect appeared to have one eye upon their knitting, or some other light work, while the other, glistening with moisture, was peering after the dear little loving creatures, their tiny wards and adopted idols. In some family groups were infants borne by servants, — the former of whom appeared not unapt emblems of the approaching spring, just budding into a hopeful existence. In the Champs Elysées, thousands of elegantly dressed people, with countenances beaming with agreeable sensations, were gaily promenading the wide avenues, or indolently sauntering under the majestic elms that line the walks, or gazing with delight upon the groups of statuary with which this paradise is graced, — or, perhaps voluptuously reclining upon the seats, watching the varied throng, and yielding to the delicious sensations which the scene and circumstances induced. From the Triumphal Arch, that fit emblem of the Great Captain, I took my course by chance off to the northwest, and was almost immediately in an extended and charming grove. The ground here for any extent is as level as an artificial lawn. The trees of oak, locusts, and other varieties, and of less size than half-grown forests, had been carefully trimmed to present a neat and uniform appearance. No undergrowth was permitted to obstruct the view of the passer, or to entangle the feet of the loiterer. This prim and smiling area of wood is handsomely intersected in various directions by wide avenues bordered by stately locusts, and presenting to the eye pleasing vistas narrowing off in the distance to the merest point. These avenues were everywhere thronged with neatly or elegantly attired promenaders, with countenances glowing with grateful emotions and the exhilarating effects of the genial atmosphere and the brisk exercise, — while there would occasionally roll past some pleasure-vehicle or family carriage, bearing steadily on, perhaps, some world-exclusive individual, or perchance a pleasure-dreaming couple, or more likely, a dignified family circle. Not unfrequently the scene was animated by a single equestrian or troop in graceful and chivalrous costume, sweeping proudly on. Here and there upon the road, or in the woods, might be seen or heard groups of country beaux and lasses in their rustic but picturesque dress, chatting in lively mood, and occasionally making the silent woods ring with their peals of laughter, so clear and silvery, as well nigh to startle the wood-nymphs from their cozy retreats. As I proceeded on, there frequently gleamed through the slim trunks of the trees, a silvery sheet of water, or burst rapturously forth a fine château, beautified with the treasures of nature and art. I never experienced anything more delightful in the way of rural scenery; and if I had been suddenly translated to the veritable Elysium, I could not have felt happier for the moment. Doubtless the change from the city, and other circumstances, had much to do in heightening the effect of the agreeable in the scene.

On emerging from the *Bois de Boulogne*, on my return I spent a brief hour in observing a portion of the magnificent new fortifications of Paris. The plan of the work consists of two distinct features, — a continuous enclosure, bastioned and terraced, around the whole city, with a line of wet ditches in front, and a system of detached fortresses, fourteen in number, outside. The detached forts are furnished with mortars that can reach the limit of a circle more than six thousand feet in diameter; and they are so situated as to command every street, place, and house in the capital, except a space containing the palace of the Tuileries, the gardens, and a passage leading from the palace towards St. Germain, affording the royal family or government a way of escape, in case the fortifications should fall into the hands of an enemy. It is believed by military men, that they would not prove an impregnable barrier against an invading army, although most efficient in demolishing the city, or reducing it, by cutting off supplies.

In 1841, one hundred and forty millions of francs, or about twenty-eight millions of dollars, were reluctantly appropriated by the Chamber of Deputies, for this grand war-measure; and how much more has since been absorbed in the ambitious project, I am not able to say. From the commencement, the works were prosecuted amid strong opposition, with an energy unparalleled in the history of human exertion. The late king took a personal interest in their speedy completion, choosing to meet the expense of contracts from his private purse, rather than suffer any delay in their execution. It seems that the several rulers of France have sought to leave some grand monument of art, to illustrate their reign,—each vieing to surpass those who had preceded him, in grandeur and magnificence; but these efforts here, as elsewhere, have often served to surround their memory with associations different from what was intended by their authors. The enormous cost of St. Peter's church at Rome, ushered in the Reformation in Germany. The countless treasures expended on the Versailles Palace, was among the principal causes of the Revolution of 1789; while the fortifications of Paris, the grandest of the works of Louis Phillippe, proved but a treacherous power to expel him from his throne, to die in a foreign land.

It was evening before I reached the Champs Elysées. A vast throng were silently sweeping along with me through the Avenue de Neuilly, as if eager to regain the fascinations of the voluptuous capital. The scene now on my return, though different, was hardly less striking than before. The gray folds of evening had invested the various prominent objects along the route, with a new aspect of admiration. The double row of lights along the avenue, gradually descending and narrowing in the distance, appeared like continuous ranges of glittering golden balls, suspended from the soft branches of the majestic elms above, through which the vesperian zephyrs were sighing with mellifluous cadence. Reaching the Place de la Concorde, I could not but pause and enjoy awhile the surrounding beauty. This magnificent spot combines a varied and powerful interest, arising from the unrivalled beauty of the place itself, its touching historical associations, and the splendid views of which it is the radiant focus. In the centre, upon the identical spot where was beheaded the good Louis XVI, as well as his lovely and lamented queen, rises the beautiful Egyptian obelisk, eighty feet high, a memorial of ages merged in the oblivious past, upon which mortals, separated from us by the abyss of time, had gazed and thought. This justly admired shaft, consisting of a single block of rose-colored granite, was cut and erected by Ramases I. and II., and the shaft is covered with hieroglyphics extolling the actions of that king or Sesostris. On either side were two magnificent fountains, thought to be the finest in the world, throwing up their pearly jets into the air from the mouths of sporting dolphins, swans and fish, held by swimming Nereids and Tritons. Interspersed around were groups of statuary allegorical of the different towns of France, — from which the lights gleamed, heightening their effect. Through the trees composing the forests of the Champs Elysées were glimmering and flashing brilliant gas-lights of palaces and theatres, and of hundreds of moving carriages. To the east was the garden of the Tuileries, faintly illumined by the streaming light from the palace-windows. At other times you may see, now the superb colonnade of the Garde-Meuble, again the façade of the Madeline, or the magnificent portico of the Chamber of Deputies.

Turning off from the Garden of the Tuileries, by a gate on the north, I was soon in the open square of the Palais Royal. A flood of light streamed from the windows of the numerous cafés and restaurants of this delectable spot. Entering one of the latter of humbler pretensions, I readily had my sharpened appetite appeased, by a frugal meal, but of delicious quality, and served in the most elegant style imaginable. It consisted, first of a plate of soup, second of fricaseed chicken, third of veal, and fourth, of fish; bread at discretion; for desert, was a plate of cakes served in cream, and all accompanied with a half-bottle of wine. The charge for the whole was but thirty-two cents. The dishes were brought in separately, and appeared to have been prepared expressly for the meal, the moment before. To be sure, the quantity served on each plate was nicely small; still, when I had eaten of all, I was quite satisfied. I do not think the same meal could have been procured in Boston or New York for double the sum, notwithstanding the price of provision averages a third more at least in Paris, than in the United States.

The estaminets, the restaurants, and the cafés, of Paris, are marked features in the capital. The traveller may search Europe throughout, and he will find nothing to correspond with them; and as for the United States, whatever may be found there, are but sorry imitations. The general distinctions between them are these: An estaminet is a place where tobacco is smoked, various sorts of beverage are drunk, and generally cards and billiards played. A restaurant is one, where breakfasts and dinners are eaten. A café is another, where breakfasts are taken, dominos played, and where coffee, ices, and all refreshing drinks may at any hour be enjoyed.

There are some four or five hundred cafés in Paris alone. Their different grades answer to the different ranks of society, from the cabinet-minister to the nameless *sans culottes*. In the quarter of the Sarbonne are cafés, frequented principally by the class of students; others by professors; others still, by cabinet-ministers. Every theatre has in its vicinity a café. At these cafés, and likewise those of the Boulevard du Temple, principally congregate the actors, the actresses, and the dramatic authors of the time.

It is thus that the cafés answer in a measure the purpose of clubs; and some, where the literati congregate, are still associated with the name of Voltaire, Rousseau, and others, who with their professional friends, used there to assemble, and uncork their spirits and humor.

These establishments are frequented by ladies, as well as gentlemen. In the best of them may frequently be seen elegantly dressed and well-behaved ladies, either alone, or in company with friends, husbands and children. This mode of living is convenient, agreeable, economical, and gratifies their taste by enabling them to see the *beau monde*. The families of many of the respectable classes of merchants and professional men, and others, live in this way. They doubtless share a larger amount of social enjoyment in this way, than they could in any other. But the evil of the system is, that the Parisian has no *home*,— and even has no word in his language to express the endearing place; — although *social* beyond all other men, he is yet not at all domestic.

The Palais Royal is a quarter of the magnificent cafés. Some of these vie with the most gorgeous saloons of royalty, in taste and splendor. Let me attempt to introduce my reader to one of these. If it be the first time, you are at once dazzled with the view which presents itself. The room is spacious. The decorations in various parts are in such gorgeous profusion, that it recalls whatever you may have read of Persian magnificence. The ceiling and walls are elaborately wrought here and there into the most lovely frescos of birds and flowers, — fawns, nymphs, graces, and images in all fantastic forms. Four immense and gilded chandeliers hang from the ceiling. A tall candelabra rises in the centre of the room, and two beautiful lamps stand on the comptoir. These lights, illuminating these colors and this gilding, make the scene brilliant beyond description. And then the mirrors, so located as to double and redouble, yes, twenty times to reflect what has been described. It is not one café that you have seen to dazzle and enchant, but a *score* of them.

As you enter, you politely raise your hat. The token of courtesy is recognized by the dame-de-comptoir by a gentle inclination so graceful, easy, and complaisant as not to be surpassed. This fair personage occupies, in another part of the room, a seat covered with velvet fine enough for a throne, behind an elevated desk with a marble top. She is the queen, the divinity, the presiding genius of the fairy place, and attends to its affairs, receiving strangers, directing servants, and arranging accounts, with a grace and promptness that no human being but a French woman could attain. This lady sits stately behind her comptoir. Two large silver vases stand in front of her, filled with spoons. At her right hand are several elegant decanters, and at her left a score of silver cups, lumped with sugar. There is, moreover, a little bell within her reach, to summon the garçon, and wide-open before her are the treasury-boxes of the café. Her influence, by her graceful presence, tends to refine the whole scene. The lady in question is dressed in exquisite taste, a mellow serenity beams from her countenance, and there is an unconscious dignity and inimitable finesse in her whole bearing, that places her beyond corporeal life. Many a one of these café divinities is young and handsome, too, attracting thousands who flock thither, first to look at her; secondly, to talk with her; and thirdly, to enjoy the delight of sipping Mocha in her presence.

You select a large or small table, according as you are alone or with company. It is of white marble, and your seat of rich plush. In a moment the garçon is at your elbow; he inclines to your ear, and catches the word *demi-tasse*. He instantly reappears, and places before you a snowy-white cup and saucer, and a little dish containing three or four lumps of sugar. Another garçon now appears. In his right-hand is a huge silver pot, covered, and in his left, another of the same material, uncovered. The former contains coffee, the latter, cream. The balmy liquid is clear, strong, and highly concentrated, and when tempered with the sugar and heated cream, it becomes the finest beverage in the whole world. It agreeably affects several of the senses. Its liquid charms the gustatory nerves; its savor rejoices the olfactory; while even the eye is delighted with its sparkling hues. Yielding a moment to the pleasures of anticipation, you have time to survey the *tout-ensemble* of the garçon. In his sphere he seems to you a *beau ideal*. His face has a balmy expression that enchants you. His hair is polished into ebon. His cravat is of purest white, and his shirt-bosom is equally elegant. His round-about is the pattern of neatness. Upon his left arm hangs a clean napkin, and his lower extremities are quite wrapped about in a snowy apron. His stockings are white, and he glides about in noiseless pumps. He is a physiognomist of the keenest perceptions, for at your slightest intimation he is at your elbow.

To prolong the delight of your cup, you employ the intervals between the sips, in perusing the journals. All the most notable are there; and by mentioning the name of your preference, it is speedily brought you.

Having finished your coffee and journals, you spend a moment or two in surveying the company present. There may be fifty in the room, dressed with elegance and in the highest taste. They converse in a subdued tone, and you may hear all the languages in Europe.

Tapping your cup with a piece of coin, the garçon approaches, and taking the money, advances with it towards the dame-du comptoir, saying at the same time, "*huit-cent.*" The dame-du-comptoir abstracts eight sous. The garçon returning your change, invariably looks forward to a small *pour-boire* for himself. If you leave *one* sou, he merely inclines his head; if you leave *two*, he adds to the inclination a *mercie;* finally, if you generously abandon *three*, he not only bows profoundly, whispering *mercie*, but respectfully opens the door to your departing. On going out, you will always look at the lady, and raise your hat. The quiet self-possession with which she responds to your civility informs you that she has bowed to half the coffee-drinkers in Europe.

On returning to my lodgings, I passed the door of one of the more common dancing-saloons of the city. Parties were thronging in, some in masquerade, others not; and I could not resist the temptation to look in upon the sight for a moment. It was the height of the carnival season of Paris; and, as a consequence, the dancing-rage of this dancing people. They had evidently become worked up to the spirit of their favorite exercise; and a traveller will select the most favorable period for his observations. The admittance was ten cents. The company were entirely young, and of the inferior sort of society. The spacious room was partially divided into several compartments, but wide central spaces were left for free communication. The dancing, which was already going on, was energetically brisk. All spaces were quite filled, partly with sets in motion, or lookers-on, standing. The orchestra, in which violins greatly preponderated, were working their instruments as if life depended on impetuous movement. They changed their tune often, running through perhaps twenty favorite airs in a single dance. The dancing was even more unique than the music. There were no systematic figures, — but a promiscuous assembling and changing, each moving as fancy led. The twirling, spinning, leaping, twisting, gliding across and around each other in babel-confusion, but without coming in contact, was fantastic enough, but not altogether unamusing. Each young man held his female partner firmly in a waltz-like embrace, leading her rapturously into the spirit of the exercise, moving whither whim listed, and changing his step or movement at the caprice of impulse. Indeed, it seemed often to be the part of the beau to surprise the other in some sudden turn of the body, exposing the lady unexpectedly to some immodest attitude. I more than once detected a crimsoning on the already flushed cheek of some of the fair ones from this cause. There were, however, two or three buxom wenches among the crowd, who vanquished their partners in all their arts,— sometimes turning the joke. The whole scene struck me as inelegant, distasteful and debasing; though, of course, it cannot be mentioned as a specimen of how the divine art is generally practised in the graceful city.

Feb. 15th. I spent the day in the "Conservatoire des Arts et Métiers," Rue St. Martin 208. It corresponds, in a measure, to the Patent Office at Washington, presenting an interesting collection of specimens of machines, instruments and tools employed in the various kinds of manufactures and fabrications. It was devoted in 1798 to the industrial arts, and has since contributed most singularly to their advancement. I observed there, among many other curious and interesting things, a simple, but beautiful mode of representing geometrical solids, by means of thread-wires. By the slight movement of a spring, the form was easily changed. It struck me as an improvement, and deserving of being introduced as a valuable apparatus of the schoolroom.

In the evening, I set off to witness the drama on the great national stage of France, the Theatre Français. Arriving early, I whiled away the spare moments in making a tour in the square of the Palais Royal. The delightful place was filled with groups, promenading, lounging, or reading the journals, hired of the little *boutiques*, so accommodatingly scattered near all the public promenades of the city. Children of the lower class were venting their joyous nature in juvenile sports. Miniature men, they showed the same spirit of rivalry and passion as persons of greater stature.

Determined on a choice seat, I was still early in the *queue*, within the barricade leading to the entrance of the theatre. In the tail were some women, well dressed, but the most respectful demeanor prevailed. When the door opened we passed in comfortably, and I took a richly plushed seat in the *parquet*, separated only by the distance of a foot, or so, from the narrow space in front appropriated to the nobility.

The first play was entitled "The Mother-in-law and the Son-in-law." It was a pretty piece, and neatly played; but observing nothing striking in its character or performance, I very happily reserved my admiration for the following play, and with one eye surveyed leisurely the beautiful room and select company.

The room, of elliptical form, is surrounded by three rows of Doric columns, grouped in the first row, isolated in the two others. From the centre rises the statue of Voltaire. Beautiful and appropriate carvings, gildings, and frescos, lend a classical elegance and charm to the entire room. The company appeared intellectual and of easy manners, but not extremely dressed. Indeed, their manner and costume bore an elegant negligence, characteristic of the more independent classes. But they practised one custom not easily reconciled with their otherwise evident propriety of demeanor — that of staring at each other in the intervals of the scenes. For this purpose, each was provided, not with a small, neat, golden-rimmed eye, or quizzing glass, such as may sometimes be seen in the delicate hand of some acknowledged belle, at public assemblies in the U. States, but huge, double-barreled spy-glasses, from two to four inches deep, strongly connected, called *lunettes.* With this, the double-eyed starer would often stand upon his feet, direct his artificial eyes at different persons in the galleries, surveying the company with all the coolness and deliberation of a naval quarter-master. It was a little peculiar to notice luxuriant-looking mammas with their blooming daughters in the galleries, thus broadly gazing at the opposite sex below and around them. A stranger to the practice might have been led to ask himself, if the same action without the *lunette* would have been considered by these genteel people within the pale of good breeding? — O! no, indeed! — but then, it is the fashion, and there is no disputing the empire of so supreme a ruler.

The orchestra was small, but apparently extremely select. The performers were all very young, — mere boys, seemingly, — and violins prevailed. The music was consequently soft. They seemed chary of their efforts, favoring the company with but few pieces during the evening, but when they *did* play, ample amends were made for their silence. I have no words that, — however dexterously placed upon this unsounding sheet, — can more than faintly symbolize its exquisite character — its ecstatic effect upon the heart! As they struck up, my every nerve was thrilled. The silken, leaping strains came stealing into every pore of my soul. So graceful, so touching, so tremblingly inspiring were the cadences, that the music often seemed but the silver echoes of some far off melody. I had never heard anything so fine.

The second piece was entitled "The Puff, or Mensonge," an inimitable satire upon the amiable and conventional deception pervading all classes in Paris. It was one of Eugene Scribe's happiest efforts, and the public had acknowledged the successful hit by giving it a run. I had previously purchased the play, and conned it by heart, with the view the better to mark nice points of pronunciation. I thought I was familiar with its beauties; but I soon found, that reading a good French play, and hearing it admirably performed, are quite different things. Soon after the performance began, my pencil dropped to the floor, and the printed pamphlet soon followed; the absorbing interest of the performance holding me quite entranced throughout. I do not know how successful the French are in tragedy, but I am sure that in the higher comedy they are inimitable, and beyond praise. The felicities of thought are so intermingled with felicities of language, as not to be peaceably divorced. There is, moreover, in the style of the performance a piquancy, a raciness that is quite enchanting. In this play, each of the artistes seemed a star, and went through his part with a propriety, ease and self-possession, truly wonderful. I have seen nothing, at all to be compared to it, in a similar performance in any other nation. The whole scene was to me a *beau idéal* of genteel discourse and elegant manners, enlivened with the most pleasingly pointed wit.

The costume of the players was the perfection of simple elegance. There was not throughout the entire performance a single posture or gesture, that would not have graced the most fashionable and elegant saloon; and, with a single exception, not a word or phrase that would have offended the most fastidiously modest ear. The whole scene was thoroughly divested of the rant, the strut, the affectation of manner and language, the leers of double-meaning, the coarse wit and artificial tone which characterize our American boards, and render, with us, the theatre intolerable even to the passionate lover of the drama. I left strongly impressed with the beautiful picture of French character embodied in French forms, French voices, and French gestures; but I remembered that this was the Royal Theatre, and that the purity and excellence of its performance might be traced to the refined and elevated taste of the family of Louis Phillippe.

Feb. 17th. I spent most of the time of the preceding two days in attendance upon the lectures at the Sorbonne. These lectures are in the same style of perfection in which everything is done in Paris.

The lecturers, who are professors, are chosen from among the most eminent men in their several walks of learning. They are furnished every facility for perfecting their knowledge, and allowed every means for illustrating their subjects. The courses cannot, therefore, but prove highly instructive, powerfully interesting, and deeply valuable. They are, also, entirely free. Hence, the rooms are thronged with eager students from all parts of the world.

One of the most interesting of these lectures was upon the life and character of Christopher Columbus. I had read any number of accounts of the world-renowned Genoese before, but it is needless to add, that I received a clearer perception of his life, and a higher appreciation of his character from the hands of the French historian. The noble discoverer received, without doubt, a well-merited tribute to his transcendent genius, unparalleled daring, unconquerable perseverance, humane spirit, and generous and lovely qualities of heart; but it was the way in which the subject was treated which gave the discourse its peculiar power and beauty. The plan was so perfect and so scrupulously adhered to, the principles of action were so philosophically developed, the various adventures and incidents were so artistically grouped, the propitious circumstances so consummately arranged, and the whole enlivened with such matchless felicities of thought and expression, as to form a bright, living picture, — distinct, vivid, glowing; delighting the taste and fancy, and filling the heart with good and noble aspirations.

Another, more striking still, was by M. Frank. His course was upon the modern social systems, and the one I heard, upon that of the celebrated Fourier. When I entered, the room was crowded. Lively expectation was depicted on every countenance. In a moment, the lecturer darted in, and instantly was in his seat, speaking. A burst of fervent but subdued applause greeted his entrance. He was comparatively a young man, — his talents and industry having evidently outstripped his age, and brought him in favor with the government. His attenuated limbs revealing a form bringing to mind shapen bundles of nerves, — the long, skinny fingers of the hand, the sharp, nervous features of the face, an eye beaming with the very soul of genius, and the whole person gently agitated with a nervous tremor, as if invested with a halo of thought, gave to his appearance a vivid impressiveness that enchained the attention, and heightened the effect of his eloquence. As the first word dropped from his lips, there was a hush of stillness that no eager interest and expectation could have surpassed: and, to the end, all was keen and breathless attention, save when a gleam of attic wit arrowed forth from the address; and then, the momentary excitation it produced was so brief, so suddenly repressed, as to show that each felt fearful of allowing a single word to escape, which would be like the loss of an irreplaceable pearl in a priceless coronet. His enunciation was most distinct, though his cadences were uniform and almost unvaried. He never hesitated for a moment, nor repeated himself, but marched right on with a steady, equable movement, resembling that of a train of cars at a distance, passing over a gently undulating surface.

But the peculiar fascination and power of his style lay in the wonderful concentration and concatenation of thought, and the matchless vivacity with which the ideas glowed and sparkled in the mind's eye of the listener. In this respect, his discourse was a strongly hammered chain, of which, each link was intensely welded, and the whole polished into the brightness of silver. It seized at once your mind, rivetted it by the force of association, and bore it through the argument with the involuntary power of *natural law*, and with the delectable grace of matchless harmony. Every word was so fitly chosen that its sound, even, echoed forth its sense and lent additional force to the beauty of the thought,—forming a mental picture vivid and delightful. There was something, moreover, in the very dignity and grace of the movement,—the power and felicitation of the mien,—a kind of radiant lustre, drawing in, and charming your faculties, keeping the soul in an unceasing titillation of delight.

The system of Fourier was dissected with a consummation that made you tremble. You felt that it were terrible to fall under the knife of such an anatomist. The flesh was parted, the bones disjointed, the marrow penetrated,—even the invisible soul scanned with an eye of fire, and a hand of deathless energy. Although the entire discourse was characterized by the very spirit of truthfulness and impartiality, yet there was such an inimitable skill displayed in tracing the juxtapositions and inductions of the author, and in detecting the invisible discrepancies of his subtle philosophy, that the great socialist was often seen in a light that irresistibly moved you to pity or laughter.

The hour's entertainment was more than an intellectual·feast, —it was a spiritualized banquet; and on leaving, I began to understand the meaning of the glowingly expectant look of the audience when I entered.

CHAPTER XIX.

GEN. SCOTT UNDER ARREST — PUBLIC OPINION OMNIPOTENT IN THE UNITED STATES — AN AMBIGUOUS CHARACTER — PARISIAN MORALS — LOVELESS MARRIAGES — LEFT-HAND MARRIAGES — LEGALIZED VICE — OPEN PROSTITUTION — HOSPICE D'ACCOUCHEMENT — HOSPICES DES ENFANS TROUVERS — CAUSES, ETC. — MANUFACTORY FOR THE CROWN TAPESTRY — PALAIS ROYALE — SUMPTUOUS INTERIOR — SPLENDID GARDEN — CHAPEL OF ST. FERDINAND.

THE French Journals mentioned, to-day, the trial of General Scott in Mexico, — the scientific, the gallant commander-in-chief of our armies, whose consummate military skill, crowned with splendid victories, had extorted warm eulogies from many eminent military men of Europe, under arrest, and being tried by a court composed of his inferior officers! The bare idea was enough to arouse the indignation of an American abroad!

What strange vagary of Fame and Fortune was this! The Americans were severely condemned, of course, by the English and European press, for the Mexican war; and what was really unjust, a sentiment of unscrupulous aggression attributed to the whole nation, — which, if it existed at all, was shared only by a part, and perhaps a minority, of the nation. But when our armies, under their skilful leaders, began to shed glory even upon the Anglo-Saxon race, and writers abroad were lavish of their praise of Yankee capability, one began to have a self-gratulatory feeling, that tardy justice was being done to the genius of our republic. But here was being enacted a drama so farcical in idea, as to make one doubt if the whole account given of those proudly martial deeds enacted in gorgeous Mexico, were not some splendid illusion created by that enchantment to which distance is said to give rise. It was not enough that the glorious old Taylor, after unfurling and carrying steadily forward against odds, the banner of his countrymen, and in an urgent crisis, shorn of the flower of his force, should be left unintentionally to deepen the dye of his immortality in a battle which brings to mind that of Thermopylæ of old; but here was Scott himself, who had marched through the renowned strongholds of Mexico, with a Napoleon-like rapidity of execution, and planted his standard in the very square surrounded by the halls of the Montezumas, all at once shorn of his lofty plumes, snatched defyingly away from the magnificent halo by which he was a moment before surrounded, and treated like any humble mortal. Well, it may have the effect to show to Europeans, what it seems quite difficult for them to understand, namely, that in the United States public opinion is omnipotent, — and that talents never so great, genius never so resplendent, or services never so glorious, cannot screen a man from the closest scrutiny of the public eye, or prevent his being called to the bar of popular judgment.

In going to my lodgings to-night, I was equivocally accosted in a delicately coaxing tone and manner, by a young woman, who appeared as if just issuing from an obscure court. Without bestowing upon her further attention than a furtive glance, just to scan truthfully her features and person, she did not, however, repeat her intimations. She was neatly but rather gaily attired. Her countenance, which was mild, and not altogether unpleasing, was marked with no obvious trace of a feeling of shame or guilt.

This comparatively unimportant incident would hardly be worth recording, but as being suggestive of a topic, which, if obnoxious to an *un*-senile modesty, has yet so fundamental a bearing upon the socially moral condition of a nation, as to claim the attention of the traveller who would impart valuable information touching the people about whom he undertakes to write.

If we were to credit the statements of some English tourists of name, we should be left to form a sad picture of the social morals of Paris. But it should be borne in mind, that travellers who are capable of giving to the public distorted views of society in the United States, would hardly be less reckless or prejudiced in their portraitures of a people against whom deep enmity has become firmly rooted by ages of war, rivalry, and the more irreconcilable influence still, of diverse natures.

Yet, however overshaded these pictures may have been, through the prejudice and enmity of a certain class of travellers, still the truth would make them dark enough to be greatly deplored.

It must be admitted, in the first place, that the holy institution of marriage is neither regarded nor observed in France with that feeling of pure, single devotion, which its sacredly important nature claims. Not that there are no exceptions to this remark. Indeed, I was informed by reliable gentlemen, foreigners, who had resided a long time in Paris and in the country, that in their deliberate opinion, in no other country could be found so beautiful instances of conjugal fidelity, or strong domestic affections; and that in this respect, the best French society is a delightful picture of what is most charming in domestic life. Still, it is most notorious that the violation of marriage and chastity are tolerated with a facility in France not done in England nor in the United States. It might be no easy task to trace all the causes that have contributed to form this ungracious feature in the national character; but among them may be enumerated the ardor of temperament and the facility of the French character, modified by climate, scenery, and a class of associations adapted to fire the imagination; the sensitive nature of the French taste, which repels the object of its adoration with the same vehemence that once attracted it; the irresistible influence of licentious courts and dissolute nobilities; the corrupting agency of a vitiated literature, by which genius, wedded to a classical power by the most fascinating approaches, has poisoned the well-springs of innocent thought; the removal, for a time, from the conscience, the sacred weight of Divine obligation, by the abrogation of a national religion. But a more palpable cause may doubtless be found in those ever-to-be-accursed unions called *mariage de convenance*, or as appropriately, *loveless marriages*, so common among the middling and higher classes of society. These are usually contracted by the parents, or even by the parties themselves, in view of the eligibility of the match, and with little or no regard to the affections of the parties, or even consulting their tastes and dispositions. Where there is but one true marriage, and that the union of sentiment, the reciprocal baptism of the affections, the magic welding of heart and heart, all such sordid arrangements as *mariages de convenance*, whether in France or elsewhere, could not be expected to yield else than bitter fruits. Indeed, fidelity could not be expected, if it should be desired, amid the damps of such prison mildew. It were almost cruel thus to bind the tender, the susceptible heart, yearning for a spiritual congeniality in which to lave its sickened life. Hence, marriage in France is but too often an endorsed apology for freedom according to fancy. Indeed, a married lady is almost expected to have her private lover; and this barely clandestine *commerge* has become so completely established in the mind of society as to have begot certain rules of observance — a kind of principle of honor — which would seem not unlike that noble quality said to exist among thieves.

Somewhat akin to this mode of wedded life, and infinitely more reasonable, as well as fruitful of conjugal felicity, are those temporary *liasons* or *mariages de St. Jacques*, better known to the English reader as *left-handed marriages*. In a country where fortunes are for the most part small, and where the precariousness of remunerative employment does not permit the masses of the poor easily to encounter the obligations of family, marriages must have their limits. A vast variety of single ladies, therefore, without fortunes, still remain, many of whom are naturally led to be guilty of the indiscretion of a lover, though they have no husband to deceive. They are wont to take upon themselves an affection, to which they remain faithful so long as the intimacy lasts. Many respectable young men, merchants, lawyers, etc., of moderate incomes, live until they are rich enough to marry, in some connection of this description. Sanctioned by custom, these unions of *expediency* are to be found with a certain respectability belonging to them, in all walks of life. The working classes, in particular, have their somewhat famous *mariages de St. Jacques*, which, among themselves, at least, are highly respectable. The laborer and washerwoman, for instance, find it cheaper and more comfortable to take a room together. They rent a chamber, put in their joint furniture (one bed answers for both), a common *ménage* and purse are established, and the couple's affection endures at least as long as their lease.

Another institution still lower in the scale of moral delinquencies, is the system of legalized public prostitution existing in Paris. This is not peculiar to Paris, but exists in common in the cities of Europe; and the Parisian will urge that it was not intended to sanction vice, but only to regulate what must necessarily exist still it can justly be objected, that the very fact of its being brought under the wing of the police, and regulated as are respectable institutions, gives the *sanction* of the government to the vice. The authority of law steps in to break down that acute and profound sense of morality which with us banishes from society, without the possibility of restoration, the female who has committed decidedly one false step. The public sense of morality is necessarily brought down by publicly trafficking with vice. Whatever conveniences the system may have, its effect upon the public mind cannot but be evil.

Then there is the abandoned class of females who seek a clandestine commerce. Although they are much less seen by the cursory observer, than even in the large cities of England and America, still their number doubtless is quite large.

As a finishing-stroke to the above-named customs, and without which they could not flourish luxuriantly and with grace, come in the establishments termed *Hospices des Accouchements* and *Hospices des Enfans trouvés*. The former, or lying-in hospitals, may be seen with emblazoned signs in various parts of the city. They furnish secret and comfortable resorts, where women *enciente* may find, for a moderate price, the best of care and treatment, until they are sufficiently restored from the ills and danger of child-bed, — the latter, or foundling-hospital, where infants whose parents are willing or necessitated to abandon them, are placed, to be taken care of at the public charge. Here, these little government-adoptives are nursed, nurtured, and afterwards distributed about the country to learn useful branches of industry. Many of them do well. This establishment, as well as many others of the hospitals of Paris, is under the care of the *Sisters of Charity*, whose self-sacrificing benevolence is justly a theme of praise. The founder of the latter establishment was St. Vincent de Paul. He commenced by seeking out the abandoned children of the city. These institutions divide the opinion of travellers. A stern moralist, regarding their little inmates as the fruits of illicit love, would be apt to look upon the system with horror. A practical man, viewing society as it is, might come to a different conclusion. He would, at least, see in the institution, the means of saving a vast amount of life, and of ameliorating much human suffering. That they prevent a great amount of infanticide, cannot be questioned; but that they facilitate the crime they are designed to ameliorate, admits neither of doubt.

In estimating the state of morality in the nation, Paris must not be taken as a faithful index of the entire country; for, however true the remark, that Paris is France in politics, the capital can by no means be given as a measure of the nation's morals. There are several causes that have powerfully operated to render Paris peculiar in its moral and social tone. The religious sentiment which was extinguished from view in Paris, has ever preserved at least a glimmering in the Provinces. Paris, like ancient Rome, is the receptacle of much of the inflammable elements of European society. The rich of the nations of the world throng there for pleasure, and seek much of that pleasure in vice. The centralization of the government of France, concentrates its principal functionaries in the capital, many of whom become in time mere pensioned voluptuaries.

The principal youth of the country, belonging to the rich, as well as many from abroad, resort to Paris for their education; while thousands flock thither for employment in shops, warehouses, and offices. Some seventy or eighty thousand troops are always present in the city and vicinity. The desperate in fortune, or ruined in reputation, eagerly resort to the capital, the former like vampires to prey upon society, and the latter to retreat from the circle in which they had been known, and to sink lower in the depths of degradation.

Yet, notwithstanding these hot-bed influences of moral disease in France, and more especially in Paris, illegitimacy there is, according to an intelligent traveller, Professor Laing, more rare than even in Prussia.

The easy footing upon which society stands and moves in Paris, arrests with agreeable surprise the attention of the traveller. The stranger there enjoys unusual freedom to go whither he pleases, and do as he will, by preserving the grace of politeness.

The modest manners of the French women are proverbial. They are a fragrant theme of general praise. The delightful virtue is seen both in their bearing and dress. Whatever immorality may exist in private, scarcely a vestige of it is exposed to public gaze. External decency, at least, prevails to a degree not elsewhere to be found. A stranger would never see in the streets of Paris an instance of the unblushing shamelessness, the utter degradation, that shocks the stranger in the streets of London, at almost every step, after nine o'clock at night. This exquisite decorum of mien which pervades all classes, from the voluptuous queen of the ambiguous saloon, to the washerwoman of the Seine, gilding society with a rosy tint of lustre, may be traced, in part at least, to the peculiar sentiment of virtue which exists. Not being considered a crime as much as elsewhere, incontinence does not bring down the mind to the level of crime. It is looked upon more as a matter of taste; and the fair one guilty of indiscretion, not being rejected from society, does not lose her self-respect, but evinces in all her intercourse, the usual amenities of polite and dignified life.

In this respect it must be confessed that the French are certainly more consistent than are we. We tolerate in men a vice which we unmitigatingly punish in woman, by banishing her entirely from the pale of decent society. The French, more just, extend the same privilege to both sexes.

I visited on February 19th, the celebrated manufactory for the Crown Tapestry. It is the most magnificent establishment of the kind in France, if not in Europe. Carpets are made here, which, in elegance, in correctness of design, choice and variety, rival those produced even in Persia in her palmiest days. Some of these costly floor-coverings, of no more than medium size, were valued as high as three thousand dollars. It is evident that only kings, princes, and millionaires can possess so expensive luxuries to grace the tread of the feet.

Numerous artisans were closely engaged in their indefatigable labors. The warp of the carpet was stretched in a perpendicular frame, and the filling was woven in with the fingers and a bodkin. The process is thus necessarily slow, tedious, and even painful. Hence the enormous cost of the fabrication. The gorgeousness of the fabric was beautifully heightened by the brilliant lustre of the colors imparting to it an almost dazzling splendor.

But the most interesting and wonderful application of the art consists in transferring pictures, painted upon canvas, to tapestry, and preserving, with exact faithfulness, the lineaments and shading of the original. Indeed, the transfer is so exact, that you would distinguish no difference between them, except that the copy bears the lifelike freshness of an improved edition. The process with the artisan, it is evident, is almost entirely mechanical; but it implies a nice discrimination in colors, and an exquisite skill of execution, acquired only by long practice. The art is valuable as a means of wresting, from the hands of time, fading gems of the old masters. I noticed several portraits, thus transferred, of members of the late royal family; and I should never have known, without a close inspection, but that they were vivid paintings upon canvas.

A very paternal measure passed to-day in the Chamber of Peers, after a discussion, animated to a degree not usual in that body, — regulating the labor of the working classes. According to the provisions of the bill, children cannot be permitted to labor in manufacturing establishments, under eight years of age; and between that period and twelve, they must not be employed more than eight hours in a day; and adults cannot be employed more than twelve hours. It is wise, as well as benevolent in the government thus to protect short-sighted indigence from the reckless rapacity of mammon.

Sunday, 20th. After services at the Oratoire, I made a visit to the Palace Royal. Sunday is the day, *par excellence*, for visiting the palaces and other public monuments of Paris; and I found the interior thronged with visitors of every class of society. The largest part of the company, however, were well-dressed and intelligent looking ladies and gentlemen of the traveller type; and I heard some half a dozen different languages.

It is called the Palace Royal because Louis XIV. lived here in his youth. Its construction was commenced by the Cardinal Richelieu, who improved and adorned it by degrees as his fortune improved, until he judged it not unworthy to be presented to the splendid monarch, Louis XIV, which he did in a testament at his death. The king bequeathed it, in his turn, to his brother, the Duke of Orleans, from whom it descended to the late Louis Phillippe, and was occupied by the latter as a private residence, but furnished in a style of royal magnificence.

A beautiful stairway leads to the first stage, which is divided into three apartments, namely, those of the centre, occupied by the late king and queen before 1830; the apartments of the left, appropriated to Madame Adelaide, the sister of the king; those of the right, destined for the prince royal. The left-wing comprises a vast dining-room, several grand saloons, and beautiful cabinets. The centre includes the saloon for the aids-de-camp, that of reception, the cabinet of the king, the apartment of the queen, and the hall of the throne. A magnificent gallery leading to the apartment of the late Duke of Orleans, occupies a part of the left-wing. The library, situated on the same side, is placed partly in the niterstole and partly in the first stage.

We were conducted through the palace by neatly liveried hussiers, who seemed impressed with the dignity of their office. The rooms were nearly destitute of carpets and furniture; but enough furnishing remained to show the former sumptuousness. The hall of the throne, in particular, was very rich. The floor, of hardwood, was so smoothly polished as to make it necessary to walk with care. The ceilings were richly painted and gilded.

The walls of the several apartments were adorned with paintings; some of them possessing rare merit. Among the historical pieces, were Julius Cesar going to the Senate, The Victory of Marathon, William Tell jumping out of the boat with Gesler, and several more modern scenes, in which Maria Theresa, of Austria, figures conspicuously. She is represented in attitudes expressive of strong emotion and intense energy. There are, besides, several portraits of distinguished personages; among them, those of Napoleon, Charles V, Madame de Staël, J. J. Rousseau, and the several members of the family of Louis Phillippe.

But what attracts more attention at the present time is the garden, with the exterior gallery of the palace. The beautiful enclosure formerly occupied a larger area than at present; as it comprehended, besides the present garden, the streets of Valois, de Montspensier, and de Beaujolais, as well as that space now oc cupied by the sides of the Palais, which have been more recently built. It was adorned with an alley of mulberry trees, which alone cost the Cardinal Richelieu sixty thousand dollars; but the old revolution destroyed them. The place was once infamous for its gambling-houses, and the throngs of doubtful characters that swarmed in it of an evening; but the late government banished these, and the galleries are now occupied with brilliant cafes, and small, but magnificent bazaars. These are the fashionable shops of the city; and they are rich and beautiful beyond description. All that can tempt the luxurious, or please the vain; whatever can inspire admiration for the industry of man, for his exquisite taste; his creating genius; his skill in producing the elegant, the beautiful, the magnificent; in fine, whatever can delight the eye, captivate the senses, or add charms to beauty, are here displayed. One of these small shops rents for three or four thousand francs a year. The chairs, alone, placed in the garden for the convenience of loungers, are said to give a revenue of eighty thousand francs. To see this enchanting spot in all its brilliancy you should go at night, when countless lamps pour floods of light through its delicious gardens and long arcades; when its walks are alive with gay promenaders, and its multitude of shops, cafés, and offices are in the full tide of business. It is then, indeed, a scene resplendent with gaiety, bustle and animation.

After finishing the tour of the Palais Royale, I made a visit to the Chapel of St. Ferdinand. This beautiful edifice was erected some eight years ago, to mark the spot and event of the death of the Duke d'Orleans, the eldest son of Louis Phillippe, and heir apparent to the throne of France. In returning home from an afternoon drive, his horses became restive and unmanageable, and leaping from his carriage he fell and fractured his skull, — sensibility was destroyed, and after two or three hours, death ensued.

The event was the more affecting, as the disposition and high and noble qualities of the prince made him not only greatly beloved of his family, but rendered him a favorite with the entire nation.

The estate was purchased by the king, and on the very spot where he died, this chapel was erected. It is a gem of architecture — the exterior tasteful, and the interior simple. A narrow space, beautifully laid out, and adorned with a triple row of Arborvitæ trees, leads to the entrance. On the right-hand side of the chapel, at entering, on a pedestal, is a full length statue of the dying prince, with his head lying at the feet of the figure of an angel stretching out her hands in the posture of devotion. Two clocks are in one of the rooms, — one of which marks the hour when the accident happened; the other, when the duke expired. Over the altar is a beautiful statue of the Virgin and Child. Descending a few steps, you come to a room which marks the exact spot where the prince expired. Here is a large and striking painting of the whole group brought together by that event. The livid features and unearthly expression of the dying man, are represented with fearful truthfulness. The queen is kneeling, with her head inclined upon his side; the king, too, is kneeling at his feet, with an expression of mute, but profound grief; two of the brothers and two of the sisters are standing near; the priest is administering unction to the dying man, and some of the king's ministers and attendants are in the back-ground. As a work of art the painting did not strike me as of peculiar merit; but its appropriateness for recalling the sad event is extremely effective.

CHAPTER XX.

THE GRAND BANQUET AT PARIS — OPINIONS OF THE APPROACH-
ING CRISIS — THE GLOOMY EVE OF THE FATED MORROW —
SUDDEN TACKING OF THE SHIP OF STATE — MENTAL SCENES
IN THE BOSOM OF THE GOVERNMENT — MADAME THE DUCHESS
OF ORLEANS — MONSIEUR GUIZOT — PARIS IN A POSTURE OF
DEFENCE — THRILLING SCENES OF THE 22D — THE RIOTERS
CHARGED IN THE CHAMPS ELYSEES.

To-day, that is, Sunday, 20th, was at first appointed for the holding of the Banquet in Paris; but the leaders changed the time to Tuesday, 22d, because that on Sunday and Monday the laboring classes being at liberty, would be present in greater numbers, and thus increase the probability of a disturbance. The place of holding it, too, was changed from one of the most frequented parts of Paris, to the grounds of a wealthy gentleman in the *Champs Elysées*.

At this time, the Parisian public seemed not to be particularly engrossed with the serious nature of the approaching event, or much anxious about the consequences to which it might give birth. The press, it is true, had pretty freely discussed the matter, — but the public mind had become quite used to inflammatory addresses. Besides, the tone of the press had lowered its pitch within a few days, and assumed something of a temperate and sincere style. This, to a sagacious and penetrating mind, was ominous of a conviction on the part of the leaders of the press, of the fearful nature of the pending controversy; but to the unreflecting masses, it served to dissipate the impression of danger. It was reported that English travellers tarrying in Paris, had taken occasion to leave; and that great numbers of English families residing in Paris, had precipitately removed away; but the trepidation which the English are wont to show on the slightest rumor of a political disturbance in Paris, sufficiently explained that act. These were mere eddies in the stream of Parisian opinion. The general current of trade and pleasure rolled on with its wonted volume and velocity.

I had endeavored to ascertain the state of private opinion, as to the result of the coming Banquet, by questioning freely persons of different classes of society. My teacher himself, a member of the National Guard, confidently looked forward to a collision with the populace, and a consequent revolution, in which he would ardently engage against the government. To my expression of doubt of the merest probability of his party's success, against the powerful army of the government, with an air of assurance he quickly replied, "*Nous verrons,*" "*We shall see.*" The shopkeepers seemed too much engrossed in their trade to have given the subject much attention, and would not venture on an opinion. The teachers were of deliberate opinion, that there prevailed an extensive and deep opposition among the mass of the population, but that the government was too strongly entrenched behind its rampart of cannon and bayonet, to admit of the possibility of a serious disturbance. The broker and his lady who weekly exchanged a gold-piece for me, looked up in my face with a half-abstracted, half-inquiring air, as if they had given no subject attention, except the table of weights and measures. My graceful landlady was certain there would be no alarming trouble. The speeches and talk that had been made, were mere gasconade, and would all end in smoke, — but then she was the mistress of a hotel with rooms to let. There was residing just across the way, nearly opposite to my hotel, a young man, the keeper of a little, meagre shop, for second-hand boots and shoes. He was a frank, generous, buoyant spirit, full of poetry and a love of adventure, and possessed withal deeply of that true nonchalance which sets so gracefully upon certain styles of character. I sought frequent conversations with him, not only for the amusement they afforded me, but because he was a representative of a large class of Parisians who are only satisfied with their present condition, because they cannot do better; who, in a revolution, have nothing to lose, and everything to gain; who ever thirst for a scene, and will fight for the gratification which the excitement produces. These are ever eager for a change of scenery, and rush deliriously forward to whatever promises stirring and brilliant achievements. They may be found among the foremost at the barricades, fighting desperately, but without as much aim as the school-boy who defends to the last a ruthless attack upon a snow-fort. In a recent interview with him, something like the following conversation ensued:

"Well," said I, "you are going to have a great time in Paris, next Tuesday."

"Yes, I hear of such talk."

"Shall you be at the Banquet?"

"Without doubt. I am always among the crowd."

"In case of a collision, would you fight?"

"That would depend how I should feel, sir."

On the Monday evening his humble shop was closed, nor did I see it open again. Whether he stayed among the crowd that found a common grave, or not, it would not be easy for me to say.

A few doors from me was a variety store, kept by an aged lady and her two only children, a boy about seventeen, and a girl perhaps sixteen. The woman was one of those remarkable personages occasionally to be met with in all countries, who are living encyclopedias of general and particular information. Her chapter on the life and pedigree of distinguished persons, was as full and interesting as that of any other subject; and she narrated to me with great minuteness whatever it was desirable to know of the entire family of Louis Phillippe. She lived in Paris during the old Revolution, was imprisoned, had been an eye-witness of some of the most thrilling and awful scenes that occurred then, and had taken place since; and she had, as might be expected, whole volumes to unfold, of the unparalleled events of those times. Her earnest manner and pathos of tone, gave a curdling vividness to the scenes she depicted. She felt certain that the approaching banquet would be the means of a bloody revolution. She knew the French character too well, and had watched the current of events too closely to doubt of that. She earnestly advised me, nay implored me, if I valued my life, or regarded the feelings of my family or friends, to lose no time in quitting the city; for, said she, although the Americans would not knowingly be harmed if they should not engage in the combat, still in such frightful times no one is safe. Her children, however, did not share her fears. They were light-hearted and sportive spirits, and would caper round the store, and hang upon their mother in frolicsome glee, like playful kittens. The young man positively threatened to leave for the thickest of the fight, on the first notice of an outbreak, — and with wooden sword and cockade cap, and serio-comic air, strutted the Napoleon; while his sister would second his farcical acts by playing the part of Maria Theresa of Austria, in some of the dramatic scenes of that heroine.

Feb. 21*st.* The morrow of this day was appointed for the great banquet. Anxiety was visible during the day in the countenances of all. The feeling was less profound, however, as it was generally understood that there existed a tacit agreement between the Government and the Opposition, that the former would place no obstacle to the holding of the banquet, but would content itself by merely contesting the legality of the act in the highest judicial court of the nation. In that case, there could be no serious cause of alarm. Any disturbance would be the merely casual one growing out of the igniting force of numbers, and easily subdued by the police or national guards. But late in the afternoon, the government suddenly tacked the ship of state, by resolving to forbid the assembling of the banquet, except the members of the Chamber of Deputies, and to employ the iron force of the State to secure the obedience to its decrees. This decision was announced in the *Chamber of Deputies* by M. Guizot, the prime minister, and head and front of the offending government. In an incredible short space of time afterwards, this decree was posted up all over the city; and government officers on horseback were sweeping through the streets in every direction, evidently in the fulfilment of weighty missions. The tone of the decree was severe and decided. It permitted the members of the Chamber of Deputies to Assemble, but they must hold themselves in readiness to retire on the first summons of the government. All other citizens were forbidden to be present, on severe penalties; and it wound up with this firm language: "*And the government shall know how to execute its requirements.*"

As might be expected, this sudden political turn struck the Opposition perfectly aghast, and threw them into the greatest embarrassment. It was as unexpected as irritating. Lamartine, inspired with a prescience, arose, and in one of those sublime bursts of eloquence for which he is so distinguished, broke forth in the following noble exclamation: "*By this arbitrary act the government has placed its hand upon the mouth of the nation;*

be the consequences of its guilt upon its own head." But what course should they adopt?

To deliberate upon the policy best to be pursued, and concert a plan of action, a number of the Opposition members immediately held a private meeting. The situation in which they were thus unexpectedly thrown, was indeed embarrassing. Either of the two alternatives presented them was sufficiently desperate or humiliating. To persist in holding the banquet, would be to provoke a bloody conflict, and accept the appalling horrors of a revolution by force of arms. To retreat before the menace of the government, would be to betray the confidence of the republican party, and annihilate its name. About two hundred members of every shade were present. The discussion was long and ardent, and the opinions diverse. As bitter as it was for all, moderate counsels, however, prevailed; and in a note which appeared in one of the evening journals, signed by some of the leading Deputies, the Opposition made known its resolution to its constituents: " Although," said they, " we are protected in our capacity of Deputies, yet we cannot take the responsibility of the evils that would fall upon those who might be induced to join us, nor the results that would follow to the country. We shall, therefore, stay at home; and we advise all good citizens to do the same."

When late in the afternoon, the news first spread through the city, that the government had determined to put down the banquet by force of arms, every heart was filled with anxiety and dread. All countenances bore a sad and boding expression. About dusk, at the corners of streets or in by-lanes, might be seen men dressed in blouses, gathered in knots, with sinister faces, in a low tone ominously discussing the posture of affairs, or tearing down the government decrees, while muttering execrations against M. Guizot and his government. But when later in the evening, the decision of the Opposition to retire was made known, the public anxiety was a good deal relieved. Still, there was an instinctive feeling, that affairs had already proceeded too far now to be quietly adjusted. The government, by its vacillation and perfidy, had, in the minds of the masses, added contempt to hatred. The Opposition, by its humane and self-sacrificing spirit to spare the blood of the citizens, had enkindled an enthusiasm of admiration and sympathy. The extensive preparations for the banquet were all completed. Delegates and gentlemen from the provinces and cities of France, had already arrived by thousands, to participate in the festival. The unbounded love of the Parisians for magnificent spectacles had become excited. All these causes added to that principle of human nature which ill brooks a severe disappointment, and that impulse of desire and determination which arbitrary opposition lends, would, it was justly feared, give a persistence and recklessness to the passions of the populace, that nothing short of bloodshed would stifle.

The reason offered by the government for its sudden change of determination at so late an hour was, that the Opposition, by inviting large numbers of the National Guards to be present, although without arms, had given to the occasion an unusual, if not a suspicious feature, which required to be checked. All felt, however, that this was a mere pretext, and that the true reason arose from the alarm which the unusual enthusiasm for the banquet had excited in the Parisian populace, as well as in the country generally.

This was the posture of affairs, when night enshrouded the city with a darkness increased by the momentous impending crisis. What were the mental scenes that the night gave birth to, at the palace, and in the bosom of the government! Subsequent events have thrown some light upon these. The king affected to despise the elements of hostility which were arraying themselves against his power. He would fain trust in his star, in the devotion of the army commanded by the princes, his sons, — in his majority in the chambers, in the skill of his adroit ministers, in the vast manufacturing and commercial interests which always fear a revolution; — still, in reality, it was evident that he was not without a mental trepidation; a vertigo of mind seemed to have come over him. The address with which for so long a time he had ruled France, and in some measure Europe, had at last forsaken him. This was evident from the uncalled-for language of the crown address, and his shifting course in respect to the banquets. In truth, the king had become old, and, though not wanting in bravery, had lost in a measure that persistence of will which sustains more youthful men in trying scenes. He had ever before his eyes the fate of Charles X, as well as that of the predecessors of that monarch. The terrible scenes of the revolution of '89 continually haunted his imagination. He well knew the combustible character of a portion of the Parisian population. Should an outbreak arrive, his humane heart would revolt at reacting the horrid part of the youthful Napoleon, and flooding the streets of Paris with the blood of its citizens. But after all, would his army certainly stand by him? Might they not in the trying hour hesitate to shed the blood of fathers, brothers, or lovers in a war against their own, and human rights? Of the possible disaffection of the army, unfortunately for the peace of the king, he had received already some intimation from one of his trusty-hearted generals. At this stage of the imminent crisis undoubtedly the king would have willingly yielded to the desire of the nation for a new ministry. But that step it was now too late to take with safety. It might have been done with great good fortune, to the royal cause, at an earlier stage, when it would have seemed to be a gift of clemency, and respect to the national will; but given out now, the king could not fail to perceive that it would be regarded as a right wrested from arbitrary power, paving the way for greater and more humiliating concessions.

The queen shared the mental agitation of the king. Passionately devoted to her husband, as wife and mother, and arrived at that advanced age of life when repose and tranquillity are so grateful to the human soul, when the grandeur of human ambition has lost its charm, she naturally thought more of the king's safety and the repose of his government, than of any advantage that might be gained in attempting to check the inroads of democratical influence. She, therefore, supplicated the king to grant to the Opposition their demands for the right to hold banquets, and to form a new ministry whose views should be more in accordance with the national will.

There was still another personage in the royal mansion, no indifferent spectator to the thickening scene of events. It was Madame, the Duchess of Orleans. She had been a widow about six years; her universally beloved husband was killed from a fracture, occasioned by an accidental fall, in jumping out of his carriage. The oldest of her two sons, the Count of Paris, now eight years of age, was the direct heir to the throne. With all the depth of a mother's affection, and the lofty ambition of a princess of the blood, the powers of her maternal soul were concentrated upon her dear boy, whom it had been the solace of her deep affliction to render worthy of the most splendid crown of Europe. The king and queen were soon to go the way of all the earth, where crowns lose their lustre; but here were beings just ascending the arch-way of the future. Life, in its fascinating power, was broad before them. With the mental quickness of a woman, and the keen sagacity of a princess, she perceived at a glance her danger, and as promptly took her part. She infinitely preferred the regular and peaceful transfer of the crown, however limited by constitutional rights, to the risk of contesting it with the French populace. In the Tuileries, the day was not distant, when her heart would swell with maternal pride to see the crown deck the brow of her noble boy. But once filched from the palace, and in the hands of the fickle multitude, and the greatest uncertainty would envelop its fate. The crowd pretend to little knowledge of the rights of the court. They have never been instructed in its etiquette. Once in possession of the glittering bauble, with a sacrilegious hand they would be as likely to place it upon the head of some country swain to enliven the festivities of some gala-day, as to return it to its rightful owner. The duchess, therefore, added her entreaties to those of the queen, and implored the king even on bended knees, as he valued his safety, the permanency of his power, the rights of his children, to make a slight concession, and save the crown.

There was still another in the imperial picture. It was the prime minister, M. Guizot. It was more against him than against the king and the royal family, that the ire of the Opposition populace was directed. He was regarded, either as the base instrument of a reactionary policy, or a principal agent in a misapplied power, inhumanly bartering the sacred rights of human freedom for the pride of a cold and ascetic philosophy. Guizot was esteemed politically a host in himself. The French populace looked upon him as the Nestor of European diplomacy and the Ulysses of French politics. He had been at the head of the French government so long, that he seemed the main pillar in the political edifice. Against him had been directed from time to time the keen arrows of the Opposition; but these shafts, fully steeped in the gall of political virulence, and impelled with the redoubled force of united action, flanked with the omnipotent power of Freedom and Human Progress, had hitherto struck against him in harmless impotence. Indeed, he was wont to take upon his impervious shield the envenomed missiles with the adroit skill of an unconquered hero, smiling with ineffable disdain as they dropped powerless at his feet, — or seizing them in turn, with a giant force to hurl them back upon his foes, often with destructive effect. Guizot is a man of immense talents and powerful genius. His remarkable powers of mind are only equalled by the extent and finish of their culture. So precocious was his intellect, that at the age of fifteen, it is reported, he could read in their native languages, Demosthenes, Tacitus, Dante, Goethe, and Shakspeare. He ranked among the foremost as a professor at the Sarbonne. As a publicist of the English school, his reputation was unequalled in France. As a parliamentary orator, though rarely eloquent, yet he was ever masterly. He was mailed all over, and had not a flaw in his armor through which the shaft of objection might penetrate and wound. But as a historian, M. Guizot stands out most conspicuously. Although not the father of philosophical history, he is emphatically the great discourser of the profound science of the present age. In this character he will continue to shine as a fixed star in the upper heaven of the world's career. His well-earned fame had become widely spread among the masses who always bear a chivalrous enthusiasm for great genius and talent, and created for him a prestige of influence. But nearly the entire force of the French press, able, earnest, eloquent, had changed the current of his popularity to enmity. The greater the strength of the prime minister, the more implacable became the Opposition, just as a barrier gathers the waters of a rapid stream. Public feeling, which has no conscience, and consequently knows no remorse, had become intensified against the Government's strongest supporter. Powerful influences had now set it in movement. It had often before in storms of agitation, laved even the pedestal of the government, and more than once dashed the sides of the political pillar. But now appearances foreboded a deeper surging from the tempest than had before been seen. The temporary stillness that reigned, was only the fatal hush that preceded the shock. It cannot be doubted that M. Guizot felt a consciousness of his approaching fate. His keen mental vision must have divined the end to which the government was hastening. But his policy could not then be changed with dignity or safety. Like a true hero, he would rather die a martyr to his policy,—to his cause. The misfortune of Guizot was in his principles; and the misfortune of his principles was, that they came into the world a century too late. His policy was eminently conservative. The Opposition demanded reform and progress. The two diverging principles borne upon on either side by the increasing pressure of arbitrary power and national will, were destined to a tremendous collapse. This, the prime minister foreseeing, wrapped himself in his mantle, and calmly awaited his fate.

Nevertheless, the Government neglected no means to stay its tottering power. A force of upwards of fifty thousand men had been concentrated in and around Paris. The artillery of Vincennes was to be transported, at the first alarm, to the *Faubourg of St. Antoine*. Dispositions long and well studied, had placed, since 1830, in case of an insurrection, strategic posts to different corps in different quarters. Any emute intercepted by these posts, was to be broken into fragments, and thus prevented to concentrate. The fort of Mount Valerin was to be occupied with a numerous garrison, and horse-troops stationed upon the road thence to Paris and St. Cloud. Thirty-seven battalions of infantry, a battalion of Orleans *Chasseurs*, three companies of engineers, twenty squadrons, four thousand men of the municipal guard and veterans, five batteries of artillery, formed the garrison of the capital.

Feb. 22d. The morning of the eventful day had now arrived. I took an early stroll to observe the hue of appearances. Nothing, at first, seemed to bode a sinister day. The citizens bore no arms, neither openly, nor secreted under their garments; nor was there a lowering expression painted upon their visages. All was as usual, except a deeper stillness than ordinary. A little later in the morning, however, crowds of inoffensive and curious people began to assemble upon the boulevards and quays. Mutually attracted by curiosity, they seemed drawn together to observe, rather than to meditate for action.

The students of the several schools, — the advance guard of all the revolutions — united by groups in their quarters, and then assembled upon the Place de la Madeline. Thence they sent a deputation from their number to the leaders of the Opposition, asking of the latter what they were to do, and signifying an entire readiness to execute their commands. Subsequently they swept in immense numbers through the streets, linked arm in arm, extending in tiers quite across the street and singing most animatingly the celebrated Marsellaise. The impression which their stirring melody made upon my mind, as standing in the door of a frequented reading-room they poured thus past me, will hardly ever be effaced. This movement, with the singing, electrified the populace through which they passed. Their column continually increased. Traversing the Place de la Concorde, they crossed the Port Royal, forced open the gates of the palace of the Chamber of Deputies, and then spread, aimlessly, in the garden and upon the quays. A regiment of dragoons soon dispersed them. Then the infantry arrived and took possession of the street of Bourgoyne, and established a military defence of the bridge.

24*

At ten o'clock, the hour that had been appointed, according to the arrangement of the banquet, for the *convives* to form a procession upon the Place of the Madeline, and thence proceed to the banquet, in the Champs Elysées, groups of boys and *blouses* assembled upon the square around the church, and finding there nothing to feed their ardor, moved on, and dispersed promiscuously in small knots, in the Champs Elysées and in the Place de la Concorde. Their expression and movement attracted crowds of the curious in the same direction, and the military were posted around them to watch their progress, and guard against an outbreak.

Early in the afternoon, I set out for the office of the Secretary of Legation, Rue Martineau, in order to get my passport viséed, preparatory to leaving Paris. My route lay through the quarters where the crowd had become most dense. Passing down Rue de Seine, I found the quays on the left bank of the river unusually free of people. But the other side was covered with the animated and moving throng, increasing to the Pont de la Concorde. As this human stream was moving my own way, I was swiftly swept along, hastened by the common pulsation of curiosity The garden of the Tuileries, which I crossed, was as solitary as a desert, except about the gate which leads from the garden into the Place de la Concorde, where the throng was dense, and the gate shut and guarded against passers. Here, climbing to the top of a post, I succeeded to a gratifying view of the scene farther on. The fine square of the Place de la Concorde was nearly filled. On one side was a handsome troop of cavalry posted in close column, with stately plumes, brilliant uniform, and armor gleaming in the rays of the declining sun. They sat upon their horses as motionless as beings from whom the spirit of life had departed. Their downcast eyes were turned steadfastly toward the point of danger; but their countenances expressed more of sorrow than of anger.

Two other sides of the square were filled with a packed mass of spectators, idly, but eagerly looking on, and curiously awaiting some brilliant explosion. Between these were insignificant looking blouses and boys, who appeared to be regarded as the embryo heroes of approaching events. They would occasionally unite in small detached groups, send up in the air a faint *à bas Guizot!* — then disperse and disappear in the skirts of the crowd. They appeared reckless, but perfectly good-natured. It was evident that they were not yet worked up to the fervor of action. On the side of the square flanked by rue Rivoli, was a vast and promiscuous throng of men, women, and children, — all eager, curious and anxious. This extended wave of life would at one time ebb off, leaving the space in that direction almost open, and then surge up in a dense mass, threatening to block up every nook of the entire square. As it was impossible to pursue my route farther from this point, I descended the garden to a gate opening into rue Rivoli, through which I passed, and with difficulty forced my way through the compact and vibrating crowd to the side of the Place de la Concorde, where several streets radiate. Here, contrary currents of people meeting, were suffocatingly forced upon each other, and engulfed in a whirlpool, from which there appeared no way of extraction. It was a maelstrom of lesser size. After being swept around for some time in the merciless, boiling tide, till I felt the life to be nearly squeezed out of me, a chance eddy precipitated me into a niche of the buildings of the street, where I gratefully took a long breath. Here, watching a favorable turn, I darted out with a view to thread the corner, and reach the space of the Champs Elysées, — but I had no sooner reached a point where I fancied myself out of danger, when a fitful surge came rolling full upon me, and swept me back quite down rue de Rivoli into Rue Royal, as impotently as some tiny bauble borne upon the boiling bosom of a swollen freshet. I now changed my route, and thought I might reach my destination by the Rue St. Honoré, which was parallel with rue de Rivoli and the Champs Elysées; but I found this street, too, so choked with people, that moving through it seemed quite impossible. But all these obstacles only served to inflame my ardor, and strengthen my purpose to succeed in getting the necessary changes made in my passport to enable me to leave the city at the moment I might wish. Indeed, I became almost desperate in my efforts, and tugged away with an energy and perseverance worthy of a more important cause. Reaching the wall of the street, and pressing hard against it with my back, when the jambed throng surged with resistless force in the contrary direction, and pressing and elbowing my way, a little, when the opposition slightly relaxed, I finally, with much ado, reached the office, minus buttons, and hat fit for the block of the hatter. I found Mr. S——, Secretary of Legation, tranquilly enjoying a cigar with an acquaintance-caller. Neither of them had been out for the day to see the demonstrations, and they questioned, with a slightly anxious tone, to know how affairs were moving in the streets. Speaking rather jocosely and incredulously of the puny efforts of the emuteurs against the strongly fortified powers of the Government, Mr. S——, with a gusto of sympathy recounted the heroic wish of a lady of his acquaintance residing in the Champs Elysées, that the emute might not be so soon quelled as to deprive her of the excitement and gratification of witnessing the sport,— and affording a rich reminiscence to reproduce among her friends in the United States. It cannot be doubted that her curiosity was amply satisfied.

Returning homeward, I could not well resist the curiosity of obtaining a view of what might be worthy of remembrance, by taking the route of the Champs Elysées; but I was near being dearly paid for my temerity. After reaching a post where the crowd was somewhat dense among the venerable elms of the splendid park, a group of emuteurs who had been vociferating cries of *à bas Guizot,* were charged and dispersed by a small body of light-horse. When these latter were returning from the charge, the rioters rallied, and for a moment the air was darkened with every description of missiles at hand. One of these striking a horseman upon the head, felled him senseless to the earth. Upon this, the exasperated troop turned their horses, and with drawn swords, rushed furiously upon the rioters, dealing severe cuts in every direction. Without changing my pace, they thundered past me, offering me no harm. But at the cruel scene around me, my heart sickened, and my eyes grew dim. In a moment I was wedged among the crowd of spectators, who, partaking of the general panic, received an impetus of movement which by turns completely took me from the ground, and I was swept along far from the immediate scene of action. The above act was the only one that I could hear of, in which blood was shed during the day. Among the entire population there was evinced no feeling of strong passion. The evening journals had modified their tone. The Opposition journals limited themselves to little more than detailing the known transactions of the day. The Government journals, on the contrary, were loud in support of the government, urging it to vigorous measures. The Journal des Débats made use of the following pointed language: " Advance upon the phantom, and it will vanish; fly from it, and it will increase to the sky." After gleaning whatever possible of information in regard to the true posture of affairs, with mingled emotions of expectation respecting the fate of the morrow, I retired.

CHAPTER XXI.

REVOLUTION CONTINUED — SUAVITY AND KINDNESS OF MR RUSH — CHAMBER OF DEPUTIES — M. GUIZOT IN THE TRIBUNE — GENIAL EFFECT UPON THE PUBLIC MIND OF THE RUMORED RESIGNATION OF M. GUIZOT — READING ROOMS — ALARM IN THE NIGHT — CAUSE — DEPARTURE — APPEARANCE OF THE STREETS — THE ENGLISHMAN — DEPARTURE FROM PARIS — EXCITEMENT OF THE INHABITANTS ON THE ROUTE — AMIENS — APPEARANCE OF BELGIUM.

Wednesday, Feb. 23d. The night passed without material disorder. The troops bivouacked upon the public squares, and in the streets. A few chairs and benches in the Champs Elysées, set fire to by some boys, gave a slight illumination of disorder. Yet the government were everywhere master of the pavement, except in a few narrow streets around the cloister of St. Méry, in the centre of Paris, which forms a kind of natural citadel. There some four or five hundred desperate republicans were thronged in dogged defiance. But their chiefs even disapproved their obstinacy and temerity. Another detachment of republicans, without leaders, disarmed during the night the National Guards of the Batignolles, burned the post of the barrier, and fortified themselves in a carpenter's yard, to await future events. No attempt was made to dislodge them. Early in the morning I made a stroll, and found the city calm and awaiting. The several routes leading to the gates of the city were covered at the earliest dawn with columns of cavalry, infantry, artillery, called by the orders of the government. These troops showed a promptitude of obedience, but were sad and silent. The possibility of a civil strife darkened their sun-burnt visages. They severally took positions at the grand junctions of the quarters which divide the city. During the day, armory stores were broken open, arms seized, and detached and scattering firing made upon the troops. It was nearly, however, without effect. Barricades were raised, commencing near the church of Saint Méry, and extending almost to the feet of the soldiers. But they were no sooner raised, than abandoned: for the soldiers, having only stones to fight, would not waste their ammunition.

The National Guard, composed of the well-to-do citizens of the city, being called upon, promptly responded; but they remained neutral, limiting themselves to interfering between the people and the troops, with a spirit of pacification. Many a generous act might be recorded of some young man, fired with sentiments of heroic humanity, breasting danger with his life, to stop the effusion of blood.

Early in the forenoon, I called on Mr. Rush, the American minister, who, in a note which he had left in person, the evening before, at my hotel, had promised to put me in a way to visit the Chamber of Deputies, and if possible, the House of Peers. I had been trying for this, since my arrival in Paris, but without success, — and as a last resort, had applied to Mr. Rush for assistance. He promptly lent me all aid in his power.

I found him arisen, but he had not been out. He inquired about the appearance in the streets with a feeling of anxiety, but expressed the opinion that the government could not possibly be moved from its strong position. He cordially lent me his own ticket for a seat in the Chamber of Deputies, stating that forty nately for me, it happened to be the first day it had been in for several weeks, so great had been the desire to gain access to the intensely eloquent, as well as stormy, sessions of that body, — that there were then numerous applicants for the favor, but he felt bound to give me the preference, from the importance of my mission. As to the Chamber of Peers, it was not in his power to do anything for me.

Mr. Rush was justly popular at Paris. He has a frankness of manner which places you at once at your ease, and so enters into your feelings that you are comfortable and delighted in his presence. He converses admirably, and evinces a tone of character and polish of style allied to great simplicity, that bespeak the true gentleman.

After a turn or two about the city, I appeared at the door of the Chamber of Deputies, and showing the ticket of Mr. Rush, was promptly and politely conducted to a box in the north side of the first gallery. It was half-past twelve, noon, when I arrived, but the hall was quite vacant. At one o'clock, the president of the assembly entered, accompanied by the officers of the Chamber and some members. He immediately pronounced the session open, and the proceedings of the last day were read by the clerk, but no one gave the slightest attention to the exercise. At half-past one the president rang his large bell, and requested gentlemen to be seated; but all present were too absorbed in conversing upon affairs without, to give the slightest heed to the summons; and it was three o'clock before tolerable order could be obtained. Members were continually entering the room, or passing out, for private conferences in the lobbies; or assembled in groups, in different parts of the hall, and conversing with an earnest and anxious look. It was deeply interesting to watch the ebb and flow of emotion on their countenances, as a letter would ever and anon arrive, bringing intelligence of the progress of the *revolution* without.

By this time, the boxes in the first gallery, which I could see, were packed with spectators, mostly ladies, whom I presumed to be the wives, daughters, or friends, of the members.

Another gentleman was in my box, who had come in soon after me. He bore the costume, and had the air of a cosmopolitan; and, after making a careful survey of the scene, had laid down on a plushed seat, and closed his eyes in silence. He was soon followed by another young gentleman, who could not be mistaken as a Yankee, although attired fastidiously in Parisian style. All around appeared new to him, and he continually evinced a pigeon-like trepidation of spirit. As soon as the session became a little turbulent he left, precipitately, evincing no relish for the scenes that might follow.

Members were ever passing around to each other, in familiar intercourse; but the principal interest seemed to centre around the seats of the ministers of the government, who were busy in receiving the chiefs of the legislative parties. The officer of the Chamber made several fruitless attempts to secure order and attention, for such as wished to address the house. He would sound his bell, and cry out, "Messieurs, aux bancs," — gentlemen to their seats, — which was heeded as little as would have been the most insignificant appeal. The president joined his official authority to his personal influence, and reminded gentlemen of their duty, and what was due to their dignity: but it all fell powerless amid the mortal disquietude which consumed every other sentiment. Two or three times, indeed, partial order was effected, to enable some speaker to ascend the tribune for an address, — but after the delivery of a few sentences, confusion again would break in, drown the voice of the orator, and force him to quit the tribune.

Towards four o'clock in the afternoon, a small delegation of military officers entered the hall, and one of them in a respectful manner, handed a paper to the president. While the latter was reading the communication, the members seated themselves, and there was instantly profound silence, as if in anticipation of some important announcement. The president then stated that the palace was surrounded with troops of the National Guard who had despatched a deputation from their number to request or demand a resignation of the ministry, as a measure indispensable to appease the populace, and stop further effusion of blood. This announcement was received by the house with the silence of surprise or contempt. Immediately a slender figure, a little above the medium French stature, darted from the ministers' seats and ascended the tribune, in front of the Speaker's desk. There was a slight awkwardness in his gait. As he turned to the audience to speak, his features bespoke the immobility of an unconquerable purpose; and his eye, the slumbering of a volcano within. It was M. Guizot, the prime minister.

He had uttered but a few sentences, when suddenly, — from the most breathless attention and the deepest stillness, — the entire assembly broke forth in one astounding, thrilling, prolonged acclamation or remonstrance. Loud cries of "Aye, aye!" "No, no!" accompanied by intense expression, and frantic gestures, filled the room, and came rolling up the gallery in startling effect. The very edifice seemed to quake under the impulse. The vast assembly was an immensely multiplied electrical battery, and each Frenchman an active Leyden jar. Had the heavens suddenly poured their accumulated thunders upon my ear, or played their condensed fire through my veins, I could harldly have been more thrillingly shocked. As to the gentleman, my only companion in the box I occupied, who had never changed from the horizontal posture he first assumed on entering,—he now started suddenly up, looked wildly round, protruded his head out upon the scene, and then, smiting his forehead with his fists as if in a fit of abject desperation, leaped out by the door like a maniac, and disappeared from me entirely. During this exciting scene, the speaker remained in the same posture, as motionless as a statue. Not a muscle relaxed, and no emotion was visible in the steady features and unwavering eye. Even the arm remained in the same posture of the half-finished gesture. He was saying, when the explosion took place, "that the demand of the National Guard was unnecessary, as the king at that moment was forming a new ministry." When the whirlwind of passion had subsided, he turned to the president, and remarked that the demonstration which had just taken place would not influence him to add to or subtract from what he was going to say; and then in a few words closed, and resumed his seat among his colleagues, when a repetition of the late tumult transpired. The whole scene was rich, and long to be remembered. I could never have conceived of two so strong opposites in the same character— such a tornado of intense power, vivid energy, intoxicating thrill, and lightning impetuosity enveloped in the gay, polite, amiable, and facile Frenchman.

On my way homeward, I found that the rumored resignation of the Guizot ministry had, with the winged flight of good intelligence, spread among all classes. The evidence of it beamed from the countenances of all. The sad, anxious face was changed to one of hope and joy. Men and women accosted each other with wonted freedom of spirit. A mental load seemed to be removed suddenly from the heart of the city. Undoubtedly there were desperate spirits that regretted any pacification, but the immense majority of respectable citizens shuddered at the bare idea of an insurrection. To such the intelligence came with healing in its wings. The utmost demanded by the Opposition was now accorded them.

In the evening I was in one of the public reading-rooms. These are found in all parts of the city. All are furnished with the journals, the popular works of French, English, German and Italian authors; and some with the standard works in the various departments of science and literature. For a single admission you pay about three cents, which entitles you to read as long as you choose. The delightful convenience of such an institution in a city like Paris, always filled with intelligent strangers, is too obvious to need comment.

This room, in the quarter of the schools, was always thronged. It consisted of three large saloons, with wide, open door-ways leading into each other, and filled with long tables, upon which were French, English, and German journals; while the walls were covered with volumes, arranged upon shelves. It was brilliantly lighted. As you enter, you raise your *chapeau* to the gentlemen, and then seat yourself at will. Waiters are ever at your elbow awaiting your demands. On leaving, you call at the desk, make payment, and retouch your *chapeau*. The utmost quietness ever reigns, and a good degree of politeness prevails among the devouring readers.

I found the reading-room, as usual, filled with hungry seekers for the daily news. The stillness of night reigned, and no ordinary incident could have disturbed the order; but an evening journal having arrived, the excitement of curiosity to swallow its contents, at once became so intense as to break through all restraint and decorum. Each wishing to read it first, a scene of confusion took place. It was instantly decided that one should read aloud for all; whereupon, a gentleman mounting upon the centre of a table, read the account of the resignation of the Guizot ministry the formation of a new ministry by the king, with Count Molé at its head,— with the comments of the editor. The reading was spiced with a due quantity of gestures, grimmaces, shrugs and ironic explanations by the reader, while the audience heightened the amusement of the scene by their contributions of *jeu d'esprits*.

It was now the general feeling that the contention was at an end; and as I had set the 24th for my departure, I proceeded to make arrangements for an early leave. The depôt of the railroad for the North, was at the northern limit of the city, while I was residing on the south side of the Seine. The several coachmen to whom I applied for a carriage, would not take me for any price, fearing that their vehicles would be arrested and converted into barricades.

My valises packed, hotel bill settled, a cordial leave of Madame D., and a douceur for her maid, I threw myself upon my delightful wool mattress for the needed refreshment for the morrow's journey.

I was awakened in the night from sound slumber, by a great noise and confusion in our hotel. A general panic seemed to have seized its usually quiet inmates; and the different parts of the house were resounding with hurried footsteps, slamming of doors, and incoherent voices. A moment's attentive listening, however, persuaded me that the occasion of this turbulent excitation was without our residence. The bells of the city were breaking the stillness of night with successive, hurried peals. Quickly moving lights gleamed across my window. The pavement in the street below reverberated the heavy and confused tread of passing crowds; while the wild clashing of multitudinous voices near, drowning, at times, some distant shout, faintly falling upon the ear, lent a strange and fearful animation to this contemplated scene. It was evident that some unlooked-for occurrence had aroused the city. But as there was neither safety, nor prospect of gratification in venturing out, it was better quietly to await results. The symptoms of alarm, however, soon subsided, and I fell again into slumber.

I subsequently learned the occasion of the wide-spread tumult. The intelligence that the ministry had resigned, had carried joy nearly to all hearts. The sudden removal of deep, pressing dread, had given an elastic bound to gladness. The city was partially illuminated. The suspended fetes and amusements shone forth in renewed splendor. A large column of reckless spirits of the lower order of the populace, carried away with the general enthusiasm, and perhaps partially intoxicated with success against the government, traversed the streets and boulevards in a spirit of triumphal exultation. Immense crowds floated along with this haggard force, in which was enveloped the spark of destiny. A red flag floated in the smoke of their torches, and a sinister tone was apparent in their animated expression. Arriving in front of the hotel of Foreign Affairs, they found the boulevard blocked by a battalion of the line, ranged in battle array, with arms charged, and the commander at their head. The column suddenly halted before that forest of bristling bayonets. The sight of the red flag, and the glare of the torches, frightened the horse of the commander so that he reared, and rushed toward the battalion, which opened to envelop its chief. In the confusion of the movement, a shot was heard. Whether it escaped from a concealed and deadly hand, or was the mere result of accident, is not known; but the soldiers, believing themselves attacked, levelled their muskets, and drew upon the column. A stream of momentary flame ran along the line. The reverberation from the houses and street shook the whole boulevard. The column from the faubourgs fell, decimated by the balls. Death shrieks, and groans from the wounded, were mingled with screams of fright from the spectators, and from women and children, who fled in every direction. The commander of the troops, deploring the involuntary massacre, essayed an explanation with the populace. The latter, gathering in carts the dead, made with them a funeral procession by torch light, breathing revenge on the Government as the authors of the crime. They were drawn up before the office of the National, and other Opposition journals, displayed in gory revenge, and exciting harangues made to the assembled crowds. This unlucky incident gave new impulse to the revolution.

DEPARTURE.

The fixed intention of leaving, awoke me early in the morning. With valises packed to their utmost density, I was quietly let out into the tranquil morning air, by the attentive maid, who in passing, nodded Monsieur an amiable adieu. The air was bland, and the street unoccupied, and perfectly still. It was the repentant, pensive face of nature, immediately after the destructive rage of a tempest. Passing down Rue de Seine, and around the corner of the venerable Institute, lines of soldiers came to view on the quays of the north bank of the Seine, presenting drowsy, haggard, and sorrowful countenances. They had evidently bivouacked on the pavement. In Rue St. Dennis the populace began to be a-stir; as I proceeded, the concourse increased. They were of the working classes, men and women. There was nothing of deep spite or deadly hate visible upon their faces, but a kind of mortal impatience, an indefinite movement, as when one would act without finding the means or seeing clearly the end. I asked a woman who was walking by my side, the occasion of the incipient demonstration. She replied, that the new Count Molé ministry gave but little better satisfaction than the one it displaced; and the sad event of the night had enkindled and emboldened anew the passions of the populace. I trudged along, perspiring freely, faint from want of breakfast, but sustained by the animation imparted by the enkindling scenes around. A little on, a tall, athletic, determined-looking man, issued from a lane, and with an iron bar began prying up the paving stones for a barricade. He was immediately joined by others; and, before I had left them out of sight, the pile had gained quite formidable proportions. A little further on, a large, strong, fierce-looking man, passed in custody of a soldier of the National Guard. He walked with a lofty and defying gait, and his countenance spoke a torrent of power dammed up within. Some half a dozen men stepped to his side, and offered to liberate him,—but for some reason he declined their good offices. The wide and beautiful boulevard of St. Martin and St. Dennis presented a desolate spectacle. The beautiful elms that lined the splendid avenue, had been cut down for barricades, and lay promiscuously strowed with omnibuses, coaches, carts, and other vehicles, in very babel-like confusion. Here, a double line of soldiers, stretching off on both sides of me in the distance, were standing in mute sadness. As I approached, they opened, leaving me a passage just wide enough to squeeze through, edge-wise. At another cross-street a barricade was vigorously being formed. They usually left a space for passers; but this extended quite across the street. A woman preceded me. With respectful kindness they suspended the work, and helped her to scramble over it. They extended the same favor to me. Getting over was a task not a little formidable to me, exhausted as I was, and encumbered with luggage. Another barricade of huge dimensions, formed the day before, forced me to reach the depôt by a circuitous route, in which I was aided by the kind politeness of a gentleman who persisted in accompanying me to point out the way. Several times before, gentlemen had volunteered and urged their services for the same purpose; and all along I was shown courteous and respectful kindness particularly grateful to the feelings. On the whole route, there was nothing sinister in the expression of the populace, but rather a fervent elasticity of feeling. When I had been in the depôt-building but a few moments, a stout-built gentleman enveloped in cloaks and furs, approached hurriedly, and rather bluntly accosted me in French: —

"When does the first train for the North leave, sir?"

"At half-past nine o'clock," I replied.

"Do you not mistake?"

"Not unlikely, but I am just from the ticket-office."

"How long have you been in Paris?"

"Eight weeks."

"Where are you from?"

"The United States."

"Then you speak English?"

"Undoubtedly."

"I am an Englishman," he resumed, changing to his native language, "reside in Havre, — arrived in Paris but a quarter of an hour since, and am now making the most of the time to get out as fast as possible of the city and territory. I confess the horizon of Paris looks a little too lowering to suit my fancy just now."

It is needless to say that we were travelling companions at once. I stepped into a neighboring café for a cup of refreshing beverage and a roll, but my friend would not venture with me. The windows of the saloon were closed with strong shutters, and all the doors barred except a private entrance from behind. A few gentlemen were within, quaffing their coffee in hot haste, while the waiters were running to and fro in distracted excitement. A traveller entered, laden with baggage, in profuse perspiration and extreme trepidation.

"When will the omnibus line pass here for ——?" he hurriedly demanded.

"It does not run, now."

"Can I obtain a carriage?"

"No, sir, not at any price."

"What shall I do?"

"Don't know, sir."

The unfortunate gentleman threw himself into a chair with a look of unutterable despair. On returning, I found the huge iron door leading into the enclosure of the depôt shut and bolted; and it was only after much explanation, seconded by my friend within, that I was permitted to repass. They had closed it as a precaution of safety. My companion suggested that we should take the half-past eight train, which stopped at Amiens, and there await the Brussels train; "for," he added, "while you were out, I observed some trivial movements, which make me more willing to get away. For instance, a bloody-looking chap climbed the stone wall before my eyes, and after deliberately laying beside him a long, gleaming knife, and pistol, pounded off the wires of the telegraph, and then descended. He looked ripe for any dreadful purpose." I was myself the more of his opinion in respect to making haste, as I recollected being told on the way in the morning, that I should not get out of Paris by railroad, as the rails had been taken up by the rioters, to prevent the ingress of soldiers to the city, — a report which convinced me that at least that was the intention, and that we had no time to lose. In a few moments, accordingly, we were breathing the morning air in the country, and leaving the glittering spires of the magnificent city, far behind.

There was in the same carriage with us, a small party of French gentlemen and ladies leaving the city for safety. They were in a flood of emotion in view of the uncertain fate of their friends behind, and of their own fortunate situation. It were no slight task to paint the phrenzied, yet graceful grimmacing, shrugging, gesticulating of these amiable fugitives, as each, in turn, portrayed the scenes of his own experience for the last few days, — heightening the picture by the inimitable French tone and accent. One of the ladies, herself melted to tears from the tenderness of her nature, described with such exquisite pathos as really to draw deeply upon our sympathies.

Excepting the slightly sombre tint of feeling imparted by our companions, we were in the most delightful frame of mind imaginable. The balmy glow of the morning air, the exhilarating movement on our easy and voluptuous seat, the beautiful and diversified landscape continually greeting our eyes with some new charm, rolling by like a pleasing panorama, added to a grateful relief from anxiety and a comfortable feeling of security, combined to render the morning ride all that could be wished.

We sped along, touching, among other smaller places, at St. Dennis, Enghien, Ermont, Franconville, Herblay, and Pontoise Wherever we stopped, the citizens of all classes, borne away with a fever of excitement, swarmed around the cars, and literally overwhelmed us with interrogatories touching the movements in Paris. At Franconville, an aged and maimed gentlemen hobbled towards me, and, observing that I spoke English, begged that I would favor him with the news from Paris, — remarking that his French was so much at fault, that he never spoke that language if he could avoid it. He cordially shook my hand on leaving, and with true English hospitality entreated that I would make him a visit, should I ever come again that way. He had resided thirty years in France, yet his heart still clung to the scenes of early youth, and when he spoke of *Ould* England, the tears actually stood in his eyes. The Americans, he said, were next to the English — " God bless them ! " He lingered on the platform till we were fast receding from sight, when he waived us an affectionate adieu.

On we galloped, screaming, snorting, puffing, by hill and plateau variegated with verdure, through dale and glen, and woodland, — passing through Auvers, Isle-Adam, Beaumont, Precy, Saint-Leu, to Creil; then on through Campéigne, Cleremont, Breteuil, to Amiens, — seventy-two miles from Paris, where we arrived at half-past twelve, noon.

The next train would pass in an hour; barely leaving us time to swallow a dinner at a restaurant, and, afterwards, make a glimpse-stroll through the city. The meal, which was despatched with a zest known only to hunger, was served after the true Parisian mode. We could not but regret the want of time to examine leisurely the notable objects of the place. It possesses more than one attraction for the traveller. Situated on the river of the same name, by which it may be approached by flat-bottomed vessels of forty or fifty tons, it is the centre of considerable trade, as well in its own productions, as in those of the surrounding country. It is well built; streets for the most part straight and clean ; and it has some fine squares and promenades. It has a citadel, constructed by Henry IV.; an academy of sciences and belle-lettres; a free-school of design ; a botanical garden ; a library of forty thousand volumes, and very considerable manufactures. The old Gothic cathedral, in excellent preservation, is one of the finest in Europe. Amiens is very ancient, being supposed to have existed anterior to the invasion of Belgium by the Romans. It is known in diplomatic history, from the circumstance of a definitive treaty of peace between England and the French Republic having been signed in it, on the twenty-fifth of March, 1802. It is, likewise, the birth-place of the famous Peter the Hermit, the apostle of the first Crusade.

We were at the depot in due season; but the usual hour brought no train from Paris. We continued to tarry impatiently till the hands on the public clock had indicated two, three, even half-past three o'clock, but no arrival.

The truth now dawned upon our minds. The rails had been removed from the track, near Paris, a few moments after our departure. My English companion, in a kind of childish ecstasy, now congratulated us on his lucky thought to take the half-past eight instead of the half-past nine o'clock train from Paris. We were thus saved a kind of imprisonment in the capital, the more troublesome from the uncertainty of its duration, and the ominous thickening of thrilling events. Our slight vexation at this unexpected delay was soon quieted, however, by the polite liberality of the prompt officials of the railway line, who readily brought out for our accommodation an extra train, in which they sent us on our way rejoicing. Here I was left to miss the presence for the rest of the way, of my English acquaintance, who, on the starting of the cars, rather unceremoniously slipped me, and joined, in another carriage, a small, lively party of dashing young beaux and belles, all fragrant with the perfume of the toilette, and perfectly radiant with inward gaiety and joyousness. Less confident than he, I withstood the temptation to follow, and resumed my seat amid my former Paris acquaintances, who compensated me, in part at least, for the deprivation, by their perfect kindness and free communication.

As we approached the interior of Belgium, the surface of the country became lower, and of a more uniform level. Indeed, except a ramification of the chain of the Ardennes, extending in a north-east direction, through Luxembourg, Namur, and Liege, and another off-shoot of the Ardennes running parallel with this, on the north banks of the Lambre and Meuse, between Mons and Maestricht, and a few hilly districts in the south and east, the whole territory presents a series of nearly level plains, traversed by numerous streams, delightfully diversified by woods, arable lands, and meadows of brilliant verdure, enclosed by hedge-rows, and thickly studded throughout with towns and villages.

It is well known that much of the fertile and cultivated soil of Belgium has been redeemed from the ocean, or from the stagnant waters of the rivers by which it is intersected. History states that, in the ages immediately preceding and subsequent to, the Christian era, much of the great plain which now comprises the provinces of W. and E. Flanders and Antwerp, was partially overflowed by the ocean. The soil was so marshy that an inundation or a tempest threw down whole forests, such as are still discovered below the surface. The sea and rivers had no limits, and the earth no solidity. Many of the inhabitants of this low country lived in huts placed upon the mounds of sand, or elevated above the reach of the tides, upon stakes. "Your kingdom," said Napoleon, to his brother Louis, "may be defined the deposit of the Rhine, the Meuse, and the Scheldt, the great arteries of my empire."

As we bounded gaily along, we were struck with the picturesque costume of the husbandmen already in the fields with their clumsy and unique implements, preparing for the summer's crop. The sight of women performing the agricultural drudgery of beasts of burden, brought a thrill of gratitude in view of the superior condition of my own countrywomen. The farms were for the most part exceedingly small, from five to twenty acres in extent, but cultivated with the greatest neatness and taste. Nearly a fifth of the whole surface of the kingdom is covered with forests and woods; and a general woody appearance is given even to the most cultivated parts of Belgium, by the custom of planting trees in the hedge enclosures of the fields. The principal roads are also lined by double rows of majestic lindens, and the canals are usually shaded by rows of poplars, beeches, and willows. All the common trees of Europe abound. The forest of Soignies is associated with the memorable battle of Waterloo. A thousand acres of this was owned by the late Duke of Wellington, in connection with his title of Prince of Waterloo. The romantic forest of St. Hubert is Shakspeare's " Forest of Arden."

Most of the houses in the smaller villages through which we passed, were built of red brick, with thatched or tiled roofs, producing a combination of the gay and rural, singularly unique and striking. One of our company, pointing to the fortifications of a small town, observed to me that it was an interesting feature of the smaller towns of the North of Europe. There are twenty-one of these in Belgium. They served to protect in a measure their citizens from the ravages of the numerous wars of which the country has been the doomed theatre. Indeed this beautiful country has been from time immemorial the battle field of Europe.

CHAPTER XXII.

ARRIVAL AT BRUSSELS — OFFICIALS — INTENSE EXCITEMENT OF THE CROWD — A WORCESTER GENTLEMAN — APPEARANCE OF THE CITY — LADY OF THE AMERICAN MINISTER — PALAIS DU CONGRESS — CHAMBERS OF PARLIAMENT — BELGIUM — THEATRES — YOUTHFUL PERFORMERS — RESIGNATION OF LOUIS PHILLIPPE, AND FLIGHT OF THE ROYAL FAMILY — BOULEVARDS AND CAFES — SCHOOLS — HOTEL DU VILLE — PALACE OF FINE ARTS — CELEBRATED PAINTERS.

On account of our detention at Amiens, it was late in the evening when we reached Brussels. The news of the revolution of Paris had preceded us, and we were, in consequence, surrounded by people on landing, eager to learn the latest intelligence. The officer declining to inspect my baggage, I hastened to the nearest hotel, a few steps from the depôt. Being the only passenger who stopped at this hotel, I was closely surrounded, on entering, and pressed for information. Two officials from the Palace of Laerkin, coming in, the crowd, from a deference shown officers in monarchical governments, readily yielded a small space around me. These dignitaries, with an excited manner, questioned me minutely respecting the thrilling and astounding events that were transpiring in Paris; and after thanking me for my complaisance, took a dignified and polite leave. They had no sooner closed the door, when the crowd, denser than before, actually pressed full upon me, and with intense eagerness, but good naturedly expressed, clamored for news from Paris. Questions were put to me so rapidly, and of so varied import, amid such confusion, that I was at last overwhelmed, exhausted, and could say nothing more. In this dilemma, I observed at the outer edge of the crowd a gentleman something like half a head taller than those around him, vigorously elbowing his way toward me. His erect form and bold movement showed resoluteness, while his countenance, rendered French-like by an elegant moustache, beamed with animation. As soon as he approached within hailing distance, his voice drowning all others, reached my ear, assured me a little, and thus set me on the track of answering his questions. Presently, however, perceiving my embarrassment in expressing myself readily, he stopped suddenly short, begged to know how long I was in Paris, and what country I was from. On seizing from my lips the name Boston, he burst forth in a tone of mingled delight and astonishment, but in an exclamation a little irreverent, "—— ——, just where I am from." It was Mr. G——, of Worcester, who had been in Europe a year or more,—and who, singular to say, lodged while in Paris, in the very next hotel to mine, which he left but a few days before the memorable 22d of February, without our having seen each other. As he was the more fluent in French, he yielded to my solicitation to become my interpreter to the news-devouring throng. Yet, later in the evening, when the crowd had fully withdrawn, Mr. G. and myself had a most glorious tête-a-tête. It is needless to say that it was long past midnight before we parted to retire. None, I will venture to say, but those who have experienced it, can conceive the perfect delight felt on the meeting of countrymen in a foreign land. It centres with a rush upon the heart all the dearest associations of home and country, enkindling it to a glow of fraternal enthusiasm experienced, indeed, but never described. Ceremony, the cold, dampening cloud which envelops character, is at once dissipated by the sunshine of the beaming soul, and the best feelings of our nature appear in unreserve. We had much to talk over of what we had seen, and the impressions we had gathered therefrom, besides a mutual exchange of a chapter of our personal history, as well as making sittings of persons whom we happened mutually to know in the U. States; and all this was done with the frankness and freedom of long acquaintance, though we had not known each other before that evening.

Feb. 25th. Arose early, and after a frugal breakfast, made alone my morning's promenade for first impressions of a city which I had for a long time yearned to visit. I found it not very unlike the idea I had formed from the many descriptions I had read. A large portion of the city being built on the acclivity of a hill, it presents, when viewed on the west, a picturesque amphitheatre of houses; and the great inequality of the elevation of its site has often induced a comparison with Naples and Genoa. The figure described by the outline of it resembles that of a pear, the smaller part pointing S. S. W. A century ago the city was surrounded with ramparts. The site of these fortifications has been converted into spacious boulevards, planted with rows of stately linden trees that encircle two-thirds of the city. These boulevards command extensive views of the country, and afford an agreeable promenade. The scenery of the adjacent country is beautifully diversified by sloping heights, and green valleys refreshed by the waters of the Seune. Many of the streets are wide and regular, and are paved generally with large flint-stones. The ancient part of Brussels is ornamented by many fine specimens of the florid style of architecture; and the modern part exhibits many excellent buildings erected about fifty years ago, — but there is an uniformity in the appearance of the dwelling-houses not pleasing to the eye.

After a breakfast à la Français, I passed, in company with Mr G., to pay my respects to the American Minister. He being absent, we were received by his lady in a manner natural only to ladies of Southern nativity, who have enjoyed large intercourse with elevated society. Mr. G. had already been honored with her acquaintance, and the conversation between them immediately turned upon the fine arts and the social amenities of the city. Madame the Minister read a note in French, which had been intrusted to her for Mr. G., with pure Parisian accent.

The conversation then turned upon the all-absorbing topic of the day — the insurrection in Paris; and learning that I was just from the capital, her interest in the subject acquired a most lively animation. Her voluble tongue seemed as conversant with European politics, as with the intimate affairs of court circles. In allusion to the communication being intercepted, by the removal of the rails on the railway near Paris, and the breaking of the telegraph-wires, by the insurgents, she thought that railroads and telegraph-wires were in every way excellent in countries where the people *pulled* with the government, but that these modern glorious improvements often proved exceedingly embarrassing to reigning powers in revolutions. She observed, further, that many liberal minded and right hearted people in Europe would gladly favor a general revolution for free institutions, but that so rotten did they consider the present political edifice, as not to dare laying violent hands on it, for fear of hopelessly burying society beneath its tottering ruins. She was perfectly simple in her manner, conversed with force, point, and luminous ease, and expressed herself in French with precision, and an almost native fluency and grace. She was a little below the medium stature of American ladies, of rather dark complexion, but of an agreeable countenance, and an eye, when animated in conversation, to remind you at once of the great Southern statesman, John C. Calhoun, of whom she is a daughter, and, I doubt not, no unworthy representative. There was standing a half finished portrait in an adjoining room, in regard to which she incidentally observed, that her husband was wont to spend some of his leisure hours in gratifying his extreme predilection for painting. Indeed, the duties of an American ambassador at Brussels are not particularly engrossing; and it is said, with good reason, that there is no foreign embassy more eligible, either in regard to its freedom from expense, the leisure it affords, or the agreeableness of society, than that at Brussels.

We went successively to the Museum and to the office of the Minister of the Interior, who is, also, the Minister of Public Instruction, but found them closed. At the Palais du Congres we were more successful. Here we gained ready admittance, and found the two branches in session. They appeared decorous bodies, and deliberated with a gravity hardly natural to the Belgian manners. The edifice, which is magnificent, is ornamented with fluted Doric columns and appropriate sculptures. Marble stairs on each side of a spacious hall ascend to the two Chambers of Parliament, which are elegantly fitted up for the reception of Members. The public are admitted into both chambers during the debates, females as well as males; and for this accommodation, the Chamber of Deputies contains a capacious gallery.

Belgium proclaimed its independence in 1830. It is governed by a constitutional monarchy; and the whole system of government is based upon the broadest principles of rational freedom and liberality.

At dinner we were joined by a third gentleman, whose acquaintance my companion had accidentally formed, since being in Brussels; and finding him much to his purpose, was not unwilling to continue his society, which he did by an occasional invitation to dine with him. The person alluded to, though evidently pecuniarily destitute, had the manners of a gentleman, and an intelligence very remarkable. His knowledge of men and things was really wonderful. Hardly a place, event, or person of distinction, in Europe, could be mentioned, but that he could describe readily all worth knowing about it. He was a living book of Brussels. Had he been born with the city itself, and had freedom and leisure ever since to observe its growth and changes, his information could scarcely have been more full or minute. It was rumored that he had once been very wealthy, was highly educated, and was an amateur in the various departments of learning and art, — but having lost or squandered his fortune, was now eking out a living in the only way consistent with his taste and his ideas of honor. But be that as it may, his deportment towards us was always scrupulously polite, deferential and obliging, without the slightest tint of servility. I could not but observe in him a grave and thoughtful air, from which no excess of humor on our part could draw him. Similar personages are frequently to be met with in Europe. They linger about thoroughfares, and are at the service of travellers, on terms quite easy. Some such I had met with before, but never one altogether of so elevated respectability as this.

After dinner, at five o'clock in the afternoon, the gentleman above named, handed Mr. G—— a pack of complimentary tickets to one of the theatres. They required, however, a trifling sum to be paid on them, to make them current. We were not disposed to slight so marked an invitation, and accordingly set out in lively mood. We found the building not at all imposing in appearance, and the interior quite humble, but neat and tasteful, however. The first act had already commenced. It was a kind of ballet that they were performing. Presently, our eyes were delightfully greeted with a perfect shower of dancing girls, which half-filled the stage. They might have been from eight to fifteen years of age. They were tastefully robed in white, with a garland of flowers for head-dress, and appeared charmingly pretty. They went through a series of dances in groups, with surprising grace, and precision. The wonder to us was, whence issued such a multitude of young girls. Mr. G. ventured, at their expense, a witticism upon their ambiguous origin, but the scene imparted to my own mind something of a melancholy tinge.

The second play, entitled the *Lesson of Love*, possessed really several good points, and was admirably performed. The acting here, as in Paris, struck me as vastly superior in quality to anything of the kind that I had witnessed in the United States. Here the genius of the stage appeared to be the child of Nature; while with us she seems rather the offspring of art. The scene was followed by dancing by two girls, perhaps twelve years of age. They came bounding gracefully in upon the stage, captivating our senses by their tasteful dress, exquisite form, and fairy movements, while their delicately modest demeanor won deeply upon our esteem. Their intricate evolutions and difficult steps often thrilled me with admiration; and they more than once carried surprise to the entire audience, bringing down the whole house with a perfect rapture of applause. They seemed gently to vie with each other in winning the admiration of the audience, and so equally balanced was their excellence, that Mr. G. and myself could not decide upon which to award our preference. Just as we had decided upon one, the other, by some surpassing feat of grace, would wrest the palm from her fair rival. These girls were doubtless inferior to Taglioni, and kindred stars, their limbs not having attained the firmness for long sustained effort; but we could not but pronounce them very promising candidates for the world's applause. To me, the simple innocence of their youth invested them with a charm not found with other dancers.

Feb. 26*th.* Long before daylight I was suddenly aroused from a sweet slumber, by loud raps at my door from Mr. G., who in a deep fervor of excitement communicated the astounding intelligence from Paris, of the resignation of Louis Phillippe, the flight of the royal family, the proclamation of the Provisional Government, with Lamartine at the head, the sacking of the Tuileries by the mob, and other thrilling events. The news ran through the city like wild-fire, producing in all minds an electric shock of emotion. Those who remember the startling effect the intelligence first produced upon the American public, separated from the grand scene by three thousand miles of ocean, can faintly imagine the impression made in Brussels, the capital of a bordering state, closely allied to France by an identity of interest and feeling. The queen, then residing in the city, was the daughter of Louis Phillippe. The language of all the better classes is French. All the best French works, in every department of science and literature, are reprinted in Brussels with equal neatness and accuracy, nearly as soon as they appear in Paris. Paris and the Parisians are the models which the people of Brussels are ambitious to imitate. There is an anxious observance of French manners and fashions among the wealthy classes. The grand features of Paris, namely, its circumambient boulevards, its splendid cafés, its palace garden, its grand theatre for the operatic drama, and the smaller one for Vaudervilles, and many other similar points, find faithful copies in Brussels, and have gained it the significant appellation of "Paris in miniature." It is not surprising, then, that the intelligence from Paris should have produced a fermentation in all minds; for with some reason it was feared that a revolution in Paris might be a revolution in Brussels, if not a continental insurrection.

I called, after breakfast, upon M. Boeuf, the Minister of the Interior, for information in respect to the schools. He received me cordially, and complied with my wish with the utmost readiness, — appearing gratified at the opportunity of making me acquainted with their system of instruction, and evincing an emotion of pride in view of the Belgian schools as standing among the first, if not themselves the very first in point of excellence, in Europe. He undertook to draw up for me on the spot a list of the schools and literary institutions that I should inspect, in order to understand fully the scope and character of their system. In doing this, he evinced so great trepidation, frequently leaving off and pacing the room in uncontrollable mental excitement, that I ventured to ask the cause of his agitation. He frankly owned that the news from Paris had completely unstrung his nervous system.

His office was in the quaint old Hotel de Ville, in the grand place, or central market place. It is one of the largest and most remarkable of those civic palaces, in the florid Gothic style, that are to be seen in perfection only in the Netherlands. It was erected in 1400. The architecture is Lombardo-Gothic, with a great profusion of quaint sculptures, pointed turrets, and other fanciful and intricate ornaments. In the front are forty windows, and in the lofty sloping roof, eighty more. At a point remarkably distant from the centre of the front, an elaborately ornamented pyramidal tower, open throughout to the summit, rises to the height of three hundred and sixty-four feet, and commands a fine view of the surrounding country, including the battle field of Waterloo. It is surmounted by a colossal copper gilt statue, seventeen feet high, of St. Michael crushing a dragon, which turns about to serve for a weather-cock. The interior of the building is entered by a spacious flight of steps, and the lofty halls and saloons exhibit many curious old paintings, gilded carvings, and specimens of fine tapestry.

During the day, Mr. G. and myself made a visit in company to the Palace of Fine Arts. We first looked in at the gallery of paintings. The collection comprises about five hundred, by the great Flemish masters from Van Eyck to Reubens and his numerous pupils. It was indeed a rich treat, — those sublime mortal productions. I stole there ever afterwards, whenever an hour of leisure afforded me an opportunity, and lingered spell-bound with delight. Mr. G., who evinced a peevish fastidiousness upon French and Belgian matters in general, was glowing in his admiration of many of the paintings. We were both struck with a head by Rembrandt. It is an old painting, but the features were as soft and fresh as life itself. The light frizzled hair stood so mellowingly out from the canvas, that you were tempted to run your fingers through it. I gazed often and long upon a Descent from the Cross, by Vandyke. The agonized features of the dead Saviour, and the painted anguish of Mary at his feet, were rendered with a deep truthfulness. There were several large paintings by Reubens, which strikingly illustrate the grandeur of his genius. The canvas is crowded with figures thrown into all possible attitudes, but so natural, that the most careful study of each reveals no fault. There is, also, a boldness and ease in the drawing, a strength and firmness in delineation, and brilliancy and contrast in coloring, which impart life and majesty to the picture. The paintings bore, too, the apparent negligence of great genius. They appeared as if executed in extreme haste, some of them looking as if scarcely finished. A heel, for instance, which at a distance became symmetrical with the body, when examined near, looked as if made with the single daub of the brush. It required, however, little attention to perceive that the surpassing excellences of Reubens are accompanied with striking faults; one of which is that of women without beauty or grace. The female faces all resemble each other, and bear almost a vicious expression.

Belgium has had the rare honor of producing two different schools of painting. The first arose under Hubert and John Van Eyck, or John of Bruges, about the year 1440. The ruling spirits of the second school, were Reubens and his pupil Vandyke, who flourished about 1600. At the present time, the Royal Academy of Fine Arts at Antwerp is the principal school of painting, and it produces every year several artists of the highest distinction. It is supported by the public, and is usually attended by at least a thousand students.

Brussels possesses a Royal establishment for *lithography*, and an excellent school for engraving, where designing is taught, and the different kinds of engraving on copper and wood.

From the Gallery of Paintings, we passed into the Museum of Natural History, surpassing in extent every other in the kingdom. The departments of Zoology, Ornithology, Entomology, and Mineralogy are especially replete with rare and admirable specimens, including animals from the Dutch East Indian Colonies, Russian minerals, and all the volcanic products of Mount Vesuvius.

We next walked through the great public library in another part of the edifice. It contains nearly 140,000 volumes, and 15,000 manuscripts. The latter were collected at a very early period, by the dukes of Burgundy, and are esteemed of great value; many being richly adorned with miniature paintings of exquisite beauty, by the early Flemish artists; and the greater part are splendidly bound in crimson morocco. Above two thousand volumes of the books were printed in the fifteenth century.

This spacious building serves, also, for public lectures, which are delivered gratuitously every day by the most eminent professors, on the various branches of learning.

On my return, I found at my lodgings a spacious envelope, with the broad seal of the State, displaying the Belgique Lion, — enclosing two handsome letters of introduction to the Principals of the Norman Schools at Liege and Nevelles.

CHAPTER XXIII.

SYMPTOMS OF REVOLUTION IN BELGIUM — COMMUNAL SCHOOLS — CATHEDRAL OF GUDULE — RELIGIOUS SECTS — LAMARTINE — MARRIAGE, IN EUROPE AND THE UNITED STATES — ACADEMIES — BOTANIC GARDEN — INFLUENCE OF LAMARTINE — CARNIVAL — HERO-WORSHIP — SHOPPING — CARPET AND LACE FACTORIES.

Feb. 28*th.* I was slightly disturbed the last night by a turmoil in the square under my window. I was afterwards told that it was an unsuccessful attempt to get up an émute after the style in Paris. The whole affair, however, was promptly quashed by the government-police, who had, from the first, exercised the utmost vigilance. Ordinances were posted at every corner, forbidding, among other things, the assembling of more than five persons at the same place. The police last evening closed the doors of one of the principal theatres, on the pretext that the play contained some passages of a seditious nature. The excitement was very great in the city; still, the most enlightened minds did not think there could be a revolution in Belgium. There was but little to reform in the minds of the people. The masses of the nation were contented and happy. The government was strong, and the king enthroned in the hearts of his subjects generally. By one of those happy movements which frequently give a favorable turn to the current of fortune, he forestalled any discontents of the populace. Calling around him his ministers, he formally announced to them, that he would not have a drop of blood spilled for him,

— if the nation desired his abdication, he was ready to tender them his crown; but if they should choose to adhere to his reign, he would lead their armies in person wherever it should be necessary, — ready at any time to lay down his life for his country. Both branches of the legislature promptly replied to this generous resolution of the king, assuring him of their warm and unanimous adhesion; and when it was spread on the wings of the press through the country, the heart of the nation responded by petitions numerously signed from all parts of the country, begging him to accept their devotion and sympathy.

I visited, to-day, one of the city primary schools. The director at first stated that it would be necessary to obtain a written permit from the minister. On presenting my letter, he cordially invited me in, giving me politely and readily all the intelligence I desired. The school was composed of eight hundred day scholars, and three hundred evening scholars. They are separated into divisions of one hundred, each of which occupies a separate apartment. To each division there is a master and an assistant. The boys, who are kept separate from the girls, are taught by males, and the girls by females. The superintendent, who had enjoyed large experience as a practical educator, who had travelled in the German States, and had read much and written upon the subject of education, was decidedly of opinion, that schools taught by men are superior to such as are instructed by women. He stated, on his personal knowledge, that the experiment had been made on a large scale, under fair circumstances, — and the result proved, that while women of high intellectual character and strong energy may do for girls and small boys, only male teachers can be employed to the greatest advantage for lads and young men. So far as I could learn, a similar opinion prevails among educationists in Germany, England, and France. The rooms here were commodious and well ventillated by means of the windows. The forms, or benches, were long enough for several pupils, and provided with inkstands. Some of them had slates set into the tops of the forms. Every room was supplied with outline maps, and a table of weights and measures. The black-boards were arranged to slide up and down in a case, very conveniently. The alphabet was taught from little blocks with the letters painted upon them, ingeniously arranged in a case, before which the class stood at recitation. A novel apparatus was pointed out to me, for teaching pupils to count. I witnessed a most gratifying exercise of a class of pupils about seven years of age, who wrote readily, and generally with correctness, sentences on the black-board, as they were dictated to them by the teacher, who assured me that they all commenced learning the alphabet but three months before. It should be observed, however, that the orthography of the French is more regular than that of the English. All the pupils were carefully instructed both in French and Flemish. The boys are taught drawing, the girls, needlework and embroidery. The materials and text-books are furnished by the city; and the articles of fabrication are distributed among the more deserving scholars. The order of the school was good. All corporal punishment was forbidden by law. A register of deportment, scholarship, and absence, was kept with exactitude, and exposed to public examination. The doors of the school-room were closed precisely at the time of the commencement of the school, and no pupil admitted after that hour. The best teachers received about four hundred dollars per annum. In addition to the salary, they usually have a room at the school-building furnished with lights and fuel. Provision is also made for the sickness or old age of teachers, and for their families after their decease. The director, who had been a long time connected with the schools of the city, informed me that I was the first American, to his knowledge, who had actually inspected their schools.

March 1st. For franking a single letter as far as England, they charged me to-day at the post-office, thirty-nine cents! At that rate, all travellers would be sincere in wishing a revision of the postal laws of Belgium.

Took a final leave, to-day, of Mr. G., who was to set off immediately for Paris, to witness the scenes of the thrilling drama being enacted there. His curiosity and adventurous spirit had become wrought up to the highest pitch, and he was often murmuring at his ill-luck for having missed seeing the entire affair. To leave Europe without having had a personal view of the revolution, and having tasted the stirring emotions of the rapid events of the great capital, would be indeed a misfortune. He therefore left in a great excitement of interest, intending to go on the railroad to the break, and then trust to his energy and fortune to reach and enter the capital. This spirit of heroic enterprise shone in marked contrast with the effeminate temerity of a young Parisian gentleman who chanced to be sitting near us at table at dinner the day before. The conversation naturally turning upon the present revolution in Paris, he stated that his wife and two children were in Paris, for whose safety he expressed deep solicitude, but did not hesitate to declare that the danger was too great to think of going there after them.

Going homeward, I stepped into an estaminet for a lunch. The garçon not comprehending exactly my demand, his hesitancy was relieved by a young gentleman near me, partaking of a frugal collation. He was enveloped in a rather pedantic-looking cloak, but possessed an intelligent and agreeable countenance. This incident led to an intimate acquaintance between us of decided mutual advantage. He proved to be a Belgian by birth, but had resided sufficiently long in Germany and France to speak the languages of those countries with purity and ease. He was now ardently employing his leisure moments in the acquisition of the English, which he already read quite well, and could even speak with remarkable accuracy and correctness of pronunciation. He was employed as clerk in an extensive silk store, and spent a part of his evenings in instructing a small class of young ladies in the German language,— one of them the daughter of his employer. To my inquiries for learning the secret of his great success in acquiring languages, he observed that he owed much to two principles to which he rigidly adhered. One was, to master if possible every point as he came to it, and the other, to retain fully whatever he learned. He was in the practice of making a note of all difficult idioms and new words, as he met with them in reading, putting the list in his pocket, and recurring to it sufficiently often to indelibly impress the whole upon his mind. We struck up immediately an arrangement by which he met with me daily in my room. We there spent an hour in conversation, and then made a stroll through the city, he expressing himself always in English, and I in French. So great was his desire to visit the U. States, that he assured me of his intention of making the tour as soon as he could honorably disengage himself from his employer. But since he has not, to my knowledge, fulfilled this design, I am more than half led to suspect the influence of some gentle treachery among the members of his very beautiful class.

March 2d. Weather moist and fitful, as usual at this season. At one moment, the sun smiling gladsomely through the bursting clouds; at the next, the streets being drenched with rain. It were not safe to leave your hotel without an umbrella, however serene might be the sky.

In the afternoon I visited another of the Communal schools.

As before, the director gravely asked me for my permit. On presenting it, his scruples readily gave way, and he most kindly showed me over the school. It did not differ materially from the one previously visited, except that the order was quite indifferent. This teacher was of the same opinion as the director of the school before-mentioned, in respect to the comparative merits of male and female teachers. Music was generally taught in the school; and I witnessed an exercise with very young pupils which I thought highly creditable to their musical powers and to the skill of the teachers. My conductor himself did not fail to commend warmly the excellence of parts of the school, and showed very significantly that he expected that I should do the same;—no uncommon way of challenging admiration! I observed here and elsewhere, in Belgium, the pronunciation of the French é mute, to be more open than the sound given the same letter in Paris. The power of the letter prevailing in Brussels differs not widely from the way it is represented in Bolmar's Levizac's Grammar, which, by the way, is not the true Paris pronunciation.

I afterwards looked into a girl's school. It, like most of the schools of the same class, was conducted by the Sisters of Charity — a fraternity resembling in dress, manners, and meekness of spirit, the Friends. Their benevolence and devotion are proverbial. They either receive no compensation for their arduous services, or the merest pittance, just to suffice their simple needs. If any class on earth seem imbued thoroughly with a Christian and humane spirit, it is the Sisters of Charity. Their life-deeds best bespeak their eulogy,— but their humane expression, also, gives clear evidence of a consecrated heart. The pupils are taught the common branches, in which they gave evidence of having been well instructed. A division of the school were taught embroidery, and various kinds of more common handicraft, and the specimens of their work shown me were neat and beautiful. This branch of female industry is more commonly practised in the European schools, than with us. The under-directress of the establishment received me with an air of unaffected politeness; and without requiring a letter of introduction, as did the former teachers, took me leisurely and kindly over the establishment. The rooms and interior arrangement were neat and comfortable, but plain and useful, — nothing expended for mere ornament. All the girls were taught sewing, both the fine and the coarser styles; and some specimens were shown me that I thought would have done credit to the skill of a practised seamstress.

March 3d. Sauntered out with the view to continue my researches in the public schools; but it being Thursday afternoon, — in conformity with the usage, a *congé*, or afternoon-holiday, had emptied the rooms of their contents of youthful life. At the Palace of Arts and Industry I learned that there is no machine in Belgium, — and I had previously learned that there is none in France,— for knitting seines, or nets. The immense quantity continually needed must still be all knit in the old way, by hand. My young friend, in Massachusetts, who has labored for years, so perseveringly in inventing a machine for knitting seines, may be cheered with the assurance that, if he succeeds in his undertaking, he will thereby not only confer a lasting benefit to human industry, but gain a name among the distinguished, and a comfortable fortune.

I afterwards looked into the cathedral of St. Gudule, the largest and finest in Brussels. It was founded 1010; and here the first chapter of the chivalric order of the Golden Fleece was held by Phillip le Bon, in 1435. There is an aspect of imposing grandeur in its spacious front, that impresses profoundly the mind of the beholder. The church is surmounted by two large, square towers, from the top of which Antwerp is distinctly visible at a distance of twenty-seven miles. One of these contains a bell that weighs 1435 pounds. In the interior, against the pillars which divide the lateral aisles from the nave, and support the lofty roof, are placed finely sculptured statues of the twelve apostles, ten feet in height, at an elevation of twenty-five feet from the floor The pulpit is certainly curious and striking. It is formed of wonderfully carved groups of figures the size of life, representing the expulsion of Adam and Eve from Paradise. The glass of the principal window displays a magnificent representation of the last judgment, by the celebrated Flemish painter, Francis Flors; and several other antique-painted windows of this noble cathedral are exceedingly brilliant and beautiful. Its altars and sumptuous mausoleums of sculptured marble, and numerous fine paintings, are objects worthy of especial note. The organ, too, is remarkable for the depth and power of its intonations and perfect unison; but that which most attracts a curious spectator is one of the side chapels — a large and splendidly ornamented oratory — called *St. Sacrament des Miracles*, from its being the sanctuary in which are preserved three miraculous consecrated wafers, said to have been stolen by Jews in the fourteenth century, and miraculously recovered. These wafers are still annually paraded with great pomp through the principal streets.

Brussels contains several other grand and venerable cathedral churches, erected in the middle ages. Four only of sixteen are considered primary, and belong each to one of the four arrondissements into which the city is divided; the others, although little inferior in appearance, are secondary in rank.

At the summit of the lofty spire which surmounts *Notre Dame de la Chapelle*, is stationed a watchman, who sounds a trumpet every quarter of an hour during the night, in proof of his wakeful vigilance; and on seeing a fire, he blows a shrill and incessant blast to hasten the attendance of the engines.

The inhabitants of Brussels are Catholics, but all religious tenets are tolerated. The Church of England service is performed in several Protestant chapels, for the accommodation of the numerous English residents. And their Lutheran king, Leopold, attends Protestant service in his private chapel. And, besides, the Jews, of whom there are ten thousand in the whole kingdom, have their general consistory in Brussels, and a handsome synagogue.

I found the evening journals in my frequented café, filled with incidents of the revolution, and with speculations upon its results. Some of the royal family, after many cruel vicissitudes, had reached England, that generous refuge of exiled royalty. There were numerous conjectures as to the fate of the king. As I mused upon his checkered life, I felt sad at the fickleness of fortune, that had sported so wantonly and unfeelingly with its favorite. Lamartine was now the bright particular star, beaming with resplendent effulgence upon the chaotic darkness of a troubled sea. He was powerfully concentrating all the energies of his noble heart and grand and richly cultivated genius, to combine the elements of order, and give stability and harmonious movement to civil affairs. His efforts were really incredible, and his success was proportionably commensurate. The dread of the conservative mind of the nation, that some excess would deluge society in blood, had hastened many to yield their adhesion to the new government. Mr. Rush, our American minister, in the just spirit of an enlightened forecast, was the first of the foreign ambassadors. Among the journals, the Journal des Debats, the Government paper, had quite turned round to the support of the new régime. It must be confessed, that the somerset it had to make, was most gracefully and adroitly done. To the praise of the new government, one of its first acts was the reforming of the school law. To the credit of the French character, let it be said, that in the momentous crisis of February, 1848, the heart and intelligence of the nation seemed to comprehend the necessity of mutual forbearance, union, harmony.

Spent the remainder of the evening in a most gratifying tête-a-tête with Madame, my amiable landlady, and a particular friend of her late husband. The favor was granted me in consideration of my being a foreigner, and especially an American. She had been a widow but a few months, but was fast regaining her wonted vivacity of mind. The morning of a brighter day was just gleaming forth from the night of her late widowhood. The soft twilight of radiance invested her with a subdued but rather fascinating charm. Her elegant figure gracefully robed in black, her raven curls, long, dark eye-lashes, and smile tempered with slightly sombre hue, imparted a chastened and sweet expression to her spirited and forcible character. She was, perhaps, thirty years of age. She spoke freely of her late husband, whose memory she respected; but their union had been unfortunate. Slight bodily ills had rendered him unfit for active pursuit, but had not taken from him the relish for society and love of pleasure. He was accordingly wont to spend the most of his time from home, in the cafés and other places of public resort, lounging and whiling the hours in vapid amusements. Their joint patrimony being soon squandered, his loving and devoted wife sprang the resources of her fertile character, to relieve the embarrassment. She opened a hotel for letting rooms to travellers, at the same time keeping herself a variety-store in one part of the same building. She thus not only supported comfortably a family of small children, with servants, but was enabled to hand over something to indulge the habits of her husband. I could not but regard her as a fine illustration of the capability of woman to rise superior to fortune. She seemed completely master of her circumstances. With a nursing child in her arms, she might be seen at one time superintending the affairs of the house, ordering the servants, or receiving company; at another, in her store, in her peculiarly engaging manner, winning largely from the purse of her customers; and at all times equable, gracious, animating. She honored matrimony, and yearned to confide in the generous and noble heart of another, but she had found man weak and ungrateful, and the world hard and unsympathizing; she would not, therefore, marry again, — ah, frail resolution of woman! The gentleman just mentioned, was wont to visit her evenings, and remain till a late hour. He was as constant, too, as the vesper-star in the heaven of Hope. He claimed the favor of her society, to condole her bereavement, out of the intimate regard he bore her late husband; but a careful eye might detect a motive of another kind. He was no unworthy son of Apollo. He might have been thirty-five; but his clear and ruddy complexion had only softened into the mellowness of the peach. His tapering and voluptuous fingers betokened no rougher partnership than a gentle union with a delicate kid glove. He was attired with superlative elegance, but not fastidiously fine. Without possessing marked personal beauty, there was yet about him an air of lofty simplicity, and a nonchalance of refined ease that was absolutely winning. He seemed familiar upon all topics of conversation, and spoke the best Parisian French with extreme precision and ease, and with an accent silvery and liquid. How could Madame resist so many insinuating amenities? She was evidently losing, by degrees, that entire self-possession which ordinarily marked her queenly bearing. Not that she was struck with the noble mien of her visitor, or admired the traits of his manner, or was charmed with his glow of character; but alas for her woman's heart, her tenderness of nature, and, above all, that sympathy which, wrested late from an accustomed object, flowed out too readily upon the first new devotee that sought its homage. This gentleman was the representative of a class in Europe by no means small in number, who are willing to offset their personal accomplishments against the money or business capital of a wife, to secure their life from the pinchings of pecuniary embarrassment, — that most uncomfortable of feelings, especially to such gentlemen. Thus fairly seated in the matrimonial car, they pass over the road of life most delectably to themselves. Leaving at the stopping places of the way, their better-half — better, true enough — to the graver duty of looking after the luggage of the journey, they are wont to spend the protracted intervals in regaling the sense with other views and scenting the fragrance of other fields. Woman, thus wedded, has the husk of matrimonial endearments, and the dregs of the wine of life, as penitential fruit for the seductions of heart over the guidance of reason. Yet it is a lesson hard to learn, — that of prudence against habit and inclination. How strange that the burnt child does not dread the fire, — that the sailor will turn again to the perils escaped by a hair-breadth, — that the soldier will reënlist for death-devouring fields of carnage, — and that woman will plunge again into the corroding waters of a same wedlock from which she has but just safely emerged, still dripping with the waters of bitter experience. Thus, Madame, who would often mournfully recount the unequal burden of her late married life, and would freely declare her determination as the result of her judgment, not to wed again, was yet evidently being lured into the very net that so appalled her judgment.

Marriage is, in many respects, quite a different thing in Europe and the United States. In the former, among the middling classes, there is one feature particularly noticeable. When a couple come together in wedlock, each of the parties retains, often to a ruinous extent, his individual habits and tastes. If the bridegroom is a sort of idle gentleman, wont to sport his time on the boulevards and in the cafés, and the bride an industrious body inured to the profession of gain, a similar course will continue after marriage. He will spend his evenings and days abroad, pursuing the phantom of his own amusement, — while she is attending assiduously to the domestic affairs, or devotedly pursuing some calling of gain. How different is it with us! A young man, for instance, of independent means, marries a girl who may have been a very respectable domestic. At once a notable transformation takes place. She immediately assumes the dignity and imitates the airs of a married lady in the highest circles; while the husband, something of an idler before, now finding his small income insufficient to meet the growing expense of his new state, engages industriously in some branch of business which he pursues with the pertinacity of a martyr.

March 4th. In the afternoon, visited one of the communal schools, which will not require a particular description, as in organization and appearance, it did not differ materially from those already described. The salary of the teacher was about one hundred and twenty dollars per annum, — a remuneration slight enough, I thought, for the apparently severe duties of his place. For the instruction of youth of both sexes in all departments of scholastic knowledge, and every elegant accomplishment, there are in Brussels many excellent academical institutions, both public and private. One of the teachers very kindly offered to conduct me to one of these latter. It was under the direction of J. Pietersz, and kept in a part of the buildings of the University.

As we passed through a basement room of this edifice, I noticed several students seated around a table, upon which was a human corpse undergoing dissection. A sight which caused within me an involuntary sensation of horror, was completely an indifferent object to the jolly-faced disciples who were working away as if carving a turkey, cracking their jokes in the most easy good humor imaginable. Around another table were pupils engaged in sketching from patterns before them. Adjoining this room were several small apartments occupied as cabinets, filled with many curious and interesting objects. In one was an entire family charred by fire, and in a complete state of preservation. They were among the victims of a fire that took place in the city several hundred years ago. In another apartment were pointed out to me several heads of criminals executed by the guillotine but a few days since. The sensation produced by viewing them was such as I cannot describe. That instrument of death whose bare name calls up such dreadful and affecting associations of the old French Revolution, was still in use in Belgium for capital punishment. Indeed, a gentleman minutely narrated to me the circumstances of an execution inflicted by its irrevocable stroke — of which he was a personal witness — and the sensations it caused him. The victim is placed in an angular position in a perpendicular frame. At a signal, not seen, the massive, gleaming steel descends noiselessly in a grooved frame, separating the head from the trunk with as much facility as a keen knife would the small end of a smooth beet.

Mr. P. received me graciously, and conducted me through all the apartments of the school, allowing me time to examine personally, and ask questions. He wore slippers, and generally spoke to me in a whisper, especially in the school-rooms, appearing scrupulous about disturbing the teachers. The school comprises some four or five hundred pupils, and twenty teachers. There was considerable difference in the degree of stillness in the several rooms, — but the pupils throughout appeared studious and interested; while the mode of reciting showed the school to be of superior character. I was particularly struck with the extreme degree of stillness in one room containing perhaps eighty or a hundred pupils. The slight ticking of the time-piece was distinctly audible all over the room, while the teacher, moving noiselessly around in the softest slippers, spoke in a note little above a whisper. Still this part of the school did not strike me as superior to that in other rooms. Indeed I was bold enough to imagine it inferior There seemed to be an unnatural restraint which stiffened the mental ardor of the pupils. The beaming eye and flushed expression of enthusiasm appeared wanting. Mr. P. spoke of the school, as if it was regarded as one of the very best in the city; and there was in reality a tone of enterprise and spirit pervading it that, to the eye of a practical teacher, bespoke unusual excellence. Mr. P., the director, receives about six hundred dollars per annum, with room, lights, and fuel. His duties are those only of a superintendent, not being required to teach himself. He has thus left considerable spa·e time, which he has wisely appropriated in preparing text-books for the primary schools of the city. He had the goodness to present me with his series of readers, in which the lessons are graduated in a most admirable manner. Some of the other teachers are paid about four hundred dollars per annum. Their teacher in English, I was told, was from Boston, but I did not get the favor of an interview.

March 5th. Took a turn to view the Botanic Garden, near the Observatory, on the outer side of the city wall. It contains an extensive and beautiful collection of indigenous and exotic plants, and is allowed to be one of the finest public gardens in Europe.

The public journals were discussing the probabilities of a coalition by the powers of Europe, to put down republicanism in France. It was evident enough that no such thing could take place. Public opinion had made a long stride since the time of Napoleon the Great. Liberal sentiments had pretty thoroughly impregnated the masses. The treachery of the governments, in not fulfilling their engagements to the people, after getting their aid to crush Napoleon, was still fresh in the public ear. Then each government evidently had enough to do to manage the affairs of its own kingdom, and prevent the wave of freedom just issued from Paris, from rolling its demolishing waters over entire Europe. If work they must against the dangerous propagandism, it would be secretly, by diplomacy, and after the first wave had receded.

Lamartine, with almost superhuman energy, was endeavoring by the fiat of thought, to elevate and harmonize the French mind to the true idea of freedom; while, at the same time, he was instructing foreign governments as to the course France would pursue. To the latter, with the power of eloquence, he held out in one hand the sword, and in the other, the olive-branch of peace. His bulletins, messages, and ordinances, were issued with a prolificness almost incredible, and were spread immediately on the wings of intelligence all over Europe; while, at the same time, he was at brief intervals haranguing the French populace, until nature being exhausted, he was obliged to be held upon his feet, to give utterance to his peace-inspiring thoughts. Let the gratitude of the world be awarded Lamartine for his noble and powerful efforts for peace at this tremendous crisis.

March 12*th*. To-day was the last of six days of Carnival which was being celebrated in the city. These religious holidays passed off peaceably enough, although the authorities, in the revolutionary panic, had taken the utmost precaution to prevent disturbance. The term is derived from the Latin *carni vale*, farewell to meat. It occurs during the week before the commencement of Lent, and introduces the great fast of the church. It is celebrated in all Catholic countries, but more particularly at Rome and Venice. It is looked forward to with happy anticipations, and is accompanied with much merriment and revelry. On these occasions business is considerably suspended, theatres are in full glow, masquerade balls reign in profusion, and a withdrawal by common consent of the lines that divide society, takes place. Young men and girls in the most ludicrous costume, parade the streets and perpetrate jokes, and take innocent liberties with each other and with the bystanders, which would never be tolerated at other times. But custom is the law of society. On the last day they had a *course*, or as we should say, procession, in which the authorities and more dignified citizens joined. It was escorted by a band of musicians dressed supremely droll, and throwing off the most fantastic airs imaginable. The side-walks were lined with people; and parents everywhere took out their children, neatly dressed, to witness the amusing spectacle.

In the forenoon I looked into several churches. They were celebrating mass, and the ceremony was imposing and novel. The meetings were unusually thronged, generally of the middling classes. The personal beauty of the females did not strike me with admiration. I could not be mistaken in thinking them inferior in that respect to the same class in the United States. Almost every woman bore the appearance of physical distortion, arising, no doubt, from the undue bodily toil imposed upon the masses of females in Europe. It is very clear that a certain amount of physical exercise is favorable not only to health but to personal beauty; and it is quite as unequivocal that severe protracted labor dwarfs the body and mind, which is perpetuated in the offspring. Hence, one looks in vain among the lower classes in France, Germany, and Belgium, for that classic symmetry of features, and rounded, graceful form, so common among us. It is not pretended that there are not striking exceptions to the prevailing rule.

I sought in vain at the bookstores, for a copy of Lamartine's History of the Girondists. The work, sufficiently popular before, had actually entranced the public mind, since the elevation of the noble poet to the head of the French government. The furor for this, his latest writings, was so great, that the teeming presses in Paris and Brussels could in no way supply the eager appetite of the public. We in America are accused of extravagant hero-worship, but our enthusiasm in that particular, pales by the side of the intensity of European homage, when the public imagination there makes to itself an idol. Some are disposed to ridicule this trait as a weakness. They would eradicate it from society. They will succeed, doubtless, when all that is noble and beautiful dies out from the human heart. The truth is, we are all benificently constituted to worship goodness and loveliness. Each has his *beau-ideal*, which he instinctively adores. When a public character appears, invested with the traits of our ideal image, our heart flows out toward him by a law of our nature. It often happens, indeed, that our souls are cheated. The bright jewel of our heart's affections is but a base coin, falsely made to glitter before our soul's eye, by some master-lapidary. But who would venture, after all, to alter the arrangement, on the score of human happiness and human good? We surely get the blissful emotions of loving the beautiful, if but in imagination; and the strengthening of our affections, by exercise, for the disappointment of the deception. Who shall say that in this sordid age, when the artificial powers of society tend to debase the soul, and strangle all the purer and nobler affections, whether our Barnums are highway poachers, or benefactors to society.

Shopping is an agreeable business in Brussels, as in Paris. You are waited on by young ladies of personal beauty, easy and engaging manners, and dressed with elegant neatness. You find none of the coarse bantering so common with us, which renders shopping an irksome affair, making you feel that you cannot pass through it without losing something of your personal dignity and manliness. Our republican manners often appear very strange to them. I one day made a purchase of a small article; and as I was going from the shop directly to my hotel, I proposed taking it along with me, — when the young lady of whom I made the purchase, insisted that I should not. As I gently persisted in my determination, she referred the matter to her mother, in an apartment below, — whereupon Madame came tumbling up stairs into the shop, in considerable excitement, and warmly entered her protestations against so mean an act. To forestall the necessity of my doing so, she called a servant, and sent him to my side. Wishing to see how far a prejudice would carry an honest and kind-hearted woman, I firmly stated that my mind was made up, and made a movement to go. The good woman first throwing up her eyes and hands towards the ceiling, then dropping them on her dress in a pathos of despair and mortification, ejaculated, "Mon Dieu, Monsieur, a gentleman take his goods with him through the streets!"

The Belgians are hardly behind any people in the variety and excellence of their manufactures. The carpet manufactory of Messrs. Schumacher & Co. at Tournay, is said to be the most extensive and important in Europe. It produces all kinds of what are called Brussels carpets, from those which adorn the sumptuous palaces of kings, to such as are used for the floor of the cottage.

Constant employment is given to sixteen hundred workmen, who occupy from eighty to one hundred looms, and produce annually about one hundred and twenty thousand metres of carpeting,—seven-eighths of which is exported. Manufactures in other departments are highly prosperous, but the most noted is that of lace. The manufacture of this article, though not so prosperous as formerly, has yet nothing to fear from foreign competition. "Brussels lace," the thread of which is made of the finest flax of the country, is superior to every other description made in Belgium or in foreign countries,—and the demand for it is kept up in all parts of the world. Its peculiar qualities are, delicate fineness and a great elegance and variety of design. The patterns are all worked separate, and stitched on. The flax employed grows near Hal, and the best at Rebecque. The finest description costs from three to four thousand francs a pound, and is worth its weight in gold. The spinning is performed in darkened rooms, with a beam of light admitted only upon the work, through a small aperture. This expensive luxury may be seen ornamenting the dress of all classes of females. It is made a *sine qua non* of wardrobe; and those who cannot afford the genuine article, wear an imitation more or less perfect. I found no gloves even in Paris, equal to those in Brussels, for softness and elegance.

Belgium was inhabited before the Christian era, by numerous tribes of the German race, who lived by hunting, and by rudely cultivating the earth. They consisted of two classes, chiefs and slaves; and Druidism from Britain was universally predominant. In stature and bulk they surpassed the Romans, whom they fiercely encountered, and nearly destroyed Cesar's army of the best disciplined troops in the world. They subsequently amalgamated with the Romans,—and many of Cesar's victories, especially that of Pharsalia, were decided by the cavalry and light infantry of Belgium. In the third, fourth, and fifth centuries, the character of the Belgians was greatly changed by successive invasions of Salian Franks from the North. In the time of Charlemagne, A. D. 800, the physical state of the country had become much improved. At the end of the ninth century, the Normans commenced a series of piratical irruptions into Belgium, and continued to plunder and devastate the whole country during one hundred and fifty years. At the end of the eleventh century, the fanatical phrenzy of the crusades induced many of the nobles to part with lands, and to grant privileges and political powers, in order to obtain the means of equipping armies to fight the Saracens. The people, conscious of power, gradually extorted from the nobles, their rulers, so many concessions, that the provinces formed in reality, a democracy, and were only nominally subject to France and its nobles. When the rest of Europe was subject to despotism, and involved in comparative ignorance and barbarism, the court of the counts of Flanders was the chosen residence of liberty, civilization, and useful knowledge; and when the ships of other nations scarcely ventured beyond the sight of land, those of the Flemish merchants traversed the ocean; and Bruges and Antwerp possessed all the commerce and wealth of the north of Europe. Under the Burgundian dynasty, the commercial and manufacturing towns of the low countries enjoyed remarkable prosperity. The famous Order of the Golden Fleece was instituted in 1430. Bruges and Antwerp were the great marts of the commercial world, and contained each about two hundred thousand inhabitants. In the Flemish court of the Duke of Burgundy, named Phillip the Good, about 1455, luxurious living was carried to a foolish and vicious excess. The wealthy were clad in gorgeous velvets, satins, and jewelry, and their banquets were given with almost incredible splendor. Many instances of the immense wealth of its merchants are recorded; among others, it is said that when Charles V. once dined with one of the Chief Magistrates of Belgium, his host immediately after dinner threw into the fire a bond for two millions of ducats, which he had received as security for a loan to that monarch, saying that he was more than repaid by the honor of being permitted to entertain his sovereign. This luxury produced depravity and crime to such an extent, that in one year fourteen hundred murders were committed in Ghent, in the gambling houses and other resorts of debauchery. The arts were cultivated with great success. Most of the magnificent cathedrals and town-halls in the country were built in the thirteenth and fourteenth centuries. History, poetry, and learning, were much cultivated; and the University of Lovain was the most celebrated in Europe. In 1477, Belgium passed under the dynasty of the empire of Austria. In the reign of Charles V, the influence of the Burghers attained its highest point. The Scheldt at Antwerp often contained twenty-five hundred vessels, waiting their turn to come to the wharves; her gates were daily entered by five hundred loaded wagons; and her exchange was attended, twice a day, by five thousand merchants, who expended one hundred and thirty thousand golden crowns in a single banquet given to Phillip, the son of Charles V. The value of wool annually imported from England and Spain, exceeded four million pieces of gold. This amazing prosperity experienced a rapid and fatal decline under the malignant tyranny and bigotry of Phillip II, son of Charles V. He established in its most diabolical extravagance the inquisition, and persecuted the Protestants to the death. He is known to have boasted, that in less than six years he had put to death eighteen thousand men and women by the sword, the gibbet, the rack, and the flames. Commerce and trade in Belgium now dwindled away, many of he rich merchants were reduced to beg for bread, the great cities were half deserted, and forest-wolves often devoured the scattered inhabitants of desolated villages. In 1706 it changed from the Spanish dominion to the Austrian; and having been several times conquered by, and reconquered from, the French, it was incorporated in 1795, with the French republic, and divided into departments. In the centre of Belgium was fought the great battle of Waterloo, in 1815. In fact, so often has it been the scene on which the surrounding nations have settled their quarrels, that it has long been styled the cock-pit of Europe. By the Congress of Vienna, the provinces of Belgium were annexed to those of Holland, to form the kingdom of the Netherlands, which existed until the revolution in 1830, when Belgium became an independent nation.

The Belgians have been successively subjected to the influence of so many different governments — French, Austrian, Spanish, Dutch — that they consequently possess no distinctive and peculiar national character. The apathy and persevering industry of the Dutch is blended with the vivacity and self-assurance of the French. The most obvious peculiarity by which the Belgians are distinguished, is their devout observance of religious rites and ceremonies. In the rural districts, the clergy are regarded with fanatical veneration, and everywhere exercise, and endeavor to maintain, a powerful dominion over the great mass of the workmen and peasants. The churches are all open at five or six o'clock every morning, when every good Catholic attends to repeat his prayers before entering upon the business or pleasure of the day; and the afternoon and evening of every Sunday are enlivened by the entertainments of tavern-gardens, grounds for shooting with the cross-bow, ball-rooms, theatres, and other public places of amusement.

Music and dancing are very favorite amusements, especially with the middle and lower classes. On every fine summer evening, balls are given at the tavern-gardens, which are numerous in the outskirts of every large town. The price of admission varies from three or four sous to a franc. Music festivals are celebrated every year at Brussels, Ghent, and Antwerp, by amateur performers, who are emulated by enthusiastic ambition to win numerous prizes, which are awarded to the best performers. The musical skill exhibited on these occasions, is truly astonishing. Music, in fact, is so commonly and carefully learned, even by the laboring classes, that the harmony of the airs which are sung by groups of peasants while at work, is often delightful to the most cultivated musical ear.

CHAPTER XXIV.

DEPARTURE FROM BRUSSELS — CANAL BOATS — BEAUTIFUL APPEARANCE OF THE COUNTRY — BRUGES — CATHEDRAL OF NOTRE DAME — DIETETICS — GROUPS OF MUSICIANS — ARRIVAL OF A STEAMER — EMBARK FOR DOVER — DOVER HEIGHTS — CUSTOM HOUSE — SMUGGLING — DOVER CASTLE — LEAVE FOR LONDON.

March 13*th*. I was up early, preparing for my departure. The bill of Madame was moderate, and her kindness in various ways had won upon me. My regret, therefore, at bidding her farewell, was heightened by friendship's power. I could not but feel a sadness, too, at leaving a city so filled with ennobling objects of contemplation. If travelling is a sad pleasure, thus separating one's self, and perhaps forever, from a place endeared to the heart by glowing associations, is not the least sombre feature in the moving panorama. The raw air without, and the overcast sky, moreover, lent additional gloom. They seemed in sympathy with the rising emotions.

I had denied myself the interest of visiting the memorable battle ground of Waterloo, having seen the tragic spot in a tour through Belgium, several years before. Yet it was not so easy for me to forego visiting Antwerp, as I had planned to do, on leaving Paris, although I had already tarried there several weeks. The venerable city is too full of art, and too rich in historical associations, for one visit to satisfy. Still, inclination had to yield to circumstances, and I was soon speeding my way on the route to England, by the way of Ostend. On leaving the city, a fine view was soon presented of the magnificent Palace of Lackin, the country residence of his majesty, Leopold; while behind us stood out in clear relief, against a back-ground of impervious sky, the numerous spires and turrets of the miniature-Paris. The city thus appears huddled upon a rounded plateau of earth, slightly elevated, and presents an agreeable contrast to the verdure of the level country surrounding it.

All the cars of our train were well filled, — the result of low fares, doubtless. The motion was easy and equable, and we experienced few annoying delays. The railway lines in Belgium being under the direction of the government, greater precision is thus secured to them.

The third-class cars of our train were open at the sides, and provided with long, plain benches, for seats. These were completely thronged with coarsely-dressed, but orderly and healthful-looking people, some of them bearing along with them even implements of husbandry, or mechanical tools.

The flatness of the country in Belgium is favorable, of course, to the construction of canals; hence the country is considerably intersected by them, forming in the aggregate a distance equal to about two hundred miles. Such as we passed appeared wider and less crooked than I had been accustomed to see, and were, of course, nearly destitute of locks. As we passed along, I was struck with several peculiarities of the canal-boats. They were larger than ours, and were rigged to sail, when the wind would allow of it. For this purpose they were supplied, like a sloop, with a single mast, which, by means of a hinge, could be lowered back upon the deck, to enable the boat to pass under bridges. Whenever they came to a *reach*, that would not allow of sailing, the boatmen jumped out upon the bank, and with a tow-line tugged their ponderous craft along, till a turn in the canal enabled them to make use again of their sail. Yet I am not certain that this is the mode of canalling throughout Belgium. In proportion as we left Brussels in the distance, we lost hearing the pure French spoken,— the language in the villages through which we passed becoming either Flemish, a sort of mongrel dialect, or the flat, broad Dutch. Occasionally, however, the ear was fuddled with a mixture compounded of Dutch, Flemish, and a little German and French. The dress, too, of the common people, partook of the *melange*, while the more graceful manners of the French character engrafted upon the sturdy basis of the Dutch, was a subject of curious interest. The flatness of the country, extending like a continued prairie, enables the cities and villages to be seen at a great distance. They are picturesquely grouped upon some site slightly elevated, and appear to the eye of imagination, life-teeming oases amid a desert of habitations. Each village, however humble, has its church, upon the interior of which is lavished the riches of the district, and whose spire shoots up to a dizzy height. The interminable flatness of the surface, its lawn-like verdure, the unique form and variegated color of the edifices, the lofty needle spires of the churches, the somewhat bulky character of the people, with their fanciful costume, and irregular language, all render the picture such as is nowhere else to be met with, and one of refreshing interest to the cursory traveller.

Belgium is full of historical associations of vivid interest. There is not a village, however humble, but has hallowed recollections enough to fill a chapter by itself. It were, indeed, interesting to pause a moment and call up, from the dim shades of the past, heroic acts of a chivalrous age, — but this is a time of railroads and steam-boats, and we must *hasten* on our journey. Let my reader, however, tarry with me a little in Bruges, and take a brief glance at a few of the noted features of what was once one of the most considerable cities of Belgium. Its name is derived from the Flemish word Brügge, — which means bridges, — from the circumstance of its having fifty-four bridges across the numerous canals by which the streets are intersected. The city has a circumference of nearly four and a half miles, and is entered by six gates.

Bruges has six large squares; and many large, and noble ancient mansions and spacious public edifices present their pointed gables to the streets, and afford interesting specimens of the ornamental Gothic architecture of the middle ages. The spectacle of these edifices induces the contemplative mind to revert to the grandeur and opulence of the city in the days of chivalry, when its gorgeous halls and courts were scenes of regal pomp and pageantry, — and impress him with a feeling of sadness in contrasting its ancient prosperity with its present comparative desolation. Among the most remarkable edifices is the cathedral of Notre Dame, the tower of which is so lofty that, when the atmosphere is particularly clear, it is visible from the mouth of the Thames. The interior contains among other interesting objects, a marble statue of the Virgin and Child, attributed to Michael Angelo, and for which Horace Walpole, it is said, offered thirty thousand florins. In the great square is a lofty Gothic tower, or belfry, the most beautiful in Europe, and its chimes, or *carillons*, are esteemed the most complete and harmonious in the Netherlands. They are played upon every quarter of an hour. On particular days a paid professor of music performs. Watchmen are constantly posted at the top of this tower, to make alarm signals of fire by ringing a loud bell, and exhibiting in the day a flag, and in the night a lantern towards the point whither the engines are required to hasten.

which is further indicated by a speaking-trumpet. The Jerusalem Church is a *fac-simile* of the Holy Temple.

Bruges, in common with all towns of West Flanders, is destitute of spring-water, so that the inhabitants are obliged, as were their ancestors in the time of Pliny, to have recourse for supplies from the clouds. For this purpose, every house is provided with a cistern for collecting rain from its roof; and that which gathers in the ditches of the ramparts is conveyed, by means of hydraulic machinery, to public fountains, or tanks, whence it is distributed in pipes throughout the city.

Speaking of its former grandeur,— the records of luxurious banquets and apparel at that period are almost incredible. Not only the dresses of men and women, but the housings of their horses were of velvet, satin and gold, profusely spangled with brilliant jewels,— an extravagance which Charles V, in the following century, was obliged to suppress by enacting sumptuary laws. It is said when the queen of Phillip the Bel, of France, visited this city in 1300, she exclaimed with astonishment, "I see hundreds who have more the appearance of queens than myself."

A little incident on reaching Ostend, illustrates the efficiency of the Belgian police; and the same trait would hold, I am persuaded, in nearly all European countries. My hotel being within a few rods of the depôt, I did not take a carriage, but was walking leisurely forward with valise in hand, when a man approached and clamorously solicited to bear my baggage. I mildly thanked him for his offers, but observed that his services were not desired. Mistaking my easy manner for amiable weakness, doubtless, he laid hold of my valise, at the same time walking along with me, and all the while insisting that I should let go. A police officer observing him, stepped up, collared my new acquaintance, and, in spite of his remonstrances and petitions. hurried him off to the watch-house. The traveller in Europe is struck with a comfortable feeling of security in noticing all around the external evidences of order and quietness, and the deference and respect shown strangers, even by the officers of government; and did he not take a mental glance behind the curtain, and see the immense cost by which this security is kept up, and reflect upon the influence of arbitrary government upon the national mind, he would be half in danger of becoming enamored of Royal Institutions. And when a foreigner, long accustomed to this strictly-ruled state of things, comes to our shores, and is exposed to the recklessness of abused freedom, it is no wonder that he cries out at first against free institutions, and declares a Republican Government a weak thing, and insufficient to protect the dear interests of society.

I spent the evening agreeably in a very respectable éstaminet, observing the manners of the citizens. It was liberally patronized, and the guests, who had the appearance of regular customers, remained in general till a late hour. In dress and manners they were of the well-to-do class, advanced in years, and pursy. They hastened off the time in quiet conversation, smoking pipes, and drinking ale or strong beer; and the quantity of this beverage each disposed of, perfectly amazed me, — so great, that I dare not say, for fear of not being credited. I could not have believed, without the evidence of my own eyes, that even their bulky trunks could have taken up, and held in solution — allowing them thoroughly of the nature of sponge — such vast quantities of the turpid liquid. But the landlady informed me the next morning, when I wonderingly recounted to her the number of glasses I had observed a single person to drink, that she could relate to me even larger stories of the same kind. Well, in the face of such facts, what, thought I, becomes of dietetic theories! The Frenchman, for instance, lives in a great measure upon highly concentrated coffee: the Hollander daily soaks his bulky person in ale; the Englishman gorges his capacious stomach with roast beef; while other races live principally upon vegetables and fruit; and yet all these varieties of people span about the same length of life. Habits so different seem to effect little more than differences of personal appearance and temperament; but they show, at least, the wonderful power of adaptation belonging to the human system! We were regaled several times during the evening, with the musical efforts of humble troops of artists, who, after having executed a few popular airs, sent around the reception-board among the guests for sous. At one time it was a little brother and sister who constituted the band; at another, a family group, including the father and mother; then again, it was a more imposing array of talent, in the form of a chosen number of artists. But they were always civil, modest, and respectful. Further, their soft and stilly manners, as they glided noiselessly into the room, unostentatiously struck up their sweet airs, just at the time to cause no interruption to any one, and then quietly retired, betokened the influence of their musical strains upon their own character. It was the intuitive politeness which music ever forms in the human soul. Their humble performances formed for me an agreeable variety to the evening's occupation; and had I not been on the latter end of my route, should doubtless have given them quite liberally. To be frank, I must confess to a more than common sympathy with these strolling empirics. So grovelling are made the pursuits of life, that I have ever felt thankful at heart to whomsoever was drawing up even but drops from the ocean fountain of concealed delight, to gladden the weary spirit. If idlers we must have, let them be of no worse occupation. It must be something of a poetic soul to find congeniality in the calling. And I must say that I have listened to strains from some of these unpretending performers, which to my untutored ear, were touching and delicious. This, too, is the medium through which some of the brightest genius has found its way to the soul of the world, and gained the enviable fortune of thrilling it with emotions of intense pleasure.

March 14*th*. I had time in the morning for a stroll about the town. It has a quaint and dilapidated air. Few travellers speak of it in terms of praise, still it is regularly and neatly built, and presents a lively appearance, the houses being painted of different colors. An interesting feature is the strong fortifications, consisting of redoubtable ramparts, a broad ditch, and a citadel. Indeed these time-grizzly champions possess an historical interest. During the ever-memorable struggle of the Dutch to emancipate themselves from the blind and brutal despotism of Old Spain, this little town sustained one of the most celebrated sieges of which history has preserved any account. It continued from the fourth of July, 1601, to the twenty-eighth of September, 1604, when the garrison capitulated on honorable terms, to the ablest of the Spanish leaders, the famous Marquis of Spinola. This siege is supposed to have cost the contending parties the lives of nearly one hundred thousand men. Situated directly upon the North Sea, it is a favorite watering-place of the Belgians, and is sometimes resorted to by the royal family. This, with the passengers daily passing through here on the new line, gives to the place an animating air.

At 10 A. M., I was standing upon the breakwater, watching the approach from the offing of a steamer from Dover. She presently glided in between the piers, a thing of life indeed. The English passengers on board, encumbered as usual with luggage, made strong requisitions upon the conveyance-resources of the place. Beasts of burden, vehicles of every description, even shoulders of

men and women, piled high, presented a moving chattel-house
The ladies of the company struck me pleasingly. Their elegant
figure, rich and flowing dress, and dignified manner, placed them
in happy contrast with the Belgian women. Then my native
language in their mouth, so long almost a stranger to my ear! It
came like sweetest music to my soul. The very tones awoke emotions impossible to describe.

At 11 A. M., 1 was standing upon the deck of another of these
graceful little steamers, darting out from the capacious harbor,
upon the angry bosom of the stormy North Sea. The glorious
Old Continent, big with the riches of human culture and experience, was receding in the mellowing distance. The last page had
been turned, and the book closed, of another volume of life. But
how precious its gleaming! What a treasure of delight will it
not furnish of future reminiscences.

On we sped at the rate of twelve or fourteen miles an hour.
Our steamer, a fair sample of those on the line, was small, but of
elegant model. The passages across the bleak Strait are often
necessarily stormy, but not a single accident had yet happened to
the line, — owing, in part, to the extreme precaution of the conductors of the boats. These are well manned, and officered by a
naval gentleman; and in all the arrangements, nothing is left to
chance. There were some fifteen of us in number on board, a
mere handful compared with the thronging crowds pluming the
decks of the gay floating palaces on our Western waters. About
two-thirds of this number occupied the stern cabin, — a neat, cozy
apartment, snugly under deck; while the remainder waived the
honor of being in the best style, from the claims of economy, and
made their quarters in the forecastle. Presently a brisk breeze
sprang up from the south-west, raising up a short sea, and cresting
their breezy ridges. The sky remained clear, but blue, and the

air raw and piercing. These features of the scene, — the severe aspect of the heavens, the chilly touch of the air, and the shivering look of the wet expanse, were enough to make me remember the old North Sea with icy feelings. Our modest little boat, however, held on steadily her way, nodding over the yeasty seas with duck-like security. Several of our passengers in due time commenced casting their reckoning with old Neptune, who seemed inexorable in his exactions. Such of us as had better *sea-legs*, well wrapped in clothing, paced as best we could the deck, and, perchance, strove to draw each other out in conversation. Several of the passengers were English, but they were able to converse in French with fluency; and one of them informed me that the educated classes in England all learn that language as a common and useful branch of education. We had on board one of the Dover pilots, on his return from having taken a foreign ship through the Straits to Hamburg. This business employs a considerable class. American ships, also, in passing through the treacherous sea, not unfrequently take pilots. The navigation of the sea is justly regarded as dangerous, there being numerous undisclosed sand-bars, not indicated by beacons. Of these merciless strands, justly enough dreaded by mariners, the Goodwin Sands are the most noted. Our pilot passenger was a genial, entertaining old fellow. He possessed a ready fund of general information, and was by no means unwilling to give us a peep into his amply garnered storehouse. He was indeed none of your oyster-class of travellers. In his ambulations, the government of his own country, her institutions and society, came in for a place in his discursive survey. He acknowledged, truthfully enough, that the British Executive was an adroit power. It managed the vast empire with consummate success, ever keeping its unwearied eye intent on the main chance. National greatness was its triumphant goal, and univer sal dominion the potent spell of its genius. It had little deep, genuine sympathy with the toiling, panting masses; but its thorough feeling of self-respect, its national pride, its glowing desire of progress, forced it to a decent regard for the urgent rights of the laboring poor. As for the vigilant claims of the middling classes, this lynx-eyed government had full employment for its astute powers; but it managed, nevertheless, to keep the advancing, exacting element within control: now yielding, and again pushing forward, ever seizing an opportunity, just like some skilful champion in complete contest with a powerful antagonist. Our talkative companion let out upon the sins of the English Government with a freedom of speech that would hardly have been pardonable in the citizen of a Republic. Still, the sincere-souled old tar carried below a loyal heart,—what Englishman does not? According to him, England was, of course, infinitely the greatest country in the world; her institutions the most perfect, and her people the guiding stars in the heavens of intellectual and moral splendor.

The low, flat, French coast had scarcely merged from view below the horizon, when the bold cliffs of Dover greeted our vision. The distance across from Ostend to Dover is sixty miles, but from Dover to the nearest point on the French coast, it is no more than twenty-one miles. Truly but a narrow space separates these two powerful, enlightened nations; yet in feeling, manner, and taste, they inhabit different shores of an impassible gulf. At first view, it would seem easy for a well-appointed French expedition to seize a favorable opportunity, cross the narrow strait, make a sudden and unexpected descent upon the island, and make a conquest of it. We know that the Normans did this in an earlier age. We are told that a similar project occupied, for a long time, the gigantic intellect of Napoleon. That the English, even to this day, have apprehensions on that score, there can be no doubt. As a fact in evidence of this, let me adduce, that in the Fall of 1847, a letter written by the late Duke of Wellington to a friend, in which he candidly expresses the opinion, that the uncommon activity which happened then to be going on in the French naval yards, had, for spring of movement, a contemplated invasion of England. This letter somehow found its way into the public prints, and its contents created a sensation in England, such as had not been witnessed for many a year. To have seen the stir it made, one might have supposed that every Englishman fancied a French rapier about to be thrust into his coporeal man. One dignified London editor declared, that " no doubt there was not a Frenchman in the kingdom that would not hail, with a yell of savage delight, the opportunity to gloat his incarnate enmity in the effusion of English blood."

As we neared the English coast, the wind moderated, the sea became smooth, and a thin smoky haze hung over the verge of the land, just to place it in fine relief. The soil on this part of the coast is of chalky formation; the land is high, and the coast abrupt, giving a bold and picturesque view to the whole. A little to the north of the town, on the most elevated part, frowns the renowned castle of Dover. The entire scene was fine on entering the harbor. The placid and lovely bosom of the sea, the quiet and arrowy movement of our boat cutting the blue surface, the unique and imposing view of the land before us, the old castle up above us at the right, the thronging of citizens on the quay to greet our arrival, the thrilling historical associations of the place, all greatly heightened in my own bosom by the spell-bound tie of home, with which the soil of England is linked, gave elevation and lustre to the emotions of the moment. The harbor, which is within the town, is quite unworthy the ancient reputation of the port. It is small, and the entrance to it being narrow, between two piers, great caution is required in entering in rough weather. It is only a tide harbor, and a few years ago the bar at its entrance had accumulated so much, that it was feared that it would be entirely choked up; but great improvements have since been effected. I was not favorably impressed with the dexterity of our captain in getting our boat into the harbor. He made clumsy work of it, though the boat was small, entirely manageable, the water smooth, and all other apparent circumstances favorable. The awkward delay was the more noticeable, as in the grave and explicit announcements of the company the captain was set forth as a first-class naval officer, of high nautical education and experience. I thought any of our *green* yankee captains would have done infinitely better. On arrival, the luggage of all the passengers was immediately taken charge of by commissioners appointed by the government, and conveyed by them to the custom house depôt, there to undergo a search. The inspection over, the luggage is conveyed by the same authorities to any place in port you may designate. For this interfering care you are required to pay quite freely. For three small pieces I was taxed thirty-seven and a half cents. If anything contraband is discovered, it is forthwith confiscated, part to the government, and part to the officers who make the discovery, and the owner thereof is heavily fined or imprisoned. One of our party was so unlucky as to fall into the *limboes* of these hawk-eyed limbs of the law. He was a German, from Frankfort. His dress, manner, and intelligence bespoke him a gentleman. No ordinary observer could have thought him capable of so mean a thing, as an attempt at smuggling; but the trained vision of the officers of the government knows where to look for the rogues. While the rest of us were allowed to pass freely ashore, our German companion was at once singled out as a suspicious person. He was superbly dressed, wearing over several other garments a rich cloak, deeply trimmed with velvet and fir. As he stepped on the quay, an officer walked up to him, and found under either arm, hidden by his cloak, several thousand of the nicest cigars. On opening his trunks at the custom-house, they found more of the same precious article. The unfortunate man could say nothing for himself, and looked chop-fallen to the last degree. We called him a foolish fellow, and were disposed to show him pity. But the officers took a different view of the case. They explained his bold, and apparently unconscious manner, as a shrewd trick of the experienced smuggler. His penalty was a heavy one; but the officers, with a praiseworthy good-will, succeeded in making it comparatively light. Let me say, in justice to these gentlemen, that they appeared to take no pleasure in discovering contraband articles, nor to enforce the law in its rigor, when in their power to do so. They certainly appeared different from the character often ascribed to the class of custom-house officers. In alluding jocosely to the possibility of finding something among my own baggage of a contraband nature, one of them by my side promptly answered, "We do not expect to. We never detect the American traveller in such low tricks. They are entirely too honorable and noble minded for that."

I felt grateful for the compliment; especially, as I had no doubt of his sincerity. He told me that such attempts at smuggling were by no means rare, and the actual amount of confiscated goods in the course of the year was not inconsiderable,—and this, too, in the face of the law in all its rigor. Persons were often detected of whom better things would be expected; and more strange still, as the advantage in prospect bore no proportion to the risk. They were disposed to be accommodating to such as had with them only purchased-articles of wardrobe in reasonable quantities for themselves, and even for friends,—such as gloves, silk dresses, velvet mantillas, etc. Dover is a likely place to meet with petty smuggling, by travellers, being one of the principal places of first-landing from the Continent. Brussels lace is the more frequent article that seeks to secrete its way, and this, because of its expensiveness and the ease with which it can be hidden from view.

A stranger is required to call at the Alien Office, and take a *certificate of arrival,* for which the charge is nothing. In the delay of removing my luggage, I stepped into a small hotel for a lunch. Here I felt again, most delightfully, the idea of *home,* to which I had been a stranger for several months. The room I ate in was a kind of a carpeted parlor, with a glowing coal-fire in the hearth, and every thing about the apartment gleaming with neatness, not excepting the youthful landlady, the brightest of all — neat, rosy, and gladsome, — a most enviable looking wife, as well as dame. And here let me say, I was struck with the superior good looks of the ladies whom I accidentally passed in the streets of Dover.

On account of our protracted passage across the strait, we were too late for the express-train, which traverses the distance of eighty-six miles in two hours. This I sorely regretted, but it afforded me time to look around upon the famous Dover Castle. It is on an eminence bounding the south-east side of the valley, and comprises an immense collection of ancient and modern works, occupying an area of about thirty acres. It is approached by a bold ascent, but is itself commanded by the higher ground on the west and south-west. There are remains of ramparts, and of a temple, bath, and Pharos, supposed to be of Roman construction. Previously to the last French war, the works were much dilapidated, but they were then repaired and greatly augmented. There are upper and lower courts, surrounded (except towards the sea), by curtains and large, dry ditches. In the centre of the former is a spacious keep, built by Henry III, and now forming a bomb-proof magazine. The curtain of the lower court is flanked, at irregular intervals, by ten towers of various construction; the oldest, built by Earl Goodwin; the others, built at different times during the Norman dynasty; with these, subterraneous passages communicate from the ditch. There are, also, four or five ancient wells, excavated to the depth of three hundred and seventy feet. The modern works consist of batteries, with heavy artillery casements, covered ways, a large vault, etc., — excavated in the chalk, — barracks, etc., capable of lodging two thousand troops. The late Duke of Wellington was Constable of the Castle.

Dover comprises what is termed the "old," and "new town." The latter is built chiefly for the reception of strangers, large numbers of whom throng the place during the bathing season. It has a neat and interesting appearance. The old part of the town, on the contrary, is irregular, and the streets narrow and ill-kept; but the whole is obviously improving, and building-lots are said to be in great request. You are besieged here as elsewhere, all over the world, by porters and idlers, for the favor of relieving you of luggage. The town is made the residence of several wealthy gentlemen.

At a quarter past six in the afternoon, we left for London in the slow train, which takes four hours to make the passage. In a moment after leaving, we entered the long tunnel which leads under the bold bluff upon the verge of the coast, termed Shakspeare's Cliff. We then glided, for some time, along upon the very brink of the precipitous coast. The quiet North Channel was away down below us, and vessels on its tranquil bosom appeared as the tiny crafts which the boy is wont to sport with in the narrow streams of his home. Our company was of very respectable appearance, but sedate in their manners, — very unlike a French assembly. I was nearly deprived of the pleasing views of English rural scenery, from the lateness of our passage; but we passed, before being quite enveloped in the gray folds of evening, several charming villas, delightfully embowered in trees and shrubbery. We were at length set down in London, at half-past ten in the evening, near the south-end of London Bridge. I was directed to a kind of restaurant, where; besides meals at all hours, they furnished transient people lodgings. Here I was conducted to a neat and comfortable parlor, in the second-story, in which I met an elderly lady, well-dressed, and of highly intelligent bearing. Immediately, and without reserve, she entered into free and intelligent conversation with me; and when she learned that I was in Paris in the first of the revolution, and was personally a witness of some of its most thrilling scenes, her curiosity and interest were almost without bounds. The most trivial detail of the grand event was seized upon by her ardent nature as if it were of real importance. We conversed till a late hour upon various subjects yet, I could not learn, without subjecting myself to the imputation of rudeness, anything of her personal history, — not even of what country she was; — but by this trait alone, I should have *guessed* her to be English.

CHAPTER XXV.

LONDON — BEGGARS — TOWER OF LONDON — DUNGEON — CROWN-JEWELS — ST. PAUL'S — SIR CHRISTOPHER WREN — THE THAMES TUNNEL — RIVER STEAMERS — TRAFALGAR SQUARE — NELSON MONUMENT — BRITISH MUSEUM — WEST-END — BUCKINGHAM PALACE — WESTMINSTER ABBEY — PARKS.

March 15*th.* Really in London — the big, beating heart of the British empire, and the emporium of the civilized world! I took an early morning stroll for first impressions. The first idea with which I was forcibly struck, was the solid, massive character which pervaded every thing. The huge bridges across the Thames, the lofty public and private edifices, — even the vehicles which traverse the streets, have an air of strength and durability entirely national.

Almost the first person I met in London was a beggar. I had but just taken the last step in crossing London Bridge, when I was almost struck aghast at the appearance before me of a human form, emaciated to the last degree, and his whole frame trembling as if unable to stand erect. He seemed the dire vestige of life! He held up with his hand a thin piece of board upon which was written, in chalk letters, "*I am starving for want of bread!*" A gentleman before me handed him, in passing, a penny, which the *starving man* slipped into his pocket with an adroitness, that struck me as not natural. I handed him another, which was disposed of in a similar manner. I now began to comprehend that he must be one of the numerous professional beggars with which the city is sorely infested. And he was certainly a most consummate counterfeit.

Beggary is a marked feature in London scenery. Its sickening sight is everywhere before the eye of the stranger, and some of its details are so revolting, as to curdle the life-blood of one's nature. Mere skeletons of human beings may be seen, with barely enough clothing to hide their shrivelled forms, and that so tattered and filthy as to outrage common decency; some maimed, others deformed, or disfigured, sitting upon the cold pavement, reclining upon the steps of doors, and even crawling upon the pavement, uttering moans, and beseeching you to give something for their famishing nature; — women without shoes, or covering for the head, and with rags, for the rest of the body, barely enough for decency, — with half-naked children in their arms, out in the muddy streets, or lying in some corner with the rain pattering upon their emaciated faces.

Such is a meagre outline of a picture that is ever before the stranger, at every turn, and at all times of the day and night, in the opulent and benevolent city of London! The features of the picture receive a more appalling hue, when contrasted with the comfortable luxuriousness and splendor pervading the West End of the city, — the residence of the aristocracy. In view of the contrast, the mind is staggered in contemplating the marvellous inequalities of human condition, and one is almost led to murmur at the Divine economy which permits, that while one mortal can roll in luxury, with an utter inability to spend his princely income, another human being of the same great family of man, must live and suffer, dragging slowly out a miserable existence, deprived of the small means necessary even to protect his body from the pinching of hunger and the piercing of cold.

The most obdurate heart is at first melted with pity, in witnessing such scenes. The sympathies of his whole nature are aroused; and he gives for the first few days freely. He soon, however, comes to bethink himself, and will reason something in this wise: "Suppose I continue to give even in the smallest sums, and only to such as appear the most urgent cases, I should soon empty my own purse, — and had I the wealth of Crœsus, it would hardly suffice. And then, should I be certain of giving with prudence? Are not those appearing the more needy cases, often mere counterfeits, while the real cases of distress are hidden from view?" After appeasing the clamorings of his conscience by such reasonings, he resolves to give no more, — and ever afterwards holds tight his purse-strings, unless indeed some dreadful case thrills every fibre of his sympathetic being, and renders it quite impossible to hold back.

It cannot be denied that beggary is a broad, festering sore on the great London body, unsightly to the eye, and poisonous to its vitality. Of the actual amount of beggary, I am not in possession of accurate statistics, but it must be very great. It is distinguished into *pauperism* and *mendicity;* the former comprising the truly needy, and the latter, such as pursue it as a regular trade, or professional beggars. These latter comprise by far the more numerous class, and English authorities give it as nine to one, — that is, out of every ten beggars, nine are mendicants, or professional beggars, that pursue the calling as a regular branch of business. I am inclined to think, however, that the statement is exaggerated, unless it be meant to include only the street beggars; for many of the real cases of indigence are hidden from view. The mendicants pursue their way of life with notorious audacity. They have a saying among them, that "it is a hard street that will not yield one penny, and he is a lazy beggar who will not traverse sixty streets a day." This would make some one hundred and fifteen cents per day.

The Mendicant Society have labored usefully in exposing the impositions of mendicants; but neither their agents nor the new police have been able to suppress them. This class are gross impostors, and convicted vagrants; and of these, the very worst are the blind and cripples. Their profligacy, and the inveteracy of their idle and dishonest habits, almost constitute them so many criminals. The metropolitan police, in 1837, apprehended four thousand three hundred mendicants. The private lodgings of this class are crowded, unwholesome, and literally sinks of iniquity.

Still, admitting that much of the beggary seen in London is mendicity, there is yet enough of real suffering. Cases come to light now and then, appalling enough to make the very heart bleed with commiseration. A lady informed me, that a woman of her acquaintance, who had lost her husband some time before, found herself without means of support, and reduced to the extremity of sewing, to support herself and family. Her health, never strong, was now every day becoming more fragile in consequence of undue application. She had been forced to part with every article of furniture, and had even disposed of her bible and wedding ring, and was then wasting toward an untimely grave. The Poor House was indeed before her, and so was the grave; and she preferred the latter to the former. Reared as the daughter of a wealthy gentleman, her pride rebelled at such humbling, and her whole nature shrunk at the idea of the degradations of the Poor House.

Another dreadful case, sickening even to the contemplation, is before my mind. The two only children of a cobler died in his house. Too poor himself to incur the expense of their decent sepulture, he applied to the proper authorities for aid from the city. This was denied him on the ground of his possessing articles of personal property of more value than to entitle him to relief from the government. The few articles of last necessity actually in his possession, being of a nature not transferable for cash, he applied for permission to bury the decomposing bodies in the narrow garden adjoining his shop. But this, of course, was denied him. The offensive corpses remained in this condition in his room, until some gentleman accidentally passing, was so struck by the disagreeable stench, as to be led to enter, to learn whence it proceeded. His astonishment may be imagined, on finding two bodies in the most loathsome condition, and the little room filled with virulent miasma. To his demand why they had not been interred, the half-deranged father replied, "My good sir, I would have rejoiced to bury them in a hole like dogs, had I been permitted to do so." It is needless to add, that the case was then promptly cared for. I learned this from persons who were eye-witnesses of the scene. It was also published in one of the London journals, the *Times*, I think. This is doubtless an extreme case; but it will not be denied, there are enough others coming to light every day, which, if not so strange as this, are yet dreadful to think of. Indeed, I was assured by English gentlemen themselves, of high respectability, that no human tongue could adequately describe the heart-appalling miseries of the poor of London.

Much of this misery may doubtless be attributed more to demoralization than mere misfortune. Still, there must ever be much of the latter. Where condition of life is so strictly ruled, and struggle for pecuniary means so intense as in London, there is left the merest chance to regain a lost foothold upon the ladder of panting existence. Where society is so pressed into time-worn ruts, the vicissitudes of life fall with fatal effect. Nor is there any relief from dire extremity by flying into the country. There, every foot of land is appropriated, with no opportunity for a second occupant. No alternative is left, then, to the unfortunate, but to pine away in dejection, or to emigrate to the New World; but the greater part have not even the means for this.

It is easier to depict the mammoth evil, than to devise a remedy for its relief. To this end, wise heads and benevolent hearts have already made fruitless efforts. Individual benevolence has copiously shed its sweet pearl-drops to assuage the misery. Combined benevolence, in the form of societies, has poured in its refreshing showers to abate the evil, but all these have been swallowed up in the monstrous vortex, like the merest heaven-drops by the choking earth, leaving hardly a momentary impress. The powerful and skilful arm of the government, too, has deployed its energies, but without success, — and the evil continues to go on with appalling strides.

In the afternoon, made a visit to the famous London Tower, strongly associated in my mind with many a sad memento in the dark annals of English history. We awaited a half hour in the office where we purchased our tickets for thirty-seven and a half cents. When our number had sufficiently increased to make it an object for the attendant to show us the place, we were led on by him, and conducted through the different parts of the grim edifice, in a precise and hurried manner. He made explanations of the different objects in our way, but so rapidly as to prove nearly unintelligible. Thus to run through a place filled with so many and deep historical recollections, is the most unsatisfactory possible. The mind loves to linger around the storied spot, to contemplate leisurely the existing memorials of tragical events, and yield to the gentle melancholy which the scene awakens. The rooms of historical armory were an interesting feature. Here were ranged in convenient order, the armors worn by warriors of different grades, from the earliest period, up to the time when the use of gunpowder rendered these unwieldly coverings a useless appendage. The mails of the most renowned military characters were pointed out; and some of these were huge and heavy beyond belief. Their weight alone must have required great physical power to have borne them up; and we were told, that often these armor-clad chieftains, when thrown from their horses, were either crushed by the weight of their mail, or unable to rise under its enormous weight. We were shown, too, the weapons corresponding to the mails, from the huge battle-axe, the iron-toothed club, for merciless blows upon the head, the blunt-pointed spear for unhorsing, to the more modern broad-sword. Terrible must have been the concussion of two bold and athletic chieftains thus clad and armed, upon strong and impetuous war-horses!

We passed into a room used formerly for the prison. Here several royal personages, highest nobles, and most distinguished commoners of England awaited in terrible silence their fate, either by the hands of the executioner, or by the dagger and bowl of the assassin. We were shown here the identical block upon which Lady Jane Gray was beheaded, and the axe that separated from the body her youthful head, and sent her sweet and noble spirit direct to heaven. Neither the axe nor block is curious enough for a dissertation. The former is in the shape of a carpenter's broad-axe, only smaller; the latter, little more than a billet of wood, on end, perhaps two feet in height, of narrow form, and opposite edges scolloped to receive the shoulders of the victim. We were shown the cell adjoining this room, where was immersed for thirteen years the illustrious Sir Walter Raleigh. Here the heroic prisoner devoted himself to literary pursuits, and composed several works, among them his famous History of the World. The walls of the dungeon, we were told, are sixteen feet thick, of well-joined and cemented pieces of stone.

In the Jewel Office we had a glimpse of the Crown-Jewels. They are nicely enclosed in an immense glass case, and comprise the crown of Her Majesty Victoria, that of the Prince of Wales, one or two other crowns, the baptismal vessels of the royal family, and three swords, one of Truth, of Justice, of Mercy. The point of the latter was blunt, emblematic of "the quality of mercy which is not strained." The crown of Her Majesty had been recently remodeled, and received additional jewels taken from the other crowns. It was certainly a most "glittering bauble," and expensive enough, one would think, for the vanity of any lady. The baptismal vessels were of gold, elaborate and rich, of course. The value of the whole is estimated to be about fifteen millions of dollars. On turning away, I ventured to remark in a soliloquizing mood, How much good might not that sum do in relieving the miseries of poor, starving Ireland; whereupon, my stalwort guide bridled up to me, and in a tone swelling with wounded pride, ejaculated, "Yes, and we have spent double that sum on the miserable people within a few years."

This rude fortress is situated on the river-bank, in the east part of the city, about a quarter of a mile below London Bridge. It was begun by William the Conqueror, in 1098, and additions were made by Henry III, by Edward IV, and by Charles X. The tower was a royal palace during more than five centuries. It was long ago, and still is in fact, a state-prison. It anciently contained several detached masses of buildings, most of which have now disappeared. It is surrounded by a moat, filled with water from the Thames, and the outer bank has recently been turned into pleasure grounds.

March 16*th*. To-day made a visit to St. Paul's—the cathedral church of London, and not only the great architectural glory of the metropolis, but of the empire. The noble structure stands in an elevated situation at the top of Ludgate Hill, and towers above the other buildings, by which it is surrounded, like some giant-oak amid a grove of sapplings. In regard to the general effect of its exterior, I have little to say. It is undoubtedly fine, because good judges say so; but I must confess that I was not impressed in a high degree with its beauty. After contemplating the Louvre, the Pantheon, and the Madeline, I had little admiration left for the exterior of St. Paul's. But the interior is chaste and imposing. Still, owing to a want of ornament, it has a naked and austere appearance. Lately it has been attempted to obviate this defect by placing within the cathedral monuments, erected at the public expense, to eminent individuals, — among whom may be specified Lord Nelson, Abercrombie, Dr. Johnson, Sir William Jones, Howard the philanthropist, etc. I was forcibly struck with the expressive character beaming from the bust of the latter. But these, it must be said, do but little credit to the builder. They appear like "pigmies in vales." But there is one feature of St. Paul's that cannot but ever fill the beholder with wonder and delight. I refer to its noble dome. As you gaze from the pavement of the church up into its immense concavity, you are struck with admiration. The enormous vault seems actually poised in the air, and you are taken up in imagination beyond the confines of earth to a region of ethereal grandeur and beauty.

While walking about on the floor of the church, I encountered a couple of very youthful looking gentlemen. By their light features and restless air, I at once recognized them as Americans. Accosting them, I learned that they were true-blooded Connecticut Yankees, who were driving briskly their queer trade in the line of *Baby Jumpers*, — then a new invention in its way. Yankee like, they had succeeded in the short space of time they had been in London in bringing their hobby before the public. They were selling, they informed me, quite rapidly, had got a handsome notice of it in a learned work just issued, from the pen of one of the eminent physicians under the royal patronage, and had even been to put one up at Buckingham Palace. They were sanguine of realizing a handsome sum in a short time.

We proposed immediately making the ascent to the summit in company; and reached the whispering-gallery by an inside stairway. Here, by some principle of acoustics, a whisper, made with the lips upon the wall, is heard the entire diameter of the cupola, by placing the ear against the opposite wall. We then went into the library, where, among other interesting objects, were shown us a book in manuscript, more than a thousand years old. It was attached to a chain, which in olden times was necessary to protect property so rare and valuable. By a more difficult ascent we reached the golden gallery, which crowns the apex of the dome, at the base of the lantern. Before reaching this point we were stopped by a portly keeper, who demanded sixpence as a condition of passing him. "But we have already paid," said one of my companions, "for seeing the entire edifice." "Not for this," was the reply. "We were told so." "Can't help it." "Wont you let us pass?" "No!" "Well," said my acquaintance, "I really believe that *old daddy Bull* would dig up and exhibit the very bones of his grandfather for a shilling!"

This, as might be supposed, inflamed the ire of our guard not a little, and he retorted "But you have to pay for everything you see in Paris." "You can't make us believe that," was the reply, "for we have just come from there, and know better."

We were highly favored by the unrivalled view from the gallery. Owing to the usual density of the smoke, this splendid view is rarely seen in perfection; but by great good fortune, the steady storm which had been raging, suddenly cleared away and revealed to our delighted gaze one of the most comprehensive and picturesque views that I remember ever to have seen. The entire metropolis, vast as it is, appeared to spread out at our feet. The broad and silvery line of the river, crossed by numerous bridges, and bearing on its bosom numbers of graceful steamers, and vessels of every kind, gave infinite variety and grandeur to the scene. At this height the carriages, horses and men, in the streets below, appear so diminutive as, not inaptly, to suggest the idea of a swarm of emmets.

The edifice is built in the form of a Latin cross, and is five hundred and ten feet in length, and one hundred and ten feet in breadth. The immense dome is surmounted by a lantern, ball and cross, — the latter being elevated three hundred and sixty-two feet above the level of the floor, and three hundred and seventy-six feet above the pavement of the church yard. The two turrets, or belfries, in the west front, are each two hundred and twenty-two feet in height. The walls are decorated by two stories of coupled pilasters, arranged at regular distances, — those below being of Corinthian order, and those above of the Composite. The whole building is of Portland stone; and its massiveness and solidity warrant the inference that it will be as lasting as magnificent. It is said that St. Paul's is a close imitation of St. Peter's at Rome; but it has been truly answered, that it is an imitation that bears the impress of transcendent genius, and may be said to be to St. Peter's what the Æneid is to the Iliad and Odyssey. There are striking points of difference; and in vastness of dimensions, St. Peter's as far exceeds St. Paul's, as the latter does the common English churches. St. Paul's was completed in thirty-five years after laying the first stone, by one architect, under one bishop of London, costing only about three millions seven hundred thousand dollars, which was raised by a small impost on coal brought to London; while St. Peter's, the work of twelve architects, took one hundred and forty-five years to build, during the pontificate of nineteen popes.

This noble edifice is the work of Sir Christopher Wren, whose name is associated with all that is great in English architecture. The future eminence of this distinguished man, like that of his great contemporary, Pascal, was early foreseen. Even at the age of thirteen, he made an important astronomical discovery, which was the preluding scintillation of his magnificent genius. From this time up to the period when he commenced the lasting monument of his transcendent powers, his whole soul was actively absorbed to reach a high point of culture. He was now favored with the society of the brightest geniuses of his day; and was an active member of the various scientific societies. Nor was this part of his life barren of immediate fruits. He made, on the contrary, several useful inventions and important discoveries, and was, in fact, recognized as one of the first scientific geniuses of his time. But the great work of his life, of course, that which will last for ages as a proud monument of his genius, is the noble cathedral of St. Paul's. Yet, so great was his talent, so untiring his perseverance, that the immense labors connected with this did not absorb his entire time, but left a portion for fruitful investigations in other departments of science. The greatness of such spirits continues to elevate and delight mankind for ages untold.

March 17*th*. Effected, this morning, an agreement for a passage to Boston, in the brig Waltron of Falmouth, N. S., Capt. Davidson. The Captain, a plain, but sympathetic and kindly-natured man, seemed gratified at the idea of having me on board along with him, entered at once into familiar conversation, and proposed in a pleasurable spirit to accompany me in a visit to the Thames Tunnel. This remarkable excavation effects a connection between the banks of the river, about two miles below London Bridge; and its entire length is thirteen hundred feet. You descend to the arch-way by an easy flight of steps. Your sensations are rather odd, on realizing that a broad and deep river is flowing above you, bearing on its bosom huge, heavily laden ships. The body of the tunnel is of brick-work in Roman cement. It consists of a double and capacious archway, one side being appropriated to carriages passing in one direction, and the other to those passing in the contrary, with paths for foot-passengers by the side of the carriage-road. The middle road between the two archways was first built solid for greater strength; but openings were afterwards cut at short distances, so that each has a ready communication with the other.

In the course of the work, two irruptions of the river took place; the first on the eighteenth of May, 1827, after the excavation had been advanced to the distance of four hundred feet; and the second in January, 1828. I was told that one of them was caused by an American ship's casting anchor directly over the tunnel. These accidents were, however, repaired by filling the chasms in the river with bags of clay; and on clearing the tunnel of water, the structure was found, on both occasions, to be in a perfectly sound state, and to have sustained little injury. This work is certainly one of the most extraordinary that it ever entered into the mind of man to attempt. Its cost was more than two millions and a half of dollars. In contemplating it, we know not which most to admire, in its originator, the grandeur and boldness of its conception, or the genius and energy with which it was carried to a successful completion. During its progress, it was visited by multitudes of persons from all parts of the world; and now the sum received from the visitors who daily view it, is its principal remunerative benefit. It would doubtless prove interesting to detail the works and process of operation in its construction, but room fails.

Made, likewise, a visit to the British Museum. It is principally deposited in Montague-house, Great Russell Street, Bloomsbury; and this being a considerable distance westward from the Tunnel, I made very pleasantly the greater part of the distance in one of those little steamers which ply on the Thames, through the city, for the transit of passengers. These constitute an original feature in the city. Only think of being conveyed in a steamer, when you make a morning's call, or just step out to see a neighbor. They afford a common and convenient mode of traversing the city in an eastern or western direction,— and they are always thronged with passengers. There were three lines, and the prices for a passage were respectively four pence, two pence, and one penny. The latter was called the Citizens' Line, and the boats were equal to the others. They start every ten minutes, from different stations, and traverse only that part of the Thames which borders on the business part of the city. They are small, of beautiful model, and may be seen cutting around each other, and darting under the spacious arches of the massive bridges, like graceful Tritons. A morning's promenade by one of them is inspiring.

Stepping out of the boat, a turn took me into Trafalgar Square. The beauty of this place is heightened by the noble front of the National Gallery on the north of the Square, and the Nelson Monument rising majestically from the centre. The latter is surmounted with a fine statue representing England's greatest naval hero. There he stands in a commanding attitude, looking serenely down upon the thronging masses who, as they pass, are thrilled with emotions of pride at the mere sight of this beautiful shaft, reminding them of the national power and glory. The monument is named, of course, for the last of those brilliant naval engagements of the great commander, in which, off the Cape of Trafalgar, he purchased a splendid victory with the loss of his life. Nelson arose, by the force of his character, from an humble position in the English navy, to the highest pinnacle of its fame; and died, covered with titles of honor, and loaded with wealth. As a professional character, he possessed a mighty genius, an ardent spirit, and a resolute mind; cool, prompt, and discerning, in the midst of danger he raised all his powerful energies into action, and the strong faculties of his soul were vigilantly exerted in the midst of the fury of battle, to make every accident contribute to the triumph of his crew, and to the glory of his country. So highly established was his reputation, that his presence was said to be a talisman to the courage of his sailors, who fought under him as sure of victory, and regarded his approbation as the best solace for their fatigues and their sufferings.

The Museum equalled the high expectations I had formed of it. It is truly a national institution, and was established in 1753. It is a grand repository for books, MSS., statues, coins, and other antiquities, specimens of animals and minerals, etc., and is considered in most respects, one of the richest in Europe. The department of antiquities is certainly valuable. It comprises the collection of Egyptian monuments, including the famous Rosetta stone, acquired at the capitulation of Alexandria in 1801; the Townly marbles, purchased at a cost of one hundred and forty thousand dollars; the Phigalian and the Elgin marbles, the cost of which was one hundred and seventy-five thousand dollars. The latter includes the statues of Theseus and Ilissus, and the sculptures in *alto-releivo* from the friezes of the Parthenon. The collection here was not completely arranged, so immense are the labors required to keep up an exact system. The library is an interesting feature. It comprises a collection formed in part by various presents from time to time; but the most valuable addition of late years, is the library of George III, collected at an expense of one million of dollars, and presented to the Museum by his successor. Modern English publications are added free of expense; and about one million five hundred thousand dollars a year are expended in the purchase of old and foreign works. There are about 330,000 printed books, and 27,000 MSS., exclusive of charters. The average number of readers is two hundred and twenty a day.

The department of zoology is rich in birds and insects, but poor in other respects, especially in mammalia. I was wonderfully interested, of course, in viewing the skeleton of the huge mastidon, the picture of which I had marvelled over so much in my school-going days.

The collection of medals, which has been accumulating since the foundation of the museum, consists of about twenty thousand coins.

The collection of minerals is large. Both for size and classification, it will bear to be compared with any mineralogical collection in Europe. Fac-similes in glass of the various large diamonds in the world, were particularly shown us. This Museum, with two or three other places, were the only ones I found free to the public.

Although the weather was inclement, still there were quite a throng of persons examining the collections. Among the number was a small party of gentlemen from Ohio. They seemed deeply engrossed. One of the youngest of their number in particular, could hardly suppress his enthusiasm, but flew from one case of minerals to another in childish ecstasy.

The present building of the Museum was designed by Sir R. Smike, and was only recently completed. It is quadrangular, with a noble and splendid façade ornamented with Ionic columns.

March 18*th.* Weather fine, for the first day since being in London. Westward ho! to revel in the varied beauties of West End. London-proper is but a small place, comprising an area only of about six hundred acres, while what is now covered with buildings has an area of about fifteen square miles, or ten thousand acres. The old city is the heart of the body, whence issue the pulsations of business. Westminster, or West-End, is the head, or seat of government, — and the east part of the town, with the docks, the feet. It is not difficult to trace other features of resemblance to the human body. For instance, the Thames running through the city in an easterly direction, dividing the city into two parts, may be styled the vertebral column; the long streets running parallel with the river, and lined with stores, may take the name of the arms and fingers of the body, while the magnificent parks have been most appropriately designated the lungs of London. In the old part of the city the buildings are huddled, and have a dingy air, — the streets are absolutely thronged with all manner of vehicles and foot-passengers, elbowing their way in every direction; but the West-End, the residence of the royal family, the nobility, the foreign ambassadors, and public functionaries, presents a neat, open, and beautiful appearance.

I first took a boat from London Bridge to Trafalgar Square, and in my route thence to St. James's Park, passed the Equestrian Statue of George IV; the Church of St. Martin in the Fields, the portico of which is much admired; the building of the National Gallery; the Royal College of Physicians; the fine Equestrian Statue, in bronze, of George III; the Nelson Column; the Northumberland House; the Admiralty Office; the chief military establishment of the Horse Guards; the Banqueting House; the Treasury; Westminster Bridge, and the New Parliament House. The change of feeling on entering St. James's Park is delightful. It is the elasticity of emotion on the sudden transition from the turmoil and dust of a dense city, to the joyous and smiling fragrance of the country. There is a marked difference between the English and French parks. The latter are artificially beautiful; the former naturally delightful. The former may be more pleasing to the traveller, but the latter must be more lovely and refreshing to the citizen. St. James's is one of the smallest parks in London, being only one-fifth as large as Hyde Park; but it is hardly inferior to any in point of beauty and attractiveness. Its site being low, it was formerly damp and marshy. Within these few years, however, the central part has been tastefully laid out, and what was a dirty, straight canal, running through a marsh, has become a handsome, varied sheet of water, dotted with islands, forming the abode of numerous aquatic birds and surrounded by lawns, shrubbery and lofty trees. The park is open to all pedestrians, and on any fair day, it may be seen thronged with well-dressed people of both sexes, and all ages, promenading, loitering, reclining, — and all evincing a happier existence imparted by the animated and charming scenery around them. Royalty herself has no more delightful spot in which to recreate than this; and here the humblest citizen, escaped from his toil and lost to the misery of his lot, can bathe as freshly in the fragrant waters of nature, as the queen herself descending from her purple throne.

I here fell into conversation with an elderly man, leading a lad, perhaps his grandson. On learning that I was from the United States, he appeared seized with a kind of gladsome surprise, and began plying me with questions about my country with a youthful curiosity. The tone which pervaded his style of speaking, when referring to the New World, showed, however, that he held it not in very high estimation; and when he brought it into comparison with England, it actually dwindled into insignificance. According to him, England was the grandest, noblest, richest, and finest country to be found in the whole world. There were, he admitted, some sadly dark features on her luminous disk, but she was, after all, a glorious country, — and the Queen — God bless her — the loveliest, the most perfect woman on earth. The cannon just at that moment were booming the national joy for the safe delivery of the queen, who had given birth to another son. I ventured to ask how the industrial part of the community could consistently rejoice at an event which added eighty thousand dollars per annum to the national expense — to be wrung out of the toiling masses? He gently shook his head, and by his silence plainly gave me to understand that he *felt* the force of my objection.

At the western extremity of the park, and commanding a fine view of its plantations, stands Buckingham Palace, the town-residence of her majesty, Queen Victoria. The English themselves do not praise this edifice, and regard it as only remarkable for its extravagant cost, amounting to some five million dollars. The poorness of its effect may be attributed, however, in a measure, to its depressed situation. Indeed, the ground in front of the palace not being paved, becomes in wet weather a most offensive puddle. It was, however, undergoing extensive repairs, which were destined, doubtless, to give the royal mansion an improved aspect.

From St. James's Park I pursued my way leisurely through Green Park, — a triangular piece of ground about as large as St. James's, from which it gradually rises to Piccadilly. It can have but little pretensions to beauty, being little more than a dry meadow, traversed by walks. St. James's Palace, at the right,—

at the west end of Pall Mall, — is an irregular, mean-looking brick building, totally unworthy the name of a palace. It was erected by Henry VIII. It was the residence, if I remember rightly, of the queen-dowager, and is said to be, internally, handsomely fitted up for court-levees and drawing-rooms, which are mostly held in it.

Passing out of Green Park, I came to the road leading from Piccadilly and Oxford, and to the west of which is the famous Hyde Park, frequented daily by the royal family, nobility, and the aristocracy of the nation. It has eight entrances. At this point, you enter by a triumphal arch, surmounted by a huge equestrian statue of the late Duke of Wellington. As a work of art it did not strike me as possessing remarkable beauty, but it carries something of an imposing effect, and stands out to view a prominent object for a long distance in the park. A little to the right, stands the Apsley House, the town-residence of the "*Iron Duke.*" It is a quadrangular, plain, massive building. As I passed, a lady of large proportions, and richly dressed in satin and furs, drove up alone, at full speed, in a splendid carriage, drawn by a span of beautiful and spirited horses, and reining up the steeds, leaped out of the carriage with the agility of a circus-rider, and entered the house without ringing.

A little within the park, at the entrance just named, is a colossal statue of Achilles, placed there by the ladies of London in honor of the Duke of Wellington and his brave associates in the Continental war. It is cast from the cannon taken at different battles; is twenty feet high, and weighs thirty tons. The park originally contained six hundred and twenty acres; but now contains only four hundred. It has a large and deep artificial lake extending, I should judge, two-thirds its length, crossed by a handsome bridge of five arches. This is called the Serpentine river, and is used for sailing, and swimming, and bathing. It is under the care of an officer of the crown, and there are distinct regulations to be observed by those who are admitted to the recreations. Beautiful boats may be seen along the shores, and houses on its banks furnished with apparatus for resuscitation. The whole of the park is an open field of much beauty, dotted with trees and traversed by carriage-ways, which, in fine weather during the season, are covered with gay and fashionable equipages. It is here that Prince Albert takes his morning ride, on horseback, and where the Queen, the Princes, and Princesses take their daily airing in good weather. Between the hours of two and five o'clock, afternoon, I found to be the most fashionable part of the day for seeking thither an airing. Kensington gardens, lying west of the park, and separated from it by a trench and wall, are open to the public, and constitute a fine, shady promenade, three miles in circumference. These gardens are certainly fine, combining the grandeur and beauty of rural scenery in a high degree.

Returning, I lingered an hour or two to contemplate Westminster Abbey. And how shall I convey my impressions of this venerable pile! The edifice itself, although less grand and imposing than the great church of Rouen, that of Paris, or Brussels even, is yet a gem of architecture, and is justly esteemed the most perfect specimen of the pointed style, in England. But however beautiful and interesting its exterior, you do not tarry a moment to enjoy the fine view. Feelings of intense emotion and curiosity hurry you within the sacred walls of the vast mausoleum, to stand

"Where England garners up her great!"

And when you pass through the rude, unpainted oaken door, which leads into the "Poet's Corner," and find yourself actually surrounded by the tombs of the mighty dead, — then it is that you become sensible of the power and majesty of the place. You stand for a moment spell-bound! — You feel now in the presence of those glorious spirits with which your soul has deeply communed in ambrosial delight; noble spirits, to which you feel largely indebted for whatever of elevation you possess; mighty spirits, that have made the world what it is; immortal spirits on earth, destined to be reproduced in every age, till time shall be no more.

As you gaze upon their marble effigies, surrounded by the gloom and damp that invests the place, a kind of supernatural awe seizes you; you dread to step, for fear of disturbing the solemn, the sacred repose of the place. At least, such were in a measure my own emotions. At the eastern end of the abbey are the royal chapels, in which are the tombs of the kings and queens of England. Some of these are much despoiled, partly by time, but more by violence. Royal avarice plundered them of their sceptres and jewels; and republican violence, out of wantonness, defaced them. Some, however, remain well preserved. The stranger cannot but pause at the tombs of Alfred, of Edward the Confessor, of Henry VII, of Elizabeth, and Mary of Scotland. The last three he will find in the magnificent chapel of Henry VII, whose fretted ceiling, wholly wrought in stone, is an object of curious interest. In the western portion of the building, the long-drawn aisles are literally encrusted with monuments. But only here and there may be found one bearing a name which illumines the pages of history, or the progress of science. The names of Pitt, Newton, and Wilberforce will arrest the attention, and bring up thoughts of these mighty departed.

But he soon hurries back to the spot, where are enshrined the Poets, to revel in the glowing inspirations there afforded. There stands, in graceful majesty, Shakspeare, holding a scroll, on which is engraved these sublime lines of the poet:—

> "The cloud-capped towers,
> The gorgeous palaces,
> The solemn temple,
> The great globe itself,—
> Yea, all which in it lives
> Shall dissolve—
> And like the baseless fabric of a vision,
> Leave not a wreck behind."

I thought he might have excepted the matchless creations of his immortal genius.

Here, too, was Gay, with these odd lines engraved below his bust:—

> "Life is a jest, and all things show it;
> I thought so once, and now I know it."

There was, also, old Ben Johnson, with a countenance expressive of profundity and wit; and James Thompson, the poet of rural nature. The countenance of the latter bears a feminine and rich expression. His head was surrounded, I believe, with a garland of flowers. The following beautiful sentiment, from the Seasons, enhanced the pleasing view:—

> "The Muse, with a crown
> Tutored by sweet poetry, exalts
> Her voice to ages, and informs the page
> With music, sentiment, and thought never to die."

There were, moreover, Dr. Watts, Milton, Dryden, Handel, Garrick, and many others of the brightest stars in the galaxy of English literature, — but they cannot be even enumerated here.

Spent the evening at the parlor of my hotel, in conversation with an intelligent country gentleman. This had been my habitual mode of passing the evenings, since arriving in London. The hotel in question, as I have said before, being near the railroad terminus, was frequented by passengers on their first arrival in the cars. Many of them were country merchants residing in different parts of the island. Their society afforded a means of information which I was careful not to neglect. There are several ways of obtaining reliable information respecting a country. One is, to learn from the candid and more intelligent of the rural population. You thus obtain something of a true picture of the national opinion and sentiment. I found these gentlemen, in manner and disposition, quite different from your English traveller in general. They were open and free in conversation, communicative, of a docile and teachable spirit. They seemed well versed in politics, and evinced considerable intelligence and discrimination respecting the institutions and resources of their country; but their knowledge did not extend much beyond the island. Of the United States, they evinced almost unpardonable ignorance, not only of its institutions, but even of its geography. They regarded their government as an expensive affair, and the taxes an oppressive burden, — still, they loved the Queen, and felt as loyal subjects.

Sunday, 19*th*, attended Divine service. The denomination, I was told, was styled the Old Church of England. There were but few present, and the exercises were conducted in a formal, lifeless manner. I was well tired before it was over. Thence took a stroll in Regent's Park. This was formed during the regency, in the last years of George III. It is situated to the north

of Portland Place, on high ground, surrounded by splendid build
ings, and is tastefully laid out. Indeed, it is considered the handsomest of the London parks, and is as large as that of Hyde
The gardens of the Zoölogical Society are situated on the north
side of this park, while the central portion is laid out as a garden
for the Botanic Society. On the east side of the park, near Park-
Square, is the large building styled the Colosseum. It is a sixteen-
sided polygonal structure, with a magnificent portico and cupola.
It is principally occupied by an immense panoramic view of the
metropolis, taken from the ball on the top of St. Paul's Cathedral.

Besides these magnificent parks, exhibiting the varied loveliness of nature, heightened by the genius of art, there are a great
number of fine squares in London. In many, the houses are in
the first style of architecture, and the central gardens beautifully
laid out. Several of the best squares are decorated with statues.
The immense parks and numerous squares form a marked feature
in this grand emporium, and render it an attraction of no small
moment. Indeed, what would London be without its parks? A
vast bee-hive, rayless of the cheerful light of heaven. As it is,
they gather the incense of homage from the hearts of all classes of
citizens, and render London a very agreeable residence, largely
uniting the splendor of a rich capital with the delightful fragrance
of charming rural scenery. Here the poor man can cheer the
monotony of toil by a glimpse of nature; and the rich can lead
out his children to rejoice in the fair paradise of the omnipres
ent sky.

On the northern side of the park is a natural elevation, afford
ing from its summit a partial view of the mammoth city. There
were some fifteen or twenty ladies and gentlemen of us struggling
for some time with moist and slippery clay under our feet, to gair

the moderate ascent. The city lay stretching off interminably before our view, partially enveloped in a dingy atmosphere, while St. Paul's reared its noble dome as an object far off in the distance. None of us could scarcely realize that we were actually within the city, which seemed distinctly away from us, a distant mass of edifices.

CHAPTER XXVI.

HOSPITALITY OF THE ENGLISH — GALLERY OF PAINTINGS — POPULARITY OF QUEEN VICTORIA — DISAFFECTION — ST. PAUL'S SCHOOL — GUILDHALL — ROYAL EXCHANGE — BANK OF ENGLAND — BRIDGES — HOUSES OF PARLIAMENT — ST. JAMES'S PARK — PRINCE ALBERT — NORMAL AND MODEL SCHOOL — EAST INDIA DOCKS — ELIHU BURRITT — QUAKERS — NATIONAL SCHOOLS — HOUSE OF LORDS — SHOPKEEPERS — HOMEWARD BOUND.

March 20*th.* To-day called on and delivered my letters to Mr. E—— C——, an extensive London merchant, with a view to trace out my Welsh friend, Captain B——, whose acquaintance I had so agreeably formed in New York, just before leaving. Mr. C—— received me with an easy, unaffected cordiality, which is one mark of the true gentleman, — begged that I would make his house my home while in the city, and gently insisted that I would accept his carriage and company for an afternoon ride to see Captain B——, some fifteen miles out of the city. From this and other experiences, I obtained a most favorable opinion of the hospitality and politeness of the English, especially with the better classes. It may be true that the national temperament begets a certain habit of reserve towards strangers, and a punctiliousness in the mode of introduction; yet, when a stranger is presented according to their idea of propriety, and has become their guest, every attention is bestowed to render him comfortable and happy.

Visited the National Gallery of Paintings. The building is situated on the north-west side of Trafalgar Square, unquestionably the finest situation in the metropolis. It has a front of five hundred feet, with a portico and dome in its centre, supported by Corinthian columns. The pictures, amounting to some one hundred and seventy, can only be looked upon as a nucleus to what may hereafter be worthy of the country. About half the pictures belong to the Italian school, and of these Ecce Homo and some others are most esteemed. The works of the two Caracci, N. Poussin, and Claude, may be here seen in their highest perfection. There are also some fine specimens of the English school, by Reynolds, Hogarth, etc.; also of the Flemish. Of the latter, I noticed gems from the pencils of Reubens, Vandyke, and Rembrandt. But one has little patience to tarry long amid so meagre a collection, after having revelled in the Elysiums of Art in Paris and Brussels. This collection must not be taken, however, as the true index of taste for art in England. For there are numerous small collections containing choice pieces, in the possession of private gentlemen, and not open to the public.

The late *accouchement* of the queen, though an event of no unusual occurrence, had yet taken possession of the public mind to an extent that we Americans can hardly imagine; and the most trivial intelligence relating to her convalescence, was sought with avidity, not only by the court-circles and aristocracy, but by the humblest citizen. On the morning after the propitious event, I fancied to perceive in the street-thronging populace a brighter countenance even, and a more elate movement. Ere proceeding far, my way was interrupted by a dense crowd hanging around a corner, all eager to peruse a large hand-bill conspicuously posted upon the wall. From the lively interest among the throng, I thought it no less than some government revolutionary decree, of vital import; and it was long before I could press near enough to read the paper. It was, indeed, a State paper, signed by the Queen's physicians, and several noble cabinet lords, in which they condescend to inform all her dutiful and loving subjects, and the London world in general, that her majesty, at such an hour and minute, was safely delivered of an infant, and that at half-past seven o'clock, A. M., both the mother and child were doing well. The bold and stately manner of thus communicating a species of intelligence which I had been accustomed to see conveyed only by whispers and knowing smiles, struck me at first so oddly as to draw forth an involuntary ejaculation, little respectful, I imagine, to loyal ears, — which being heard by a sturdy, well-dressed gentleman at my side, he darted on me a look so full of virtuous indignation, that I almost trembled in momentary expectation of being summarily called to account for rudeness so unwittingly shown. Squeezing out of the crowd, I pursued my way, a little humbled in feeling, and pondering upon the strange vicissitudes of life, upon the inequalities of human condition, and the marvellous aspect of the national train of thought and sympathy. It did look strikingly wonderful, while thousands of females, endowed by nature with the graces of life, should be passed by uncared-for by the multitude, and left to starve amid a world of plenty, with no fraternal heart to cheer the bitterness of their lot, nor sympathizing hand to soothe the anguish of their sufferings, that a single woman should be infolded from out of the world of humanities, lifted to an Elysian throne, and made the supreme object of earthly adoration; that thus deified, she should be permitted not only to well up in monopoly the oceans and seas of delighted admiration immediately surrounding her, but to scoop dry the waters of love from the little wells and rivulets in the remotest parts of the kingdom. Still, moralize as I would, I felt that I was quite wrong, and the Londoner fully right, that the life of the queen at that time of revolutionary panic, was of momentous interest to the nation, and the safety of the sweet infant as involving maternal anxiety of no trifling import. A fatal issue of this annual event of Buckingham Palace, would have rived the hearts of a large number of relatives, enshrouded in mournful gloom the court circles, and touched to weeping the hearts of loyal and loving subjects. It would have severed a chord in the national pride, lessened the sentiment of public admiration, and withdrawn a living beau-ideal of the national glory. So appalling an event would, too, have involved a change in the course of government, and increased the apprehension of a civil war. But these were only circumstantial causes in swelling the national heart of sympathetic admiration and interest. The exercise of a natural sentiment had begotten in the bosom of the Englishman a profound esteem for his queen. Invested in public estimation with the attributes that command the homage of the heart, she had become the enthroned idol of the national affection. Now, the human soul is fashioned to admire, to love, to worship. It will have some object even beyond the family circle upon which to employ its panting energies. It craves a living ideal of power and beauty to elevate and refine its aspirations. This denied it, the soul will often chase the phantom of its imagination, or settle upon grovelling objects of thought and action. Thus yielding homage to superior characters does not degrade the nature, but elevates it, as the contemplation of the beautiful beautifies the mind. I will not complain of the Englishman, then, for loving and reverencing his queen. Would there were no more degrading objects of worship than rendering grateful homage to a noble and beautiful woman.

Becoming a little tired of my quarters, I removed to rooms with Mrs. ——, in Tower Hill street. I say Mrs., because, although the lady was living in marriage with her husband, he seemed so imbecile as hardly to merit being mentioned in the partnership. Indeed, I afterwards learned, that through his incapacity for business, their joint patrimony had become entirely sunk in trade, and they were living in the narrowest manner possible upon a very small income still belonging to the wife. This hardly sufficing, they were obliged to let the rooms of their house to travellers. The lady was naturally a noble, spirited, and energetic woman, and managed things at home to perfection. Her example, in the education of her family, may be mentioned as worthy the emulation of every mother. Though living with the utmost frugality herself, their children were at the best schools in the realm, and on the Continent. Their oldest son had already just received a lucrative appointment, and one of the daughters was spoken for to fill the place of governess in one of the best families in England. Doubtless, under the spirit of honorable ambition, inherited from the mother, they would soon rise to stations of profit and honor, and before long have wherewith not only to support in comfortable circumstances their parents, but likewise to gladden the hearts of the latter by their superiority in life. Mrs. —— was a warm admirer of queen Victoria, whom she invested with the beautiful hues of her own mind. According to her, Her Majesty was very popular throughout the entire realm, and had always been so. When only the young daughter of the Duchess of Kent, she was a public idol, and could not move out from her home without receiving in showers the fragrant incense of popular homage. Her Majesty's choice of a husband fell upon an English gentleman, an early rosebud of her heart's affection; but the Duke of Wellington and the cabinet ministers, for reasons of state, would have her select from the princes of the blood. Indeed, another course would have been undignified, and contrary to the laws of the realm. Her

Majesty, according to my excellent landlady, is a sensible and amiable woman; she is, moreover, highly educated and accomplished, able to speak at least three of the modern languages of Europe, to execute finely upon the piano-forte, and to design with exquisite art. Indeed, a circumstance occurred while I was in London, which goes fully to substantiate the fact in regard to the latter accomplishment. It seems, the queen had loaned some of her drawings to a female friend, who allowed an artist professing great admiration for them, to take the drawings home for inspection. The latter had them engraved, — and soon the shop-windows of the capital were embellished with the beautiful designs of Her Majesty. An action was immediately entered against the unlucky artist, and the circulation of the drawings stopped, but not until the good citizens of London had caught a glimpse of pictures actually executed by the delicate hand of their sovereign. The queen is also very polite to all, even to her servants, and inculcates the same principle in the manners of her children, with whom she is so particular in their education, as not to permit their reading a book without first having perused it herself. Then she is benevolent, sympathizing, and humane, giving freely to good enterprises, commiserating with the afflicted, and performing deeds of charity. With such a character, it is not surprising that she is esteemed and beloved by the entire nation.

I observed by the papers, that a meeting of the Revolutionists of the capital was to be held in the evening, to devise measures for a revolution somewhat after the style of the grand movement in Paris; but this did not seem to disturb in the least the public mind. An unsuccessful effort had been made a week or two before; but it resulted in little more than demonstrating the power of the government, and the loyalty of the citizens in general. Indeed, only a glance at the character of the English, and the condition of the nation, will show the high improbability of anything like an effective revolution in England. In the first place, the government and institutions of the country stand upon a more liberal basis than those of any country in Europe, and are little less popular in character than those of our own country. Then, the government is conducted with acute and far-seeing sagacity, by sage politicians, chosen by the queen in a liberal spirit, as holding a nice equipoise between popular will and patrician conservatism.

The queen, cabinet, and nobility in general, would never, of course, favor a revolution. The respectable, middling classes, largely engaged in manufactures and commerce, whose interests suffer disastrously in a civil disturbance, would not forsake their golden god, Mammon, to chase the unsubstantial form of Liberty. Then, the vast army, and mighty navy, the two huge elements of power for carrying on war, or maintaining peace, are disposed with great skill to identify their rank and file with the disposition of the government, and place them in willing obedience to the cabinet wires. Besides, there is a large, thoroughly organized, and powerfully efficient police extending with a net-work ramification throughout the realm, slumbering indeed, yet with eagle-eyed vigilance, and a lion force, and ever as true to their queen as the magnet is to the polar star. All these powers are immensely increased by the large, genuine, ever-beating, loyal heart in the Englishman, which oxidizes his national blood, and makes him feel the fratricidal poignancy of civil strife. Against such mighty forces, what can the toiling, panting, heel-trodden million do? They may, as they have, and will probably, again, when some liberty-shriek fans anew in their breasts the flame of mortal indignation, throw up their arms and voices in pleading, avenging clamor, — but it is but the pattering rain amid the tempest's roar, or the writhings and cries of the puny quadruped in the giant paws of the king of beasts.

Looked into St. Paul's school, situated near St. Paul's church It was established in 1518 by Dean Colet, and provides a free education for one hundred and fifty-three boys, the most advanced of whom are sent to Oxford and Cambridge. The present building was erected in 1824, and the income of the school is about thirty thousand dollars per annum. I found it extremely difficult to gain admission to this school.

Guild Hall, which I strolled through, stands at the north end of King street. The front, added in 1789, is in a heterogeneous style. The great hall, one hundred and fifty-three feet in length, by forty-eight in breadth, and fifty-three in height, built and paved in stone, is capable of accommodating six thousand persons; at least that number was present at the grand entertainment given by the corporation to the allied sovereigns in 1814. At each end of the hall is a magnificent painted glass window, in the pointed style. In the hall are statues of Pitt, Chatham, and others; and in the west end are the two wooden giants, called Gog and Magog, the subject of so many popular tales.

There are several other rooms possessing considerable interest. The walls of the Council Chamber are hung with paintings. Among them was a full-sized portrait of her Majesty as she appeared at the Coronation. The figure was graceful, and the countenance bore a sensible and amiable expression. A country gentleman present informed me that the portrait was a good representation of the queen, except that now she was grown *stouter* and more *matronly*, as he expressed it. There were also portraits of queen Caroline, the princess Charlotte, and of David Rienzi, the favorite of the unfortunate Mary, Queen of Scots. Before finishing a survey of the several apartments of the quaint and interesting edifice, a portly person, neatly dressed, accosted me in officious style, and begged in the blandest tones to point out to me something more than I had seen. After a turn or two, he left me; but, as I was going, he suddenly made his appearance, and began a series of complaisant looks and subdued gestures. Finding me slow to apprehend his meaning, he finally " popped the question " by asking that I would be good enough to hand him something.

"But," said I, "the building is free to strangers."

"Ah, yes, but then *gentlemen* commonly pay."

"How much will you have?"

"What you choose."

I bestowed my best bow. He turned on his heel, as if he was not unused to such partings. It is a lesson the traveller latest learns, to know how to treat properly such gentry.

I also looked around upon the Royal Exchange, of recent construction. It is a splendid building, and is one of the chief ornaments of the city. It encloses an open square, in the centre of which stands upon an elevated pedestal, a full-sized statue of queen Victoria, erected in 1844. The artist has managed to impart to the statue a full, luxurious, womanly deportment, which rivets the gaze of the beholder. At a rough estimate, two thousand merchants and brokers have their places of business within a half mile of the exchange, and meet there to carry on operations by which the commercial affairs of the world are powerfully influenced.

Near, is the Bank of England, a monied monster indeed. The building covers eight acres, and is irregular and incongruous enough. The affairs of the bank are managed by a governor, deputy-governor, and twenty-four directors, elected annually. The business is conducted by about nine hundred clerks, whose salaries amount to about a million. The capital of the bank has been as large as £50,000,000, lent to the government at three per cent.

March 22*d*. Took an early stroll through Cheapside and the Strand, the great thoroughfare of fashionable retail stores. It could bear no comparison with similar streets in Paris, and not surpassing, I thought, Broadway in New York, or Washington street in Boston.

Made several agreeable calls on American gentlemen. Americans in Europe are eminently fraternal. Distance, which lends enchantment to home, invests with a lively charm the living object which recalls to the tenderly yearning soul, the glowing associations of country and friends. The Somerset House was pointed out to me as interesting from its historical associations. It is somewhat after the plan of the Louvre in Paris. Elizabeth and some of the other queens held levees here. Crossed the Thames by the "suspension bridge." This is certainly a great triumph of art. The Thames, averaging one thousand feet in width, is crossed by six bridges. These gigantic structures cost an aggregate of more than twenty five millions of dollars. Two of these, Vauxhall and Southwark bridges, have iron arches, the centre arch of the latter being two hundred and forty feet in width. Waterloo bridge is really a fine structure. Canova said that it was itself worth a visit from the remotest corner of the world. It is of granite, and has nine elliptical arches, each one hundred and twenty-seven feet wide. The new London bridge, whether regarded in reference to magnitude or the beauty and simplicity of its structure, is one of the finest specimens of bridge-architecture in the world. It is built of granite, and the span of the centre arch is one hundred and thirty-two feet.

From Westminster bridge, I had a fine view of the new houses of Parliament. They have a splendid river-front, nearly seven hundred feet in length, with a terrace and stairs leading down to the water. The style of architecture is gothic, and beautiful. The edifice forms a striking feature in the metropolis, and is an ornament to the city. It is very elaborate in finish and profuse in ornament, but lacks grandeur. It stands on a low site, and the edifice itself seems to want due proportionate height.

I was delighted with the scene on passing into St. James's Park. The sky was open, and the air soft and balmy. Numbers of people, young and old, sedate and gay, variously costumed, were sauntering in the serpentine walks. Children accompanied with their governesses were gamboling in happy merriment upon the verdant lawns. Birds of varied plumage from amidst the shrubbery, were enlivening the scene with their rich notes, while aquatic fowls were sailing gracefully over the mirrored surface of the impearled lake, conscious of the beauty of the scene around. Thus issuing suddenly from the dense city to the gladsome country, is like entering a new world.

At the corner of Hyde Park, I learned of Prince Albert's levee at St. James's Palace at two o'clock, P. M. I was there, of course in time to witness the cortege. The crowd of spectators was not so great as I had expected.

The carriages entered by three different ways. Those of the foreign ambassadors by one, the officers of State by another, and the Royal, still by another. Some of the carriages were splendid, but others not finer than what may be seen every day in Boston and New York. All the carriages had footmen, who were generally in livery. As the centre squares of the carriages were down, and the inmates uncovered, a fine opportunity was presented to scan the features and costume of this imposing array of the elite of the world. Some were accoutred in uniform, some garbed in gown and wig, and others in simple citizens' dress. They were, on the whole, very sensible and intelligent looking. They continued rolling past, till a late hour, and the first arrivals were departing long before the last had come. The cortege of the Prince consisted of three carriages, escorted by the "horse guards," beautifully mounted on black steeds, preceded by a spirited brass band. The prince's was the middle carriage, a heavy, but splendid affair, rich with gilding, and drawn by eight cream colored horses, with coachman, postilion, and four richly liveried footmen, behind. The centre piece was down, and from the top of the post, where I had been standing for some time, in impatient expectancy, I had a fair opportunity to look directly in upon the Prince. He was in uniform, uncovered, and accompanied by two gentlemen, one seated by his side, and the other opposite. He was of medium stature and size, something less than the average of English bulk. He appeared good looking, but not handsome; a mild, sensible, German face. He wore a neat moustache of sandy hue, but no whiskers. Not quite satisfied with this glance, I waited till his return, when I walked briskly by the side of the carriage, till it turned into the Palace Court, when I apologized for my boldness, by uncovering and saluting the royal personage, in form. It was acknowledged by the Prince, by a slight inclination. The next day, being in Hyde Park, three horsemen, in plain citizens' dress, at short distances from each other, rode past at a round trot. The foremost one, when opposite me reigned up, and lifting his hat made a graceful inclination of the head. Turning to a workman near, I was told it was the Prince. His change of dress had rendered him not recognizable by me. His royal highness is said to be very courteous and polite to everybody, and especially to strangers. Indeed, he has little else to do, but to win popularity. He may truly be considered a lucky mortal, and his lot a happy one, so far as happiness depends on fortunate condition; for he enjoys the honors, and pleasures of royalty, without its burthens and dangers.

An incident took place near me, while awaiting the cortege at the Prince's levee, which shows the eagle-eyed efficiency of the London police. Near me I saw a man suddenly seize another by the throat, and press him to the earth. A fierce struggle ensued. A crowd gathered, but there was no confusion. It seemed that information had been given that a certain person had passed counterfeit money. Whereupon, two of these lynx-eyed officers, disguised, with no other guide than a general description of the person, tracked him out, and came thus upon him unawares. The counterfeiter, when seized, attempted to swallow the money upon him,—but the gripe at his throat made with reference to that contingency, proved a successful barrier.

March 23*d.* I visited, to-day, the Normal and Model School in the Borough Road. There are upwards of three thousand pupils, who are taught by the Lancastrian system. The school is under the care of the National Society, which has its model school in the sanctuary at Westminster, and gives instruction to more than nine thousand pupils. The young gentleman whom I addressed, with a cordial, enthusiastic air bid me welcome to visit them as often as I wished, and stay as long as I pleased. "He would be glad," he said, "to have the world know of it, and see it." He regarded me with wonder, on learning that I was a school-master from the U. States, and had actually visited the schools on the continent. He remarked, that he was then deeply interested in reading a work on Popular Education, written in the U. States. I first went into the model school, composed of about six hundred pupils from the poorer classes, who pay two pence, or about four cents per week, as tuition. They are instructed by members of the superior department, styled normal pupils. The session was principally in a large hall, or school-room, with long seats running quite across the room, except leaving a wide aisle entirely around the apartment. At recitation, all the pupils were grouped in circles of from ten to fifteen in number, with the teacher in the centre.

As they recited simultaneously, some unusual noise prevailed. The exercise was arithmetic. The master gave out the problem, and all the pupils performed the same. When completed, the master questioned critically, in a cursory manner; but there was little that could be called philosophy in the manner of teaching. But there was a promptness and vigor on the part of the teacher, and an earnestness and attention in the pupil, which indicated efficiency and progress; hence many of the pupils were advanced for their age. Corporal punishment is held here as a last resort.

I visited several other rooms. In one, there was an exercise in natural history. The master, a very young man, appeared familiar with his subject, and deeply interested in the exercise. But he was most unpardonably impatient, hurried, and morose, and tumbled his little pupils around as if they had no sense of kindness, or delicacy of feeling. They gave good attention, however, and appeared progressing in the interesting science.

At half-past three, P. M., I was present to attend a critical lecture by one of the normal pupils, before a class of the " model school." Other members of the normal department were present, as well as Dr. Cornwall, taking notes. The lecturer was some time getting his class to order, to listen to his address, — scolding, pinching, cuffing them by turns, while the other normalites would frequently come to the rescue, volunteering a little authority of their own. The scene in this respect was painfully ludicrous, and reminded me of the confusion produced by a ship coming into dock under a press of canvas, to be taken in on the spur of the moment. After the lecture, Dr. Cornwall informed me that his lecture, which was to come off at four, P. M., would be suspended, to give the scholars opportunity to visit the Museum, according to their practice once a quarter; but if I would be pleased to call at any other time, I should be shown and told everything relating to the school, with great pleasure. I left with a lively feeling of the usefulness of the institution. I visited several other schools for the poorer classes, but I have no space here to record my impressions in detail.

March 25th. After breakfast, took a ride over the Blackwall Railway to the East India Docks, some three miles down the river, on the right bank of the Thames. They were commenced in 1803, and opened in 1806. As their name implies, they belong to the East India Company. There are two docks, covering eighteen acres of ground. My object in visiting these was, to see some of the East India ships, of which I had heard so much; but I must say I was disappointed. In size, model, and style, they bore no comparison to the idea I had formed of them, by the representations of my English friends. I must say that little risk is run in stating that we are in advance of the English in ship building. A little further up the river you come to the West India Docks. In one of these, six hundred vessels may be accommodated; and the whole area covered by them and their warehouses, is about three hundred acres. The extent of the Commercial Docks, further along, is even greater than those last described. Then come the London Docks; and last the St. Catharine Docks, situated just below the Tower. These are all vast receptacles, solidly and even beautifully constructed, and are one of the greatest wonders of London.

In the East India House I saw a huge meteoric stone, weighing twenty-five pounds, which was observed to fall, accompanied by a report as loud as that of a gun, and to bury itself several feet in the earth.

Elihu Burritt, the "learned blacksmith," delivered a lecture last evening before some one of the many literary societies of the capital, upon the "dignity of human labor." He was warmly greeted on commencing, and his address was reported to have been received with enthusiastic applause. The laborious student was under, it was said, the patronage of a wealthy and benevolent quaker, and was being worshipped as a prodigious literary lion by the elevated and philanthropic portion of the capital.

Sunday, 26th. Set off in order to attend a Sabbath-meeting of the Society of Friends. A four-years' residence, nearly, among these excellent people, in the United States, had so endeared to me their latent but manifold virtues of character, that I felt a strong inward delight at the prospect of again sitting with them in their humble and quiet waiting upon the breathing inspiration of the Divine Spirit. A traveller's curiosity, doubtless, mingled with the feeling I possessed. It will be recollected, that it was in England this sect had its origin about the middle of the seventeenth century, under the guidance of George Fox, that fearless apostle of a purer and more spiritual worship; and I esteemed it a gratifying inquiry to observe, as I might, how far the distant branches of the society, thrown off by a relentless persecution, still preserved the lineaments of the parent-trunk. Before proceeding far, I had the good fortune to overtake a man whom, at a glance, I should have recognized, the world over, as a veritable Quaker. Availing myself of a traveller's privilege, I at once accosted him with the request that he would set me on the way to a Friends' meeting. Without slackening his measured pace, and scarcely turning a look upon me, he sedately replied, "I am just going there myself, and thou can come along with me." He entered readily, but cautiously, into conversation with me, on matters touching his society; but when he discovered that I had myself lived with the Friends, had heard a number of their eminent preachers, and was familiar with the controversy then going on between the *Hicksites* and *Gurneyites*, his face gradually brightened up, his step became quicker, and his tongue more free, showing that the force of moral ideas cannot always fully subdue the impulses of nature. I was advised of our approach to the meeting rather by my friend's relapsing into his former calmness of manner, than from any visible indications around. We soon, however, entered a narrow archway, leading into a court, where, in front of a partially concealed edifice of humble proportions, stood some half-dozen men of different ages, awaiting the hour of meeting. Here, after a moment's tarry, the Friend approached, and in a low tone observed: " Some little affairs to be attended to in the room call me in. When it pleases thee to do so, thou can follow after." The company now began to gather, passing along by me into the room, — the men with a serious deportment, and the women, both young and old, with a steadfast, downward look, and with faces as destitute of the play of emotion as polished marble. Presently, the people having gone in, without receiving further invitation, I was led to adopt the suggestion of the Friend, to pass in unaccompanied; but I must confess to a slight trepidation, as, on issuing into the room, the extended methodical array of black bonnets and broad-brimmed hats struck my view. A seat was immediately assigned me, combining in its selection respect for a stranger, and dignity to their order. The room, capacious enough for five hundred persons, was of the style of a fashionable lecture-room, possessing not a vestige of that homely finish, and those quaint internal arrangements which characterize so peculiarly the quaker meeting-houses I have seen among us. The session of deathlike stillness and motionless attitude lasted about one hour and a half, being interrupted but once by any exercise whatever. Then, the deep-measured tones of the speaker, united with the energy and pathos of language in which he portrayed his ideal of paradise, was greatly heightened by the profound stillness of the room and the spiritual sympathy among the company. The meeting was broken up, preceded as usual by simultaneous shaking of hands among the male members. I at first set off on a route away from my hotel,— but after some five-minutes' walk returned upon my course. On arriving near the meeting-house, who should I meet at an angle of the street but the same afore-mentioned Friend, who had all the time been awaiting my coming, with a martyr's patience. He accompanied me a few streets down, when, after explaining to me minutely the arrangements for their weekly meetings, he took a cordial leave, saying that he would have invited me with him to dinner, but for the illness of his wife. What a contrast does the manner of this man form, mused I, to that of the world in general! What candor, what freedom from false-seeming! The current of his social nature has not been choked up by the shifting sands of a great city. I have often thought that the Quakers, despite their sedate, serious tone, their stiff, ungraceful manner, were really the most polite people in the world. If true politeness be kindness kindly expressed, then they most certainly possess largely of the cardinal virtue. At least, the genuine, substantial current of their intercourse is delightfully refreshing to such as are favored with their society.

In the afternoon, I made a long and leisurely stroll in the environs of the capital. I will not attempt here what has baffled the skill of more able pens, namely, to embody a faithful description of English rural scenery.

March 27*th.* Spent the forenoon visiting the National Schools, at West-End. The organization and mode of teaching were after the Normal school, already mentioned. Corporeal punishment and emulation were both employed. The teaching seemed efficient, and the scholars advanced, for their age. Afterwards, looked into the New House of Lords. The room is superbly rich, yet it did not strike my taste favorably. It was of rectangular form, instead of being semi-circular, and the seats, arranged for r ble members to face the sides of the room, instead of the speaker's desk. The throne of the queen, situated over the speaker's desk, seemed too high for appropriateness.

An incident befel me on my return homeward, so humorous that I can hardly forbear narrating it. While crossing a street, a jolly-faced mulatto approached me, bearing in his hand a finely rigged miniature vessel, and accosted me in French. By his bland tone and complaisant manner, it was evident he wished to flatter me into a purchase. At last said I to him, How happened it, my good fellow, that you knew I was a Frenchman? "Knew it, knew it," he repeated, with imperturbable sang-froid, "anybody would know *that* by your *figure*."

March 28th. Spent the day in making purchases previously to my departure on the morrow. I was highly pleased with the dignified ease, and honorable bearing of the London shopkeepers. I met with no such thing as bantering or falling upon prices; and I was informed such a thing was unknown, especially in the more respectable stores. The shops are kept by men, instead of women as in Paris; but there is a polished and quiet ease in the tone of the gentleman by whom you are waited on, that puts you in the happiest frame of mind. In one of the princely shawl stores that I had entered for a purchase, the principal shopman, on learning that I was from the United States, was delighted to see me. It seemed that he himself had been a merchant in New York, Boston, and

Albany, and had travelled extensively in the United States. He appreciated deeply the strong features in the character of the New World; and we were soon in the most glowing converse, expatiating upon the grandeur of American scenery. Some dozen of the clerks soon surrounded us, hanging with fixed attention upon our accents, when one of them broke out in this wise: "Well, uncle, I hope Heaven will spare my life to visit the United States of North America, for I really believe the whole world besides is nothing to be compared to it."

March 29*th*. At six, in the morning, we were gliding over the unruffled surface of the Thames, under tow of a modest little steamer, with the great London world receding in the distance. Homeward bound! What emotions of joy does not the reality bring to the heart of the traveller!

I would gladly extend this narrative to include the more peculiar incidents of our homeward passage, but space fails; and I do not doubt the good-natured reader who has in imagination accompanied me thus far upon our route, will now be willing to part my company for other society.

Now, in separating, let me affectionately press thy hand, dear reader; and express the hope, that we may never feel the less friendly for this journey, made together through so interesting a portion of this bright world of ours. Rather, may our acquaintance ripen into a friendship, which shall extend through the entire journey of life, and be consummated in our spiritual existence.

CHAPTER XXVII.

EUROPEAN SCHOOLS.

FEELING that a portion of our community, deeply interested in the glorious cause of education, would naturally expect something further said of European systems, than may be found in the narrative of this work, I had drawn up, in a chapter by itself, a few such conclusions upon the subject, as, after mature deliberation, I have arrived at with the clearest certainty. The manuscript of this, in being transmitted to the printer by mail, by some means miscarried; and now, after having vainly waited for the due arrival of the straying leaves, and the press being ready for finishing the work, I am constrained to supply, as well as I may in the very brief time permitted me, the accidental omission.

Let me premise, in the outset, that so different are the social and political institutions of European countries and our own, that an intelligent development of their school-systems, and a just comparison of them with ours, would require the space of a volume, instead of that of the few pages here allotted. Little more will therefore be now expected than the mere statement of my views; and it should be remembered further, that I refer, in my observations, particularly to France and Belgium.

SCHOOL-HOUSES.

I am free to state that I saw no public-school edifices superior, on the whole, to the best of the same class found in Boston, and some of her sister cities of New England. The school-rooms were, however, generally better and more fully supplied with apparatus and various ingenious contrivances for aiding teacher and pupil.

PUBLIC SCHOOL-SYSTEM.

In comprehensiveness of plan, in thorough organization, and in efficiency in execution, the European systems of public education must continue to remain, for some time at least, vastly superior to our own. The reason for this is obvious. The entire subject of public instruction is there in the hands of the government. This central power selects its agents from the most highly educated and philanthropic citizens of the state, who can be governed by no other motive, than to devise and carry out, in full consummation, the most complete system of instruction of which the human mind can conceive. And it is needless to say that this is faithfully done. Quite different is it with us. Here, the matter of maintaining public schools is left very much to the people at large. It is evident that the standard of instruction cannot, from the nature of the case, rise much above the common intelligence. By our system, then, the genius of education is constantly forced to appeal, so to speak, to ignorance for support. Now ignorance is incapable of appreciating the soul-cravings of education. Hence our school-system must continue to drag its slow length along, in snail-like imbecility. Still, there are gratifying features in our common-school system. For instance, we may feel encouraged in knowing that our public schools will continue to improve, in proportion as education is more widely diffused among the masses. The spirit of improvement will grow upon what it feeds. Again, we may feel assured that our progress is permanent. There can possibly be no reaction. In Europe, the system being immediately under the direction of the Government, may be modified or even swept away altogether, by a change of Government; but here, springing directly from the bosom of the people, it is as lasting as the granite of our everlasting hills.

INTELLECTUAL PROGRESS OF THE PUPIL.

Notwithstanding the greater efficiency of their school-system, the pupils generally, in such of the common branches as are duly taught in our schools, did not appear more advanced, for their age, nor to have been better instructed, than scholars of a similar class with us. For this, there are several reasons; two of which I can hardly forbear naming. One arises from the fact that there, the children of the better classes more generally attend the private schools, than with us. Their public schools are thus made up more fully of the children of the lower orders, and are consequently, to a greater extent, deprived of that efficient home-influence, for which nothing can make amends in a school. The other reason arises from that condition of European society which renders it next to impossible for a person to rise to a superior social position from the one in which he happens to be born. Thus the European pupil feels that, in a great measure, his social fate is sealed; that however studious he may be, there is but little chance that any ordinary intellectual superiority he may acquire, will enable him to advance from the situation in which the accidents of birth have placed him. This conviction constantly hanging over him, like an incubus, freezes his mental ardor, and paralyzes a powerful incentive to study. On the contrary, the pupil in our republican school-room, is, in this respect, quite differently and more happily situated. He is constantly made aware, by thousands of bright, living examples, that the path of honor and emolument, in his country, is open to the humblest; and that however obscure and unpropitious may have been the circumstance of his own birth, he has only to put properly forth his inborn energies, and he may reach the highest station withing the gift of the people This animating thought naturally awakens the latent forces of his being, supplying in a great measure the place of books and teacher. Hence, our common-school scholars will accomplish more, by less means, than the same class in European schools.

PRIVATE SCHOOLS.

It cannot for a moment be questioned that the private institutions of Europe afford by far more ample means for a full and complete education, than do the educational establishments of our own country. This naturally arises from the higher standard of education among the educated classes, the fostering care of Government, the munificence of individuals, and the ampler means at hand for illustrating educational subjects; but it is owing (more than to anything else), to the principle of the extreme division of labor which is so fully carried out in every department of life in Europe. In a private school of any pretensions in Europe, there may usually be found a Professor for each branch or department of instruction. It is needless to say, that a school thus circumstanced, affords advantages for careful instruction in the several branches, which cannot exist where, — as in many of the academies in our own country, — the principal is obliged to teach several or all of the various branches of his programme. Still, even here, we enjoy a compensating advantage. For instance, the principal advantage of a school is its moral influence, — the moulding, transforming power of the teacher over the pupil. The European professor, though more learned, is but partially developed. Many of his powers have been neglected in order to afford a fuller growth to others. He is thus an incomplete man, and however competent to give instruction in his favorite branch, possesses not that fulness and completeness of character, which constitute the highest form of man, and whose magic influence lies in his indefinable manner, tone of voice, beaming of the eye and fervor of expression. Now, the American school-master, from the necessity of being obliged to attend to many branches of learning, thereby gets a more general intellectual development, and from being forced into the practical relations of life, obtains a more efficient bearing of manner; and this advantage may compensate for his inferiority in some one chosen department of learning.

ORDER.

As I have elsewhere said, corporal punishment in the public schools is prohibited by law. In the private establishments it is treated as an obsolete idea. In our own country, the majority of intelligent educators have come to the conclusion that it should be used only as a *last resort*. But the French and Belgian authorities seem to have imbibed the idea, that if allowed at all, the trouble is, that this *last resort* will come too soon; and instead of being made the exception, it will gradually become a principal means of government. Hence, they have banished it entirely. Whether their school-masters would succeed equally well with our scholars, who are under less parental restraint, and so early become imbued with ideas of independence, I will not undertake to predict.

DRAWING.

Drawing is made an indispensable branch in all schools, public and private. It is pursued not only as a means of improving the taste, and cultivating a love for the beautiful, but as having an important relation to the practical business of life. An artizan would hardly expect to attain to superiority in his calling without a good knowledge of drawing. Undoubtedly, the superiority of the French, in the grace and beauty of their fabrications, may be attributed in a good degree to their thorough knowledge of this branch.

SINGING.

Singing is taught in all the schools. It is made essential, and is as common as reading. Children, from an early age, are thoroughly drilled in the elements, and the practice is made a concert exercise to enliven and gladden the air of the school-room. And further, it is deemed of vital importance in softening the manners, refining the feelings, and preparing the soul for the impression of noble and elevating sentiments. No singing exercises to which I have listened in the schools of this country, will favorably compare with such as I heard in European schools.

SEPARATION OF THE SEXES.

It is a marked feature in the European schools, that the sexes are not taught in the same school, as is often done with us. At least, no such schools came under my observation. Nor could I learn of any arrangement of the kind. Females are generally employed for teaching girls, and gentlemen, for boys. I believe the opinion is gaining ground among the more intelligent educators in this country, that a mixed school, of boys and girls, of limited number, taught by males and females, unites the more favorable conditions for healthy progress. At least, it seems more in accordance with nature; and, if permitted to speak, I would add my own observation and experience in its favor. Such a school requires, it is true, a firmer character, and more skill in the principal.

MORAL AND RELIGIOUS INSTRUCTION.

This is recognized in the plans of instruction, and its importance clearly enforced upon the teachers. In most schools, the pupils are weekly, and sometimes oftener, accompanied by their teachers to the churches, where they receive religious instruction from an ecclesiastic appointed for the purpose, while exercises of a religious character, in many schools, are a daily exercise.